Beyond Tolerance

Beyond Tolerance

The challenge of mixed marriage

A record of the International Consultation
held in Dublin, 1974

**Edited and with an Introduction
by Michael Hurley**

GEOFFREY CHAPMAN

Geoffrey Chapman Publishers
an imprint of Cassell and Collier
Macmillan Publishers Ltd.
35 Red Lion Square, London WC1R 4SG
and at Sydney, Auckland, Toronto,
Johannesburg.
An affiliate of The Macmillan Company
Inc. New York.

ISBN 0 225 66093 8

ed 1975

Printed in Great Britain by
Hazell Watson & Viney Ltd,
Aylesbury, Bucks

Contents

The Contributors

Björn Björnsson (Lutheran): Professor of Christian Social Ethics in the University of Iceland at Reykjavik and Dean of the Faculty of Theology; author of *The Lutheran Doctrine of Marriage in Modern Icelandic Society*.

John Coventry (Roman Catholic): Lecturer in Christian Doctrine, Heythrop College, University of London; member of the Academic Council of the Irish School of Ecumenics; co-chairman of the Association of Interchurch Families (England).

Kenneth Cragg (Anglican): Reader in Religious Studies at the University of Sussex; author of many works on Islam and on Christian-Muslim dialogue; formerly Assistant Bishop in the (Anglican) Jerusalem Archbishopric.

Gabriel Daly (Roman Catholic): Lecturer in Theology at the Milltown Institute of Theology and Philosophy (Dublin) and at the Irish School of Ecumenics.

G. R. Dunstan (Anglican): F. D. Maurice Professor of Moral and Social Theology at King's College, London; editor of *Theology;* member of the Anglican/Roman Catholic Commission on the Theology of Marriage and Mixed Marriages.

Paul Duffy (Roman Catholic): Director of the Centre for the Study of Social Issues in Canberra, Australia; author of several sociological and socio-political studies.

John Fulton (Roman Catholic): Research Lecturer in the Sociology of Religion at the Irish School of Ecumenics.

Adrian Hastings (Roman Catholic): A fellow of St Edmund's House, Cambridge. Author of several studies on theological, African and ecumenical topics, including *Christian Marriage in Africa*.

John Hayes (Roman Catholic): Teaches at University College, Dublin. He was Research Lecturer in Social Ethics at the Irish School of Ecumenics until September 1974.

Alasdair Heron (Presbyterian): Teaches at the Faculty of Divinity, University of Edinburgh. He was Research Lecturer in Systematic Theology at the Irish School of Ecumenics until September 1974.

Joseph Hoffman (Roman Catholic): Lecturer in Systematic Theology at the Faculty of Catholic Theology of the University of Strasbourg.

Michael Hurley (Roman Catholic) is Director of the Irish School of Ecumenics.

Joachim Lell (Lutheran): Head of the Institute for Confessional Studies of the German Evangelical Church at Bensheim in West Germany.

Enda McDonagh (Roman Catholic): Professor of Moral Theology and Director of Postgraduate Studies at St Patrick's College, Maynooth; member of the Senate of the National University of Ireland and of the Academic Council of the Irish School of Ecumenics.

Felix Trösch (Roman Catholic): Student chaplain at the University of Basle; a member of the Basle Synodal Commission for Ecumenical Questions.

Geoffrey Wainwright (Methodist): is Lecturer in Biblical Subjects at the Queen's College, Birmingham; member of the World Methodist Council and of the British Methodist Faith and Order Committee; author of *Eucharist and Eschatology*, etc.

Introduction
Michael Hurley

The difficulties involved in marriages between Christians of different denominations pale into insignificance when seen, as they must be, in the perspective of the vast challenges and problems which the churches face today in every sphere of life and not least with regard to the future of the institution of marriage itself. These mixed marriage difficulties, however, deserve careful consideration because they are at present preventing the churches from addressing themselves together, more credibly and effectively, to the larger issues of our time. For this reason among others the subject of mixed marriage has been under discussion since Vatican II, not only in a number of individual countries, but also by two international commissions. The Roman Catholic Church is involved in each of these. Its partners are the Anglican Communion in one case and, in the other, the World Alliance of Reformed Churches and the World Lutheran Federation. Unfortunately, the results to date of much of this work are disappointing and, as Professor Dunstan (a member of the Anglican/Roman Catholic Commission) states in the following pages, "our public, if we have one, must be rather bored with waiting for a practical outcome to our discussions".

The papers contained in this book were, with the exception of the final chapter, prepared for the International Consultation on Mixed Marriage held by the Irish School of Ecumenics in Dublin from 2-6 September, 1974. The aim of the Consultation, which is now the aim of the book, was to open up new approaches, to add new dimensions to the study of the mixed marriage problem in the hope of making the Churches' current discussions more fruitful. (The full text of the Minister's address is given in Appendix II, p. 188.)

The School, which sponsored the Consultation, is an interdenominational institute for research and postgraduate teaching in the interdisciplinary science of ecumenics. It is not an official organ of any church or of any Council of Churches.

The Consultation was attended by some 120 participants, half of them Roman Catholic, half Anglican and Protestant, with about one third coming from outside Ireland. The proceedings were formally opened by the Chairman of the Irish Council of Churches, the Rev. John Radcliffe, of the non-Subscribing Presbyterian Church of Ireland. They were closed by the Minister for Foreign Affairs of the Republic of Ireland, Dr Garret FitzGerald, who addressed himself in forthright fashion to the political implications of the problem in Ireland and who remarked that "as one of the progeny of a mixed marriage . . . it would be hard for me to assent to a proposition that asserted that such marriages are inherently undesirable, for by doing so I should, in a sense, be negating my own existence".

This book begins, as the Consultation began, by considering the exogamous character of marriage, its role in bridging divisions in society, and by studying the possibility of interfaith marriages, i.e. marriages, not just between people of different traditions within the one Christian faith and religion, but between people of different faiths and religions, in particular between Christians and Muslims. The effect on the participants was to enlarge our horizons, to help us to see how relatively unadventuresome and innocuous intermarriage between Christians really is and how unwholesome a generally negative attitude to such intermarriage must be judged. These considerations were a novel feature of the Consultation and it is hoped that they will now impress the readers as much as they did the participants and lead towards the more positive attitude to marriages between Christians of different denominations which is suggested by the title of this book: *Beyond Tolerance*.

A second noteworthy and novel feature of the Consultation was its acceptance of the methodological principle that orthodoxy must often be preceded by orthopraxy, its attempt to bring to the discussion an emphasis on the experience of Christians who are, themselves, involved in a mixed marriage. As the President of the School's Academic Council, the Reverend Cecil McGarry S.J., stated in his opening address of welcome:

> During this Consultation we will be sharing our theological, social, political, psychological, cultural insights. And because it is a consultation and not a conference we will be recognising the interrelation of *theoria* and *praxis* in any search for truth. Too often we take it for granted that theory always and inevitably comes before practice and totally defines practice. We are recognising that practice has much to say in the development and understanding of theory. We are accepting that reflection on experience has a great deal to contribute to understanding and to truth. We are also recognising that God speaks to us in our lives, in our homes as well as in the studies of scholars and students; that the teaching Church is not separate and distinct from God's believing people.

This dimension of the Consultation marks in various ways the papers collected in this book, but it found its most memorable expression in a symposium (not recorded here) on "Living an Interchurch Marriage" when, at a public session, two couples, Ruth and Martin Reardon (a Roman Catholic and Anglican from England) and Gay and Seán Hogan (a Northern Ireland Presbyterian and Southern Roman Catholic living in Dublin) spoke of what their marriage meant to them. According to the latter:

> We could have ducked the whole problem, if one of us had "turned"; but neither of us believed that this would be right. Instead, we chose to face up to the fact that ours was going to be a two-church family. This meant learning about each other's religious practice, going to each other's churches, and re-thinking beliefs which we had always taken for granted. The result has been a heightening of our religious

awareness, which is central to our whole relationship, and has deeply enriched our lives. This new understanding has spread to our own families as well. It's as though we had become a bridge and a point of reconciliation between two cultures, as well as two churches.

Part of the price which the churches and their Commissions on Mixed Marriage are paying for putting theory before practice, for putting themselves and their doctrines in the first place in their discussions and mixed marriage couples and their experience only in the second (if in any) place is that the changing nature of mixed marriage is escaping them. For an increasing number of mixed marriage couples today, their situation, as in faith they experience and try to live it, bears little, if any, relationship to what the churches are talking about. In the lives of these couples a new reality is being born: the new reality which the new term "interchurch marriage" is attempting to express. These couples experience themselves as belonging to both the churches which are represented in their persons and they wish their children like themselves to come to belong to both these churches. For those who have it, this experience gives an air of unreality, of meaninglessness to Roman Catholic *and* Protestant talk about, for instance, the denominational upbringing of the children of a mixed marriage. Instead of ignoring this experience, much less denying it or rejecting it as inauthentic, the Consultation gave it pride of place. In this it broke new ground.

The papers prepared for the Consultation and here collected with a final essay to make a book, bear witness in different ways and with differing emphases to the primordial importance for the churches, as they address themselves together to the problem of mixed marriage, to listen to the experience of interchurch couples and to devote themselves to the task of helping these couples to deepen and develop their religious experience.

It remains for me as editor of these papers to record my indebtedness to my colleagues in the School of Ecumenics, to those who helped us to prepare the background materials for the Consultation, to all those who participated and made the Consultation such a profoundly moving experience and, last but not least, to my secretary, Ruth Moran. I also wish to express my thanks to the staff of Geoffrey Chapman, in particular, to Sarah Hedley for her interest in the book and for the skill and speed with which she saw it through the press, and to Gerard P. Hassay, S. J., for help with proof-reading.

A statement was issued by the Consultation at the conclusion of its deliberations and is included in this book as Appendix I. A Report commissioned by the Consultation was prepared by the School and published in *Doctrine and Life, One in Christ, The Furrow* and *Theology* (February 1975). Other Reports and comments on the Consultation have appeared in various theological journals.

Interfaith Marriage

1. Intermarriage and the Wider Society

Adrian Hastings

A Midsummer Night's Dream is, perhaps, more than any other of Shakespeare's plays, a celebration of marriage – of marriage seen as a social as well as a personal covenant whether it be entered into for reasons of State or intense private love. The whole structure of the play suggests that marriage is of much more than personal interest; it is the public bonding at every level of society (as it is in *As You Like It*) of the two deeply distinct halves of the world. It is a social union replacing the skirmishing of the sexes manifest in war, in avoidance, in pursuit, in joking relationships. With Theseus and Hippolita's wedding war comes to an end; Oberon and Titania's reconciliation provides for the re-uniting of the two halves of the elves. The loving and bedding of the wooing and wedding of Hermia and Helena are seen in this context to be but the tip of the iceberg (to use an inappropriate metaphor) as regards the full reality of marriage.

Marriage, in fact, is the inter-sex covenant, the social institution which brings together most closely and most deliberately in a relationship of communion and creative tension two such dissimilar partners as man and woman. It is better to marry than to fight, much better. But it does involve the sacrifice of much of that predominantly one-sex society to which one has hitherto largely belonged; it draws the boy from his primary loyalty to football club or hunting companions, the girl from weaving or the typists' pool. Each, of course, has sallied out from those one-sex fellowships frequently enough, but now it is different – the balance of life is to change. The stag party expresses this change with a symbolically final celebration of the past. An "alliance" has been arranged – a covenant between two parties with their different attitudes, education, occupation. It is to be a bridge, establishing a new focal point of fellowship and loyalty, but one which does not eradicate earlier clusters of fellowship and loyalty upon either side; it will weave them together into a new pattern affecting a great many people within whose lives bride and groom already belong.

In the perennial tradition of Africa, Asia, and Europe too, marriage has been seen as an alliance, not just of two individuals, but of two families, two kin groups, at times even of two cities or kingdoms; today, often more significantly, of two friendship networks. The rules of incest,

endogamy and exogamy are complex, varied and much disputed as to
their full meaning and origin. Occasionally, and we shall come back to
some instances of it, a society builds up firm rules of endogamy (marrying within one's group), but generally the primary concentration of
custom was rather upon exogamy (marrying outside one's group).
Incest is the greatest marital crime but far beyond the boundaries of
incest are the "prohibited degrees", the clan or village groups one must
avoid. By a rule of exogamy one is driven out to create new relationships not only for oneself but for one's blood relatives, the whole society
of one's kindred. One is allying the group with another group. Even
today the arrival of a French daughter-in-law, for instance, is sure to
affect a whole nest of people in their attitudes to another group of
people if in fairly unformalised ways. Much history, social and political, can be written as a record of the consequences of marriage in the
interweaving of traditions, the reshaping of loyalties, the expanding
network of friendships, the creation of new responsibilities to offer
support. In many an African society the affinal obligations consequent
upon one's kin after marriage are precise, complex, recognised of right.
Elsewhere such things may be more implicit, but they do not disappear.
Indeed in certain historical cases, political marriages – as of a French or
Spanish princess with an English king, as of Isabella with Ferdinand –
express and bring about a politically altered relationship involving
millions of people in the two societies somehow united by the marriage.

It is perfectly true that the danger here is for the personal relationship at the core of marriage to be veritably crushed by the political
significance: the girl becomes but a pawn in the diplomacy or terri-
torial aggregation of her father or bridegroom. And such was often the
case. Yet it does not have to be so: social and personal significance are
not antipathetic but complementary; the social bonding possible
through marriage is no substitute for the personal relationship.
Separate either wholly from the other and you get a recipe for disaster:
either the total politicisation or the total privatisation of marriage
negates the deep sense of the covenant which is, even naturally,
sacramentum. The social and political dimension must grow out from
the personal bond – sometimes almost technically, more often by its
symbolism and the further opportunities for new social links doubly
weighted that this particular household, constituted in the way it has
been, now affords. Thus, to take once more a royal and large scale
example, Albert and Victoria did, in their union, both symbolise and
stimulate the Anglo-German understanding of the mid-nineteenth
century.

All this points to the inherent social function of marriage as something which makes a person face out of his or her own society to
achieve the deepest relationship in life with someone until now of a
different society, in order that subsequently they will not only be themselves joined together, while still belonging to a greater or lesser extent
to each former group, but their union will affect the social horizons and
obligations of many other members of each society as well. These
consequences are not the odd and almost regrettable accidents of
marriage, but form a large part of its central purpose; they are conse-

quences of which most societies stand from one point of view or another in serious need if they are not to become ghettoes of blood, culture, class or creed.

Such is the challenge of marriage as a public reality, a challenge it has to meet in appropriate form in many a different social milieu. It is quite true that society in the past was structured in most places very much more by marriage and kinship than it is today; marriage today has a relatively secondary role to play in the shaping of society; indeed the consequent over-personalisation of marriage (and the theoretical justification for this provided in works such as those of Fr. Schillebeeckx) can be part of the whole modern problem. Nevertheless the social role of marriage today is not nearly so slight as many might assume. A very considerable proportion of one's leisure activities, enduring personal relationships outside the household, social responsibilities, letter writing are related to the wider family; and then there is the whole pattern of one's non-related friends depending upon the character and loyalties of the two people who first make up the family. That character and those loyalties may be such as to cut across significant frontiers or, on the contrary, to remain entirely inside them. In any society which includes such frontiers it will be dangerous if almost all the marriages fail to leap the frontier and remain instead endogamous in regard to the issue which is here precisely the significant divide; it may be a class divide, an international divide, a racial divide, or a religious divide. It will be still more dangerous if endogamy of such a sort be erected into a moral obligation.

The essential pattern is always much the same. Two groups of people with decided differences are living side by side and in considerable contact. Without some genuinely close personal relationships and the achievement of at least a measure of institutionalized solidarity misunderstanding and tension are inevitable, open conflict probable. The situation calls for friendship and the weaving of a network of relationships; if this be allowed, alliances will follow, inter-society marriages providing the sacramental expression of that human fellowship now admitted between the two groups as in the reconciliation song from *Oklahoma*:

Cowboys dance with the farmers' daughters
Farmers dance with the ranchers' gals.

But inevitably inter-society marriage will threaten the purity of the tradition, the identity of either group. And so groups frequently frown at such marriages or ban them entirely, and as soon as they do so the openness proper to a human society faced with other societies has to be replaced by the sense of the *lager*, the besieged citadel: the purity of race or faith is held to be in danger. They go endogamous. The blue blooded must not marry the peasant; a Hapsburg may finally find himself unable to marry anyone but another Hapsburg; Montague must not marry Capulet; nor white black; Catholic must not marry Protestant; nor Christian non-Christian.

The tendency here is, first, to exlude large blocks of our neighbours from the possibility of being a group with whom it is possible to make a covenant alliance, and secondly, if someone slips through the net, then to insist that a person marrying from another group must wholly enter into one's own. Marriage is acceptable only with a prior "conversion" which – if complete – is really to deny the nature of the covenant. In true marriage the unity of the bride and bridegroom does not exclude a continuing relationship with either side, though understandably one or other will frequently be the dominant one. To which kin will the children chiefly belong? In a patrilineal system we get one answer, in a matrilineal one another. It is interesting to see how in Africa, where there are inter-church marriages, the religion of the children tends to be settled by the kinship pattern of the tribe: in a patrilineal society they will follow the religion of the father, in a matrilineal society the church of the mother.

There are patrilineal marriage patterns in Africa where the bride actually enters the clan of the husband, but far more frequently she remains in her own. While the children take their father's clan, they will still have particular obligations – a special relationship – to their mother's clan. This suggests that a mixed marriage too can indeed be structured in a number of ways; and it is clear from experience that this is so. One cannot insist that there be no "conversion"; to some extent, at least, there should indeed be one upon either side: a quite new approach to and communion with the society represented by one's partner and the values it cherishes. On the other hand if one side insists that there be a quasi-total conversion, then the marriage loses its function as a social covenant. It becomes not a bridge but a new cause for antipathy and division. And this, alas, is what civil and church authority has at times made of it. There has been the endeavour to nullify its bridging power by the inequality of terms on which the two partners enter it in relation to their former status. As a consequence Jessica's alliance with Lorenzo can only be one more item in the alienation of Shylock. Bob Williamson in the song marries Bridget McGinn but "turns papist" and consequently has to "flee to the province of Connaught" from his native Ulster. If somehow he hadn't had to flee, been allowed to remain orange and Bridget papist, then perhaps there might have been no bullets of the Provos and the UVF. If two groups live cheek by jowl and there is no marriage, then there will be war.

Of course, even though the individual, wife or husband, does enter the clan, church or political allegiance of the other partner, he or she has still a whole family behind him whose proper links with the new generation are intended to assert the under-valued side. The role of grandparents is an important one and, while it is understandable, it is mistaken for parents to resent the bond between children and grandparents. This and the multiplicity of other relationships with uncles, aunts and cousins are the particular links which make real the wider implications of the social covenant of marriage – links which in any "mixed" situation weave back and forward across the borders of faith, class or race.

Clearly there are limits to the ability of a marriage to be a bridge without disaster; this depends both upon the capacity of the partners and the willingness of the two societies to be so linked. The hostility of Montague and Capulet was such that the attempt to unite them came to immediate disaster, though in doing so it pricked the whole absurd bubble of their hostility. The incompatibility of the two was annulled in death. Some societies are murderously opposed to mixing; others will simply stone-wall. But the capacity of two people to bridge the divide can only be discovered in the trying, and it should be allowed to do it in its own way, though of course people may rightly be warned of the difficulties. The basic principle remains that true human unity is never a unity of uniformity.

Human communion is always the bonding of the diverse. But how far in a single household can the diverse be acceptable, even tolerable? What is possible for some will appear quite impossible for others. There must clearly exist some deep sharing of conviction, beyond any division of loyalties, but such a sharing is quite achievable across many divides. One must always start from the position that marriage does not and should not end previous loyalties, though it may materially alter them. A husband in taking on commitments to his wife does not withdraw from those he already has to parents, sisters and others. These commitments will then be shared; but others, more elusive or spiritual, will remain the possession of one alone, though respected by the other. A degree of cultural, political or religious division within the household which would be intolerable for some, is in fact found acceptable, and even stimulating, by others. In reality one does not have a single model for "the perfect marriage"; and marriages, anyway, are all imperfect: over the years achieving more or less according to one or another model. It may seem to some ideally desirable that a husband and wife should agree upon all fundamental matters, and with some people and in some societies that may appear easy enough. But in the world as a whole, and in many parts of it, there is no such agreement, and it is both unreal and undesirable to require it for marriage. On the contrary, it is socially dangerous, as has been suggested above, to have such divisions in society, and not to have them also within marriage: not to allow marriage to cross them. It is in marriage indeed that they can be challenged, overcome in a deeper unity, but only through accepting the possibility of continued tension and disagreement.

One obvious and common example in modern western society is marriage between the Christian and the "modern pagan". It does in fact frequently work out very happily; it would be highly undesirable socially if it did not exist; and yet the basic religious gap here may be immense – far wider than between two Christians of different churches or between a Christian and an African adhering to a traditional religion, or a Christian and a Muslim.

People are often only very inadequately aware of their predicament in this area or others; they are within a social situation which they have not analysed and do not very closely foresee the pressures it will exert on them, the demands it will make. As time goes on they may respond in a positive manner, they may survive for ever largely uncomprehending, or they may be overwhelmed. This woman has married this man: they love one another. In fact a cluster of circumstances, attractions, preferences, the leap of personal trust, all this has brought them together. They need one another and want to put this relationship in some way first, but seldom (and then somewhat unnaturally) intend to abandon the vast network of relationships and loyalties already woven into their lives. Yet one is a Christian, the other an animist, a Muslim, a modern non-believer. Probably neither is consciously prepared for the intensely difficult task of growing into a deep personal union with someone with whom much of what is deep in one's own life cannot just like that be shared. But such is the nature of life, and marriages do in fact achieve different sorts of harmony and cooperation; they can succeed in different ways, while some can fail – wholly or partly. Many do fail, and for a variety of reasons. Yet seldom, probably, chiefly for this one. One may be more tolerant of religion than of many other things in the close quarters of a single household. The great majority of inter-something marriages are doubtless not lived with a great degree of deliberate vocation and self-analysis. They may not bridge the chasm theoretically, yet many do so in practice and in doing so may yet a little diminish the theoretical separation. Between a believing Christian and someone of another faith, there can in fact be much in common at the level of personal religion: faith in God, in providence, in goodness, in the need to forgive, in the obligation of loyalty, in the acceptance of the true. These are the things decisive in anyone's life and they can cross the widest theoretical divides of religion. It can well happen that a Christian and a non-Christian are more closely linked at the level of the deep things of religion than, say, a practising and a lapsed Catholic.

Many such unions which do in fact exist the Church, alas, has refused canonically to recognise. But many others it has recognised, more easily in earlier centuries, more marginally in later times. From one such Augustine was born, though admittedly his subsequent rather negative view of marriage does not speak particularly in its favour. Today there are thousands of Christians in Africa, at least, who do live in an interfaith marriage recognised by the church, for they married before they were baptised, though they may well already have been catechumens. The pattern of a Christian wife and a non-Christian husband is a common one, not only in Africa but elsewhere too, notably Japan. Doubtless in its tidy and canonical way the modern Church has not much liked such arrangements, but equally it has to a large extent accepted them, recognising (despite clerical reluctance) that the world largely makes itself, that marriage is – first of all – a natural fact which one has to live with in all its jagged splendour rather than construct on *a priori* lines.

The duty of the wise man, the understanding legislator or pastor or parents in State or Church, is not to outlaw the outlandish marriage, to fling out boy or girl because he or she has married beyond the frontier, but rather to celebrate the event while endeavouring to provide in an unostentatious way the additional support of which anyone in a somewhat exposed position may stand in need. One should acknowledge that this is marriage at its most meaningful, its most sublime, and that some people at least must be called in this way even if – as normally happens in human experience – they have themselves not perceived half the significance of that to which they have personally set themselves. A society in which this is absolutely not acceptable is sure to be a society in a bad way psychologically. For here indeed marriage is being most true to itself, God's chosen instrument within man's own order for social reconciliation, made in Christ into sacrament of the final reconciling covenant. If its nature, in all its personal and fleshly particularity, is to signify the intensely improbable marriage alliance of infinite God and a finite people, it will do so authentically the more it really is an alliance between the unlike, unlike in spirit, unlike in flesh, drawing the diverse into an authentic unity. Nothing is more truly sacrament than a loving, persevering marriage covenant which crosses the bounds of faith or race. This is rather the ideal of human and Christian marriage than the *Catholic Fireside* union of boy and girl from the same parish, the same street, the same sodality: as a model of marriage the latter may appear to border on the incestuous.

Of course marriages vary, as do ministries. The rich diversity of purpose within this one institution cannot be fully realised in the particular instance. In hard fact it is perfectly acceptable that some be more endogamous, some more exogamous; and their characteristic life styles, their mode of relating the household fellowship to wider society, the virtues they most noticeably substantialise, will vary accordingly. Within the complexity of human nature and of modern society, one certainly does not want to declare one particular pattern normative.

All I wish to suggest here is that the "traditional" Catholic concentration upon the importance of avoiding a religiously "mixed" marriage, or at the least controlling and next to nullifying its bridging capacity, implies a restrictive and inadequate understanding of the very nature of marriage, both socially and theologically. Adherence to religion and the state of marriage are alike social realities; and that side of the social purpose of marriage which can be covered by the word "alliance" (relating to a wider group of people than bride and groom) is as relevant for a religiously divided society as for one divided according to any other criteria.

There is no gap in human society which cannot be bridged in marriage or which, in principle, should not be bridged. Such is the nature of mankind. We must affirm most emphatically that it is and should be an intermarrying society. To the extent that we exclude intermarriage we exclude the full recognition of our common humanity, and we deny too the adequate sacramentality of marriage itself: we would be admitting that its covenant power has inherent limitations, and that it is not, even with the added grace of Christian faith, up to being an appropriate sign of ultimate reconciliation. We must not accept that. Marriage is always difficult and dangerous. No man or woman can commit him or herself inter-personally and inter-sexually to the extent that marriage demands without difficulty and danger. Covenants always cross frontiers and all frontiers are perilous. But if the Church of Christ is committed to working in truth within the hard realities of social fact and human division for the realisation of a communion, a *koinonia*, of mankind, and has two blessed instruments to bring about and symbolise such communion: the eucharist covenant and that marriage covenant which she did not make and which did not begin in Christ's life but has been with us always "from the beginning", then she must welcome and use these where and as they are, not imposing limits at odds with their meaning. Where division is deepest, there the pioneer is most needed to step out: to establish that inter-personal covenant which yet somehow draws the kindred with him. Leaping the sex barrier, he will leap too that of class, of race, of religion. Instead of excommunicating the mixer, it is surely the role of the Church to bless the pioneer who thus steps out to extend the frontiers of fellowship.

2. A Christian-Muslim Perspective

Kenneth Cragg

Our purpose is to see broadly how Muslim and Christian faith and practice have understood and expressed the married state and to consider three patterns of interfaith marriage which seem to emerge from experience of it within these two communities. This intention necessarily carries us beyond the range of problems and factors obtaining in the Christian locale, in Ireland or elsewhere. But the Consultation has been invited to include this consideration, if only prefatory to its own immediate complex of concerns, in the belief that the larger geographical and spiritual dimension involved in moving beyond the borders of Christianity may be significant both for perspective and direction. For our part, those of us who are deeply engaged in the themes of inter-religious theology look both for precedents and stimulus, in that task, from the temper and quality of inter-Christian wrestling with issues of marriage and community. We cannot, however, take time in this context to discuss the large questions which arise in any instinct to find in Christian ecumenism guidelines and criteria for the still more daunting business of a more general *oikumene* of religions – if such there be.

Marriage has to do with almost ethereal joys, but also with very mundane liabilities. If "heavened" in benediction, it has to be "earthed" in its realism. We have to hold together both the utmost concepts of vocation and the modest, maybe even warped, possibilities of achievement. This being so, it will be well at the outset to allow ourselves a brief focus of reflection on how critical the human stakes are. All our thinking has to do with a relationship that is deeply vulnerable because it makes the partners uniquely liable. It is the commitment within which there is no immunity because there is no reservation. What is, in truth, life's most steadfast adventure may for that very reason, become life's most dismal misery.

Thomas Hardy, with his keen sense of joy and pathos, caught the alternative when he wrote:

Face unto face, then, say,
Eyes my own meeting,
Is your heart far away
Or with mine beating?
When false things are brought low
And swift things have grown slow,
Feigning like froth shall go,
Faith be for aye.

9

But chained and doomed for life
To slovening,
As vulgar man and wife,
He says, is another thing. . .
Yea, sweet love's sepulchring.

There is nothing more intimately and mutually "existential" than wedded-ness. "Through marriage," wrote Bonhoeffer of a bridal pair, "you are placed at a point of responsibility toward the world and toward mankind." So, he went on, we salute the "occasion of joy – joy that human beings can do such great things, that they have been granted the freedom and power to take the rudder of their lives into their own hands". From that sense of exhilaration – so spontaneous in a "right" wedding – comes assurance such as that which Mark Twain described in a letter to his fiancée two months before the day:

Our wedding will be the mightiest day in our lives, for it makes two fractional lives a whole. . . . It will prove a new revelation to life, a diviner depth to sorrow, a new impulse to worship.

That, indeed, is "the truth of troth". But if its vision is to be steadily translated into fact, it must know, measure and surmount the odds which confront it in this human world coming both from self and from society.

In that sense, every marriage, we may say, has marriage itself in trust. Just as freedom is at stake in every claim to it and justice at issue in every plea that seeks it, so every husband and wife, in their pledged-ness to each other, are in personal, social trust with marriage itself, with its meaning both as status and achievement. In this divine universe of human obligation, is it not in the nature of the divine law and of the human dignity that we should be responsible, as it were, for responsibility itself? The intention of the Creator is within the making of the creature and the design of God a co-operation with man.

"Receive ye one another to the praise of God."[1]

Where such "receiving" comes to birth across the confines of creed or culture, its fulfilment in due "troth" makes for a specially exacting relation of each to the other and of both to God. Where active or passive sources of communal estrangement have not debarred the personal bonds of love, something of a reconciling quality is released into the wider world. The intimacy of marriage may then become the proving ground of communal attitudes, where faiths are tested in the necessity of co-existence.

Or, contrariwise, the suspicions of the larger context may bedevil the private purpose to transcend them and marriage may founder in the stress of tensions it can no longer elude or subdue. Or, again, and perhaps more likely, some acquiescent complacence or pedestrian tolerance will do duty for genuine exchange.

If "receive ye one another to the praise of God" is to be the ruling principle through all our thinking, both theological and pastoral, then we had better start with this mutual "receiving". The marriage of persons is, of course, the marriage of personalities. When they come from disparate backgrounds there is to some extent a marriage of their cultures. When the marriage service enquires: "Who giveth this woman (should it not be also "this man"?) to be married?" implicit in the often unvoiced, merely gestured, answer is the matrix *whence* she, or he, is given. For birth, heredity, home, nurture, maturing, are all culturally identified. The resulting "identities" of the marrying parties, though still malleable, and certainly not "fated", are none the less definitive and, in some measure, unalterable facts of the situation. Bride and bridegroom become the *locus* of a new relationship between their cultures and the faiths that have shaped their growing years. Interfaith or interculture considerations which, elsewhere, may be discursive, academic and abstract, become for them a living and a lived reality. They may well be inarticulate about many of the themes which scholars writing papers (or pundits in consultations) wish to ventilate. Married troth, by contrast, lives these, has to come to terms with them, in an actual, personal equation. Having chosen marriage as the sphere of their love (as distinct from the casual escapism in which sexuality can be pursued) they have, we may say, married, within themselves, the patterns and concepts of the married state that obtain in their respective religions and societies.

Though, as individuals, they may be far from representative instances of the cultures that have "given" them to each other, they, nevertheless, embody those cultures in a quest for compatibility in the most intimate and testing enterprise of life. Except on rare occasions, that situation belongs, not with highly sensitive, deeply perceptive exponents of their faith-culture, but with flesh and blood folk, having foibles, qualities, blemishes of their own which affect, in a score of ways, what they may or may not make of the harmony they propose. It may often be that the love which enterprises marriage, perhaps in rather sanguine terms, across the divide of religion, has with that very readiness an easy-going or superficial sense of loyalty and so an unlikely capacity or disposition to bring to the venture the temper it essentially requires. That is not to say, of course, that the deepening may not come in the proceeding, especially in the context of ensuing family and the longer haul.

Or, on the other hand, the will to undertake inter-race, or inter-faith, marriage may denote a quality of inter-penetrating trust which has understood the stakes and in the sealing of commitment is confident in the ability of love to "make both one" and so is deliberately aware of the taxing mediation that its partnership must practise. Relatives, and society around, will obviously be a powerful factor in their task, just as they are in the other direction where one-sided or superficial marriages fail, by capitulation, to be really inter-religious at all.

For all communities, in their collective tradition, tend to be tenacious and possessive of their own and too readily bring an active or a passive sanction to bear upon defaulters or trespassers. Secularity, no doubt, is doing much to break down absolutist ideas of religious solidarity. Personal religion may be the freer and truer for what some have called, in this liberating context, "the left hand of God". Secular liberation, by the same token, may also put the religious sense of marriage on its mettle in a livelier way than authoritarian religion inspires.

But, either way, it is out of the dual heritage of nurture and religious order that the separate parties come, with their personal identities communally conditioned and schooled. Their wedded-ness is, then, the inter-acting of that past in the new personal present of their troth. It follows that we should study the ethos, and doctrine, of marriage in the two faiths with which we are primarily concerned.

Marriage according to Islam

Muslim law and practice in relation to betrothal, marriage and divorce is a vast and complex theme. But it is entirely clear that sexuality is only properly expressed within the contractual bond of matrimony. Aside from the phrase of the Qur'ān about "that (fem.) which your right hands possess", (i.e. female slaves) – a point hardly operative in our context of discourse – the marriage pledge, though in revocable form, is the only valid condition of sexual exchange. Woman only becomes a consort when she is given the honoured status of wife. Witness the abhorrence of *Zinā*, or adultery, in Islam (cf. Surahs 4.15-16 and 24.2-26). Only marriage legitimatises sexual relationship. There must be this contractual standing of the parties, to which also, in the Islamic way, the safeguards and provisions of divorce in Islam bear clear witness. Marriageability on the female side is rigorously conditioned by due contractability.

It is true, of course, that such marriageability is not limited by plurality, until traditionally the number of four is reached. But plural wives are, veritably, wives and not paramours, and their status is contractually defined. Plurality, anyway, is scarcely germane in our present context, since the interfaith marriages which are our concern (except perhaps in Africa) are likely, in their sophistication, to have been firmly and instinctively "singular" in their genesis. In any event, even while plurality remains legally feasible in traditional law, monogamy is increasingly coming to be both the legal norm in many countries and a growing consensus of the exegetes. The operative passage of the Qur'ān, on this issue, is that in Surah 4.3 f. Here, plurality of four wives is authorised, but only with the much debated proviso, "if you can do them justice . . ." or, "if you can be even-handed between them". If this clause is taken to mean equal rights in material and sexual measure, it is an attainable condition, and it was for centuries so understood. But if it requires a constant quality of emotional regard, this is clearly humanly impossible. Then, the proviso being unattainable, the permission lapses and the passage should be read, as moderns insist, as a virtual prohibition.

This exegesis, which is widespread, ranges the Qur'ān firmly with monogamy, in response, no doubt, to external pressures – economic, social and spiritual – but, none the less, also sincere and inward. But *virtual* prohibition of plurality, if it finally prevails, is still eloquent of the contractuality we are expounding. For, on the Christian basis of the "estate", or "sacrament", of marriage, plurality is ontologically false to the married state itself, where thought of duplication, far from being a matter of *de facto* experiment in which failure may be presumed, is *ab initio* excluded from a true self-giving.

What is relevant for us at this point, however, is the firm and sure dignity of the married status within Islam in the legal sense – a status which is a significant potential element in any Christian "engagement" with it. It is, of course, only too sadly true that that legal status has been socially (and indeed also legally) eroded by the ease of male divorcing without need to show cause, and by the hard fact that Islam has been traditionally a man's world. Nevertheless, that freedom of divorce is hedged about in the Qur'ān with provisions about restraint, fairness and compassion. Surah 2.226-7, while not stipulating any necessary grounds for dismissing a wife, lays down a waiting period of three menstrual periods for the woman, and four months for the man. She must be "dismissed with kindness" (2.228) and there is always the hope of reconciliation (*loc. cit.* and 65.18).

This legal contractuality of marriage in Islam, revocable truly, but increasingly also unilateral in changing law and gathering custom, may, and does, grow towards the Christian concept of the sacramental. It is very important, for our inter-faith task, to sense and enforce the Qur'ān's potential here. There is, for example, the striking passage in 30.21, which sets sex among the "signs of God", meaning that it ought to be the occasion of reverent awe and thankfulness. It continues: "He (God) has created for you from your own selves wives (or "partners", as it were, lit. "marital ones") that you might live in joy with them and he planted love and tenderness between you". Here a deep, perhaps almost sacramental, mutuality is implicit. Surah 4.21 seems to echo a similar sense, seeing in the married experience something too sacred to allow of casual rupture. "How can you take it back (i.e. a dowry) when you have lain with each other and entered into a firm covenant with your wives?" Is it not arguable that there are more essential things than dowries to which the same argument might apply?

Perhaps the greatest potential of all is in Surah 2.197: "They (your wives) are a garment (*libās*) unto you and you for them". This word *libās* would seem to be close to the Biblical: "Adam *knew* his wife . . .". The mutual intimacy of sexual experience, as marriage hallows it, provides the seemly setting, the mantle, the reciprocal completing, which "clothes" and "justifies" what otherwise would be "uncovered" and so gross. It comprehends, say the lexicographers, "everything that a man desires of his wife".[2]

"Women are your fields: go then into your fields as you please", says Surah 2.223. Fertility, virility, ardour – these are properly Islamic values. But "keep in mind", continues 2.223, "the fear due to God". In the circumstances that are likeliest to obtain, these days, in the context we are discussing, it is deeply possible that these hints of the Islamic Scripture may be ripened by mutual Muslim-Christian aspiration into the sense of fidelity within an undivided covenant, where "the fear due to God" has come to mean the wholeness of self-giving in once plighted troth. For is not the undividedness of sexual love, arching the family in a sure unity, the true counterpart of the undividedness of worship which acknowledges that God is One? Enigmatically, Surah 33.4 observes: "God has not given to any man two hearts in one breast".[3]

These, then, are our theological resources in reckoning positively with the Muslim Christian marrying that is, or may come to be, ready to implement the potential that is in them.

The Christian "Estate" of Marriage

"Estate" is, no doubt, an archaic word. But it serves. A son, a daughter, a brother, are not contractually so. That is their estate. Husband and wife, likewise, albeit by a different road. The contractual element is there, but with it and around it the hallowing into "one flesh", which is at once a "coming to be" and a "being to become". There had better be, at this point, a deliberate economy of exposition, the more so as no doubt the Christian theology of marriage will be more explicitly discussed elsewhere in this Consultation. The vital point, *vis-à-vis* a Muslim partner in intermarriage, is to make vivid – and, as far as may be, definitive – this other and Christian dimension of what we understand wedded-ness to mean. The love of which marriage is the form and fabric is understood as the unreserved commitment which, in Donne's memorable words, "inter-animates two souls", and joins their flesh into one communion, wherein they possess and pursue the divine design. For, as the Zohar has it, "the pleasure of cohabitation is a religious one, giving joy also to the divine presence".

Such commitment is really a continual "being what we are". It is at once a being and an intending to be, a status definitive and a purpose prospective. Marriage is the due and apt "form" of the spirit's nature. As form, it cannot of course "guarantee" the achievement of which it is the essential shape. The being and the becoming inter-depend, belonging together because love is troth for ever willing, and troth is love for ever active.

There obtains here – as everywhere in the sacramental relation of spirit and form – the paradox of the uncompulsive and the necessary. Due order is no automatic guarantee, or guarantor, of due reality. "Indissolubility", in that sense, is a sadly ambiguous term, carrying into harsh legality what is only truly free and creative, yet is altogether unfree, because it has willed its troth as the sure context of its intention and its sanctity. To see the troth as merely legally and externally perpetuated is to invite hypocrisy, falsehood and tyranny and to profane the troth itself. Yet married love, in its sincerity, lives by and for and through that ever trothful intention – "faith be for aye". We cannot here take up the related problem of how to hold a due balance between our care for the form and truth of troth and our care for the liberation and redemption of parties caught in the bondage of now troth-less form.

These, then, are the sacramental dimensions of Christian marriage that have to govern all our theological thinking and our pastoral relation towards mixed marriages – dimensions, as we have seen, which some Islamic attitudes may, hopefully, come to share.

...not One-Party Capitulation

Muslim-Christian, like any other intermarriage, is likely in practice to resolve itself into an actual *modus vivendi* in one of three ways. Adequate sociological survey is not here possible or intended. We focus rather on the pastoral implications. The first possibility is that of total subjection of the one party to the other in respect of institutional religion. When that happens, there is hardly any longer an interfaith marriage. But it is, in fact, a sort of interfaith "solution", and, as such, is very widespread.

It must be clear here that we are not referring to the desirability of unifaith marriage for those who have not yet been drawn otherwise. Nor are we meaning to question the urgency, at a certain early point, of clarifying and stressing to those involved the strains and hard hurdles, love-wise and family-wise, which go with marriage across frontiers of culture, race and belief. But once love and the sense of mutuality have reached a certain watershed surely that mutuality itself includes an obligation to "take as they are", to find compatible, and not to require a switch of profession, or a surrender of identity, as the condition of acceptance.

Yet, after marriage, it is just such a surrender which is so often demanded or exacted by one side. In the case of Muslim-Christian marriage it is almost always Muslim husband and Christian wife, since Muslim women almost never marry outside Islam. Though the marriage may begin in a rough equality, it all too often happens that the wifely Christian liberty is eroded, violated by relatives, forfeited by pressure, or simply denied when children arrive and must have Muslim citizenship and Islamic rearing. So it is that in the capitals and villages of the Arab, Asian, and, to a less degree the African Muslim world there are many western "Christian" wives who have been required, actually or virtually, to Islamise and whose religious independence, even supposing they retain the will for it, is precluded by social mores and religious bigotry. Though they may have been forewarned, love is always hopeful, or impatient of scruple. The sequel is often a far more pathetic, even tragic, version of "the longest journey", which was Shelley's characterization of marital tyranny.[4]

It is proper, then, to register a steady protest – necessary often in interchurch, as well as interfaith marriages – against this kind of absolutist oppression which demands a total surrender or exacts an entire capitulation. For such eventualities are finally disloyal to the nature both of religious faith and married partnership.

...nor Two-Party Indifferentism

The second *modus vivendi* (or should we say *modus moriendi?*) is indifferentism. Marriages all too often settle acquiescently into a negligent attitude which evades the difficult issues by falling back into unconcern. Religion, anyway, is a tedious business; dogmas are provocative of tension; worship, fasting, and observances focus otherness. Is it not better to lapse with the secular temper into the "tolerance" which is really abeyance of belief and lassitude of will?

So it is that in Baghdad, Teheran, Cairo, Singapore, and the cities too of the western world, one finds, as well as the submerged capitulated, the partnering indifferent – American-Turkish, German-Iranian, Anglo-Malayan, Dutch-Indonesian, Scandinavian-Indian, and many other couples – who are inter-faith in hardly more than name. Having likely met and united in the context of university study, or trade, or diplomacy, or simply of travel, they may have been liable anyway to a certain secular drift or direction, and this their marriage has accelerated or approved.

As such their situation, as a pastoral burden, merges into the larger problem of our present wistfulness for renewal under God. The sincerity, or at least the implicit concern against hypocrisy, often present in such now secular marriages, must be respected. Even without the doctrinal or symbolic and liturgical context of established faith, there may be good hope of serving such anti-institutional temper, in its integrity, by caring with them for new forms of the sacred which certainly survive within the mysteries of human, and not least of married, meaning, and because of which no indifferentism need be reckoned hopeless. It is simply that we are called, from within our faith, to a longer patience and a livelier resilience in the Holy Spirit and in the compassion of Christ.

... but Authentic Mutuality

The third option, the truly interfaith duality, is the search for authentic existence in which love inter-animates the two traditions *because* it inter-animates "both their hearts and bodies".

But how, it will be asked, can this be so, both in spirit and in practice? Does not the prayer just quoted continue ". . . in the ways of Thy laws and the works of Thy commandments"? How can these be diversely understood? Is truth divided? How is there to be concord between a faith that "the Word was made flesh" in the lowliness of Jesus as the Christ, and the assurance that such condescension (on God's part) or such pretention (on Jesus' part) are quite untenable? How is one to co-exist with the Holy Communion on the one hand, as the focus of the redeeming Cross, and the conviction that Jesus was too good and the Lord above too sovereign for such redeeming ignominy to be either necessary or conceivable? How does one relate Christianly to Muhammad as "the final prophet" out of loyalty to Jesus the Christ as the inclusive Word and revelation of the Father?

And, within all these and other issues, how does one communicate a creative duality (if creative it be) to one's offspring? And what may one do about the observances of Sunday and of Friday, of sacrament and pilgrimage, of Lent and Ramadān, of bread and wine and Qur'ānic recital which, seemingly, stand in open competition and mutual exclusion?

These are real questions and answers need to be achieved. "Achieved" is the word, for if marriages around them exist, the answers cannot be discursive. It seems clear that some at least of the impulses and suggestions in *Two-Church Families* and other inter-Christian ventures (discussed elsewhere in this Consultation) can be translated into interfaith idiom also. That enterprise is doubtless more difficult, more exacting, more tentative. But it is very much an open option.

Between spouses of differing loyalties there needs to be – as, in another idiom, between scholars in dialogue about religions – what has sometimes been called an *epoche*, a pausing, or holding-up, in the instinct to disqualify. "This . . . *not* that" doctrine and ritual instinctively say. The *epoche* is content simply to say "This", and allows another to do the same. The foreclosing simplicity (and convenience) of sheer distinction is suspended, not against, but out of, a positive loyalty to one's own, in the confidence that it can keep a longer patience, that it has no proper need to be magisterial with or for its own fidelity, that it can truly afford the magnanimity which does not "salute its brethren only", but has a will for what it hopes to reconcile.

This temper or posture of mind is surely in harmony, on reflection, with the instinctive nature of troth. But it is also a more imaginative and fitting attitude to the trust of truth. For it avoids riding rough-shod over all complexities of language and meaning. It leaves room for the judgement of God and the patience of the Spirit. It is saved from reading its own assumptions into the other's myth or rite or concept and so is open to their inner point.

As between mosque and church, Qur'ān and Gospel, sufi and saint – and all in Bradford, Istanbul, Lagos, or Lahore – it may then be seen that there are wide areas of common meaning, that even due controversies have hidden kinships without which they could not matter, and that what still divides belongs with what unites. Reference may perhaps be made here to a simple anthology of Christian-Muslim prayers in documentation of this claim.[5] This collection, made over many years and out of many lands and centuries, demonstrates the common language of Muslim and Christian devotion in praise, penitence and petition. In all honesty, it does not incorporate *all* that Muslims and Christians are in their distinctiveness. Nor does it in any way propose, or sustain, some easy identity of spirituality. But it is not to be idly condemned by the unexamined cry of "syncretism". To refuse the evidence of its contents, in rejecting the Muslim, would be rejecting part of one's self as Christian. Thus it may be seen to point a way towards such measure of common intercession as may come to characterise an interanimation between the two faiths that is more than academic and discursive – the sort of common prayer which must surely obtain in an interfaith household that is authentic in its partnership.

It is on such basis of discovered kinship of heart and of a will toward God that the vexed and vexing controversies may be broached, within the *epoche*. And here hope must be given its due rein. The Islamic attitude to Jesus incarnate is by no means so adverse as much polemic has assumed, once it is seen that the greatness of God, so precious to the Islamic mind, is not violated, that the question about that greatness is not *whether*? (so that it is doubted) but *how*? (so that it is fully held in awe). The Christian is one with the Muslim in confessing *Allāhu akbar*, "Greater is God". The question is: by what measure? That of potentate, or shepherd? Serenity above, or Bethlehem below? There are thus Islamic reasons for being Christian: we need the Islamic sense of God even to differ from it, and the onus of our controversy is the ally of our hope.

Likewise with that other sharp arena of our tension, the Cross as divine design and Jesus crucified as "the power and the wisdom of God". Here, too, there are negative misconceptions to be excluded and there are positive affinities to plead. What matters essentially for the Muslim is that the divine prerogative of forgiveness and mercy is seen to be altogether free, adequate and plenteous, needing no device, or scheme, or aid, *via* a suffering Saviour, to enable it to operate. All too easily we seem to preach the Passion as that by which "God is able to forgive" and so we play into the hands of the suspicion that we think Him otherwise inadequate. But, probing this confusion, does it not emerge that a truly untrammelled divine fiat, or prerogative, of mercy does indeed avail us, but that it is not effortless, or unconditioned – we being the sinful creatures that we are? So, again, the question about mercy in God, is not whether? (assuredly Yes!) but how? Then the Cross may come to be seen as just where that plenteous (Islamic) mercy is taking its gloriously adequate (Christian) highway into the world of all of us. And, though this is a longer story, the Qur'ānic disallowing of the crucifixion, insistent as it has been, is by no means exegetically so antithetical to a wisely formulated Christian understanding of the Cross as has been traditionally supposed by Christians and assumed by Muslims.[6]

There is much else at stake. These, though salient, are no more than examples of how the living openness and sensitivity of dialogue may anticipate its rewards of mediation and discovery with "the mystery of Christ". Is it altogether beyond expectation that some at least of the interfaith unions of authentic troth could be the matrix of such relationships on behalf of the larger wholes that "gave" them into marriage?

Probably a mood of scepticism persists. The foregoing is certainly an exacting hope, remembering all the properly mundane pre-occupations, the human frailties, the social pressures, the personal foibles that belong with married existence. But, if our business has been to trace the theological vocation and to measure the pastoral ambition that must be ours, then surely it is here. Weddings, no doubt, "fade into the light of common day". It would be idle, and not marriage, to think it might be otherwise. Yet is not the wedding's enthusing hopefulness, its ardent aspirations, the fibre even of prosaic wedded-ness? If the troth was truly "interfaith" have we misread what, however rarely or remotely, its continuity might mean?

It was John Donne who used to pray at the altar: "Make all the days of their life like this day unto them: and as Thy mercies are new every morning, make them so to one another".

Notes

1. It may puzzle some readers why the discussion here does not first deal, as a prior matter, with the question whether interfaith marriages should take place at all. Such a query may likely have St Paul's dictum in mind about not being "unequally yoked with unbelievers". (2 Cor.6:14). It is agreed that there may well be situations where it is a strong pastoral obligation to dissuade and, if possible, preclude potential unions, the more so where the odds, as determined by factors, personal and general, seem to be heavily against their viability. But, as Father Adrian Hastings argues in his paper, it would be wrong to assume, undiscriminatingly or undiscerningly, that such dissuasion was the only appropriate course. For one might then be quenching a potential of love, and arguing without the grace of God. One should beware of reading in St Paul's warning against evil's contagion as a total verdict against alternative cultures and traditions.

2. The fuller implications of this rich term *libās*, and other aspects of Muslim understanding in this field, may be had in the writer's *The Dome and the Rock*, SPCK (1964) pp. 151–161, "Islam and Sex". See also G. H. Bousequet: *Islam et Son Ethique Sexuelle*, Paris (1953), Nouvelles Editions (Islam no. 14).

3. Some readers may be inclined to protest that this brief summary is questionable, not only for its brevity, but for its "expectancy". A very different presentation, it will be said, could be made, out of wide sociological experience of the Muslim patterns of male dominance, of female seclusion and of religious rigorism – all of unlovely character. The author is in no way unaware of this sometimes dismaying picture. But the concern here has been with the Qur'ān's potential for the correction of the admitted actualities in its own societies. It is a deeply Christian posture to anticipate that any and every situation is redeemable and that hope, where it finds authentic grounds, is a truer relationship than censure.

4. The phrase occurs in one of his sharp denunciations of marriage and gave E. M. Forster the title for a novel in which he portrayed the "dreary journey" of the unloving "indissoluble". For captive wives in Islam it is the "irreversible".

5. Kenneth Cragg: *Alive to God, Muslim and Christian Prayer*, OUP (1970). The Introduction to this anthology attempts a careful assessment of the problems and possibilities of interfaith spirituality. It might conceivably provide a framework of family devotion in so far as this can be expressed in a common vocabulary and common concerns of praise, penitence and petition.

6. Interested readers may refer, *inter alia*, to the English text of Kamil Husain's Arabic *City of Wrong, a Friday in Jerusalem*, Djambatan, Holland (1959) and Seabury Press, New York (1964) being, with its Introduction, an illuminating Muslim study of what is at stake between Islam and Christianity in respect of Jesus crucified. For fuller discussion of the themes that must gather around a joint

Muslim Christian will to prayer and Godwardness, see *The Call of the Minaret*, OUP, New York, paperback ed. (1966) part 3 and bibliography. See also David Brown, *Jesus and God* (SPCK, 1967); *The Christian Scriptures* (SPCK, 1968); *The Cross of the Messiah*, London (Sheldon Press, 1970).

The Nature of Marriage

1. New Horizons in Christian Marriage

Enda McDonagh

In the conventional, transferred sense of new possibilities to be realised or new goals to be achieved, our era has abounded in new horizons in marriage as well as in other dimensions of human existence. How far these horizons have proved to be frustrating mirages and how far they have actually led to real achievement overall, has its own bearing on the particular dimension of marriage which concerns us but discussion of it would take us too far afield. How far these horizons could be described as Christian or at any rate compatible with Christianity will receive attention in the case of marriage.[1]

The generation of new possibilities inevitably depends on people and their creative abilities. It would be unwarranted to relate the amount of human creativity in any specialised sense to actual population figures; yet the population explosion of recent times has meant a sharp increase in the units of human consciousness, experience, reflection and possible inventiveness. The media explosion has simultaneously given a much wider voice to such experience and reflection so that at times we seem to be unable to cope with the wealth of experience, experiment, suggestion in the diverse dimensions of human living and, in particular, in that of marriage. New horizons in human living and dying pass in rapid succession across our television screens and our own individual consciousness. Marital ideals and practices from polygamy through hippy-style communes, "swinging partners", even to our own more numerous, "lack-of-due-discretion" couples, provide a dazzling array of other people's horizons when they do not entirely confuse or obscure our own.

The horizon game is more profoundly disturbing if we take seriously, as we must, the multiplicity of scientific approaches to the examination of marriage which have emerged in recent times. How much have horizons changed, through the work of the biologists, the biochemists, the geneticists, from the discovery of the ovum in the 1820s to the introduction of the pill in the 1950s? And of course other health and medical developments have reduced the infant mortality rate, extended life expectancy, increased the procreative span for most women, enlarged the population enormously and created a situation in which prospective life-together for married partners may be considerably longer when life-expectancy for both partners has greatly increased. (In Britain at the beginning of this century life expectancy for women was about 48 years, while now it is over 70). The further possibilities or threats which biological development offers (for example, through overcoming infertility or fertility, through test-tube babies, through genetic engineering, through safer and/or easier abortion) will also affect the horizons of marriage and continue to demand ethical clarification and a living response from Christians.

A different scientific viewpoint, that of the psychologists, has had, particularly in the aftermath of Freud, very deep influence on Western man's view of sex, marriage and the family. Combined with anthropological and sociological studies of the different sex and marriage patterns in primitive and sophisticated societies, psychological findings and theories have at once enlarged and threatened the human basis of our Christian understanding of marriage. The stages of sexual development as outlined by Freud and refined by his successors or the results of Kinsey's investigations into sexual habits in the United States of America, have greatly extended our knowledge and deepened our understanding. They may also have shaken our confidence in the ethical norms which we had traditionally accepted.

It is against a background of profound and continuing change in and challenge to so much of the conventional wisdom on sex and marriage that the Christian seeks his own horizon with its possibilities and goals. His response can never be simply one of flight or evasion from human developments, problems, challenges. In marriage above all he is acutely aware of the validity of the human and its development, as expressed in Creation and confirmed as well as transformed in Incarnation and Resurrection. I do not think that the theological differences between the churches on Redemption, Justification or Sacrament would prevent agreement on the basic character of marriage as a human created phenomenon which in the power of Jesus Christ has salvific value and divine significance. Because it is a human phenomenon it is subject to history with its ebb and flow of change and so Christian marriage is lived and understood in the interaction between Gospel message and human development. The story of that interaction is long and complex. The different churches give it their own nuances. However, the main structures of Christian marriage, born of that interaction, have remained constant and are agreed between the churches, although they may differ in detail from age to age. Christian marriage is based on the exclusive and permanent union of man and woman which is formed in love and open to new life in procreation. Diversity in ecclesiology, sociology, psychology or anything else has not obscured that agreement on basic structure. The horizons opened up in our own time can, for all their exotic manifestations and finally ambiguous character, only be tested, Christian-fashion, against this foundation.

With this shared background it is possible to suggest some lines of development for the human marriages of Christians in the years ahead. If I leave aside some of the more obvious problems mentioned earlier in connection with various scientific developments, biological, psychological or sociological, this is not because I underestimate their import-

ance or the difficulty they may pose for Christians. In a limited framework one has to choose and I choose what I consider to be the more positive possibilities opened up in our own time. These will, I believe, ultimately enlarge the Christian horizon more significantly.

One of the most seminal ideas of recent centuries has been that of democracy. From its original political setting it has found its way into industry and the economy, schooling, even the churches and, of course, marriage and the family. At the marriage level it is still very much in a developing condition as far as relations of husband and wife, of parents and children are concerned. The patriarchal family of yore may have disappeared for the most part in our culture but the restrictions on wives and children in life and in law are still very real. Democracy is based on a cluster of ideas deriving from the equality of all men as human beings. It operates in group form by recognising certain basic rights of all members of the group and ensuring them a say in decisions taken on behalf of the group. Confining our attention for the moment to the couple, the democratic spirit which is now ineradicable in our society (however much it may be obscured in practice at times) demands protection for the rights of wives beyond the measure afforded by our present outdated laws. For example, equal rights in family income and property with proper protection against desertion (and any other invasion of her rights) should be a normal part of our legal system and it should not require very much time or energy to provide the necessary legislation. Similar protection of children's rights is long overdue as is only too tragically obvious.

It may seem a rather harsh approach to new horizons for Christian marriage to call for such obvious legal safeguards. Legal reform will provide the necessary framework for the democratic character which modern marriage demands and which might be better described as partnership marriage. Partnership is, of course, a frame of mind before it is a framework of law. Without the mentality the law will avail little. Without the law one is unprotected against abuses arising from lack of the correct mentality. On the positive side the partnership concept of marriage ensures the mutual respect on which true unity is built. In the spirit of partnership the couple can enter on the enterprise of building a life and a home together with growing trust and security. If the partnership must enjoy at one level the protection of the law in regard to mutual rights and duties and on a basis of strict reciprocity, it must be animated at another level by personal feelings of trust and love. The partnership quality and the personal feelings will gradually encompass new members of the family in children. Recognition of their rights and increasing participation in family councils and decisions will gradually enable them to become full partners also.

The democratic ideal of partnership derives, as I said, from the political arena. It might well return there or, at any rate, be expanded both in defence of fundamental rights of the citizens and in increase of their participation in decision-making. The partnership marriage and family require a wider context of partnership in society if they are to survive, let alone thrive. The inner dynamism of the family itself, as it reaches out to neighbour, locality and all forms of wider society, will eventually lead to frustration, if such wider partnership is not guaranteed and practised. Is not all this based, fancifully perhaps, on "secular political" ideas which can hardly have very much relevance for the Christian outside their immediate sphere of reference? Not so! Marriage for the Christian is the dynamic human reality which is shared with all men. Its gospel structure, based on the interaction of the power and the message of the gospel with the human reality, is reinforced in its human and Christian character by the partnership concept. The equality of all men as created in the image of God, as redeemed in Christ, by whom all false historical barriers between men and women were destroyed, is realised more and more fully in the partnership marriage.

The Christian partners do not live in a religious vacuum either. The health of their partnership will be related to the partnership quality of their own Christian community. A patriarchal style is no more essential to that community than it is to the marital one. In the present climate it may be no less harmful to the Christian community as a whole and the married couples and families who constitute it. It is not a question of applying the criteria of parliamentary democracy to the Church (they may be badly enough in need of overhaul in the State). Yet a form of partnership with diverse functions but respect for certain fundamental rights and effective participation in decision-making should characterize the modern church in which everybody is expected to be not a passive believer but an active apostle.

Partnership between the churches is just as urgent as partnership within a particular church. In no area is this more true in Ireland than in that of interchurch marriage – the theme of this Consultation. Without genuine partnership, respect for fundamental rights and shared decision-making between the churches in this, but also in other areas of contact and conflict, the Christian message will be continually contradicted by Christian behaviour. It is to be sincerely hoped that the deliberations of this Consultation will, in a spirit of partnership, find a way to allow mutual respect and common decision-making by the churches and by the partners to an interchurch marriage, in the penultimate solution to this problem, which is all that can be expected in this sinful world. The partnership marriage then has ramifications far beyond the domestic hearth.

It can and should set the style and the standard for the various forms of social life, secular and religious. To the Christian this is scarcely surprising. At the heart of all social life in the Judeo-Christian tradition lies the Covenant, primarily between God and his people. This divine-human partnership which reached its climax in Jesus Christ forms the basis for fraternal covenant or partnership which has been established between all men and which receives its visible expression in the Church. In illustrating the structure and character of this covenant-partnership, human marriage has played a key-role from the teaching of the prophets down to St Paul. A partnership marriage not only expresses the covenanted or graced relationship which exists between the particular couple, it offers a model and a challenge to the Church itself and to all forms of human society.

character it remains a continuing and demanding task. The celebration in one flesh rejoices in the mutual gift and prepares for the common task. In its own structure it is essentially covenantal and can be the clearest human manifestation of God's covenantal love for his people. The *communio* of marriage illustrates again the communion to which all men are called in Christ. The particular marriage, its family life, its activity in the believing community and its contribution to the wider society should in word and deed extend that communion of humanity and sanctity we call God's kingdom.

Living love is always creative; it seeks to transcend itself, to expand out from its present confines to new centres or objects of that love. The loving communion of marriage is specifically directed in its creativity to the highest form of human creativity, the conception, bearing and rearing of further human beings, new centres of partnership, friendship and love. The gift of children through birth or adoption begins a new stage in the husband and wife relationship which will potentially enrich them and the wider community, but will make increasing, if also enriching, demands on their resources and those of the community. Perhaps enough has already been said about the parent-child relation – as it ought to develop in terms of partnership and friendship animated by love. Yet the horizon of parenthood may in practice be very unsatisfactory for the majority of parents and children. Too many fathers, for instance, might be opting out of parenthood altogether due to their involvement in their job. Too many parents may exclude themselves or be excluded from any effective participation in the child's development, i.e. education, once schooling starts. The now extended process of adolescence may develop into complete breakdown in communication, giving no scope for partnership or friendship. A great deal more attention should be paid to the stages of development in parenthood as in childhood, and parents should be drawn more effectively into the education of their children, which in turn should bear many more of the marks of partnership between school and home, between teachers, parents and children. The destruction, to which St Paul called attention, of the distinction between bond and free might require a little application in our educational system.

Christianity might well be interpreted or misinterpreted as a horizon game; one more utopian ideology which inspires its adherents with aspirations which are doomed to eventual frustration. Indeed many romantic couples floated into marriage on a wave of feeling only to founder on the first rock of difficulty. The difficulties, even fatalities in marriage, are notorious. How far the increasing divorce rate all over the world indicates greater marital unhappiness today than in earlier times when divorce was not so readily available, may be open to debate. At all events the failures in and of marriage are widespread and obvious. And it would be equally unchristian to shrug them off with more promises, with the Utopia this time displaced to the next life. The Christian takes suffering and failure seriously in this life. He knows that he is committed to fighting it, by seeking first of all to prevent it and, where that does not work, to overcome or at least alleviate it. His Master spent too much of his precious little time dealing with the ordinary this-worldly sufferings of his contemporaries for any Christian to feel that he can substitute a stony promise even of eternal life for genuine loving care and service of the suffering. The same Master's account of the final assessment of his disciples (Matt. 25) does not augur well for any self-styled Christian who passes the wounded by on the other side. Consciousness of and compassion for the wounded in marriage have grown apace in recent times. There remains an immense amount to be done in research, in providing trained personnel, in attracting voluntary workers, in financing social services which bear directly on marriage difficulties from case-work to home visitation to housing. The long-promised reforms in this area will not, I hope, be further delayed.

Prevention is naturally better than cure. We do have some achievement by voluntary bodies organised by the churches to provide pre-marriage education. But their own members would admit that they are reaching too few too late. For the rest, we have promises but no legislative or administrative action to help to prepare the vast majority of our younger people for marriage. The inadequate or – worse – divided witness of the churches cannot provide sufficient impetus or inspiration to ensure that the resources of society as a whole are harnessed to this essential educational and remedial work. If the new horizons of Christian marriage are not to be continuous judgment on Christian churches, some very energetic and co-operative initiatives are urgently required.

The historical horizons now opening up to human and Christian marriage are full of exciting challenges. They will meet their measure of failure in every individual marriage. Their final significance does not however rest on the rate of empirical success achieved, on the actual number of marriages which attain a high or, at least, satisfactory degree of partnership, friendship and loving communion, important as that is. For the historical horizon derives its ultimate meaning and significance from the Easter horizon revealed by the Risen Christ. And it is to that ultimate horizon that the Christian finally hopes to attain. The happiest of marriages is broken by death or it would be if we had not the promise of new and fuller life in the Resurrection. Here there may be no giving or taking in marriage but it is the charity which will in St Paul's words abide, the charity or love which receives its most intimate human expression in authentic marriage.

To highlight that further horizon, particularly in the area of sexual loving, Jesus and the churches have recognised the special call of celibacy for the sake of the Kingdom. It is the complement and not the rival of marriage, endorsing marriage's historical horizons which it does not precisely share, but joining with marriage to relate all our living and loving to the horizon beyond, yet encompassing, all our earthly horizons of family, society or church.

Note

1. This is the text of a lecture given at the first of the three public sessions which took place during the Consultation.

2. The Nature of Marriage: A Socio-Theological Critique

John Hayes

Discussion of the nature of marriage is in many ways relevant to a consideration of the problem of mixed marriage. Some measure of agreement on ideals for marriage is obviously necessary if the churches are to unite in joint pastoral care of intermarriage. This paper is intended to open up for discussion the subject of marriage ideals and to do so in the context of a socio-scientific perspective on marriage. The paper takes its shape from the parameters provided by this brief. It divides into the following parts. Firstly, the rationale for the introduction of social science data into theological discourse about marriage is discussed and, in addition, the general cultural context, social and spiritual, within which marriage is lived today, at least in the western world. Secondly, the lineaments of the contemporary intellectual debate about marriage are outlined, and the specifications for an adequate socio-scientific model are suggested. Thirdly, an appropriate model is chosen. This model is a Freudian one and was developed by Erik H. Erikson. This model is criticised on internal grounds. Fourthly, an attempt is made to specify what this model has to say to Christian theology and to the churches. Fifthly, we consider what Christian theology has to say to the model. By this means we can hope to enter into dialogue with a view of marriage that is widely influential to-day, to reanimate the theological discussion about marriage and to situate the problem of mixed marriage in a wider perspective.

I. Marriage: A Human Reality

There is considerable agreement in all the Christian traditions that marriage is a secular, a profane, a created, or a human reality. This fundamental truth about marriage is complemented by another truth: that the human reality of marriage is to be seen in some pattern of relationship to a sacral, a sacred, a redeemed order or to a divine saving mystery.[1] This is not to say that each and every Christian tradition,

or any theologian within any tradition, subscribes to all the poles mentioned here: sacral and secular; sacred and profane; grace and nature;
order of redemption and order of creation; human reality and saving
mystery – or even to a polarisation at all. Traditions and theologians
have their own preferred languages. A large part of the challenge and
the task of ecumenical theology is to tease out these languages and the
world-views that they embody. For the purposes of this paper however
it will be sufficient to take as accepted among the major Christian
traditions the human reality of marriage in an undifferentiated common
sense understanding of the term.

The common acceptance of the human reality of marriage can be
well justified on biblical grounds. Marriage is presented as part of the
natural order of things in *Genesis* as opposed to the exaltation of sexuality in the fertility cults of the Ancient Near East. Jesus is firmly in the
Genesis tradition, though marriage is transformed in the light of the *mys-
terion* in the New Testament theology of Ephesians 5:32-3. Again, the
history of marriage in the Christian traditions is a history of involvement
with the human values of the institution of marriage. In the early Church
and in patristic times there was no formal distinction between marriage
as a universal human institution and the marriage of Christians, except
that Christian marriage should not be dissolved. When the Church came
to acquire jurisdiction over marriage in the Middle Ages she took over
the existing Roman law and customs and largely preferred them to
Germanic customs. There was a tendency however to move beyond the
Roman model of marriage as a family affair for the upper-classes to
marriage as a personal choice open to everyone. Ideas about the
equality and freedom of men under God fostered this development.

The Middle Ages also saw the development of the theology of
marriage as a sacrament. This development should be seen not only
against the background of the growth of church jurisdiction over
marriage but also as a specific application of the general medieval
sacramental theology. For their part, the Reformers believed that such
a theology of marriage destroyed the authenticity and partial independence of the secular sphere. They firmly located marriage in the structure
of Creation and under the authority of the civil magistrate, who was
however ordained of God. The Roman Catholic Church on the other
hand maintained so far as possible its authority over the marriage of
Christians in virtue of its sacramental character. In this view, the state
had authority over the civil effects of marriage only.

Marriage has nevertheless come more and more under the aegis of
secular legislation. This legislation has followed out essentially the
implications of Christian ideas about marriage as a personal choice
open to all and has swept away many of the restrictions of the old canon
law against marriage within certain degrees of relationship and against
mixed and interchurch marriages. In the twentieth century, ecoles-
iastical legislation has followed this nineteenth century trend in civil
law.[2] Secular control over marriage focuses attention not only on
questions of transfer of power from ecclesiastical to civil jurisdictions
but also on questions having to do with the secularisation process by
which marriage has been affected. More fundamental than jurisprud-

ence are the ideas by which men live and the milieu in which they live them which good jurisprudence will reflect. A theology that is committed to the integrity of the human character of marriage as we have taken it here will take seriously both the ideas and the milieu. This includes as we shall see the context of idea and culture as reflected in the social sciences.

Broadly speaking, the ideas men have held concerning man and his destiny in Western civilisation have been derived from three sources viz., the Judaeo-Christian religious traditions, humanism, and science. These three have always been in tension, have "contained conflicting notions, and were never articulated with any thoroughgoing logic".[3] In the modern era the powerful union of applied science, finance, and industrial organisation together with the decline of religion and its replacement by secular ideas has tended to weight the precarious balance in the direction of science and technology.

The nature of our social life has been profoundly influenced by the industrial base and urban character of modern society. The family, as "the natural and fundamental group unit of society",[4] has in the logic of things come under pressure from and been shaped by this new society. For example, there is now a longer period of dependency of children on parents for education, a higher degree of social mobility, and better health care than before. There are many more options for women other than motherhood and the costs in bearing and rearing children are higher. It is highly probable that all of these factors enter into the decisions of couples regarding family size. One can capture imaginatively the overall trend in the philological fate of the Greek *oikos*, house. In the Roman Empire domestic self-sufficiency was both the ideal and the practice. What kept people alive was the "oeconomy" which was centred on the domestic hearth. The main purpose of marriage was to keep the ancestral fires burning in that hearth. And this was a religious task. Nowadays, what keeps people alive is the "economy".[5] Domestic life tends to serve the economy's large-scale demands and this life at home, like the system which it serves, is quite without religious meaning.

Profound dissatisfaction with modern industrial society and its effects on family life has been expressed in many quarters. Conservatives believe that the shattering of traditional society and its time-honoured customs, values and ways of life has made the achievement of social order and of individual harmonious development difficult. Radical criticism, on the other hand, tends to concentrate on the psychic manipulation practised by the political and economic agencies of modern society. Thus, from both conservative and radical fronts today the conviction emerges that "modern technology is destroying the emotional and collective life not only of those immediately caught up in it but of the entire society".[6] There is some exaggeration in this, at least on the short term. There are certain limits to the amount of pressure an industrial society can afford to bring to bear on family life if society as a whole is not to be destroyed. Given that a man's home is now one of the few places where he can recreate his spirit, and that society needs able-minded workers, it is in the interests of the managerial elites and the technocratic planners to listen to the human voice of their workers. There is however no guarantee that the pursuit of wealth and power by technocratic means will not in the end destroy man. For the moment at least there is some evidence that family life and the different political and cultural organisation of specific societies in which this life is lived out profoundly modify the way in which a modern economic order is received.[7]

One can say however that there is a compelling set of forces, material and spiritual, which makes industrial society attractive despite the difficulties. There is, after all, much to be said for the view that "our society is more humane than any that existed before".[8] Because of our economic arrangements there is now the possibility – and, in Western Europe, North America, and the Westernized East, the widely-fulfilled reality – of adequate food, lodging, health care, and educational opportunity. The long-term cost of this achievement is another matter and the debate about it is far from resolved.

The ineluctable promise and attraction of industrial society is not material, however, but spiritual. It is the promise and the attraction of freedom. Max Weber discovered this early in his studies of the agricultural labourers in the German provinces east of the Elbe. These labourers would foresake a centuries-old patriarchal system of economic organisation with considerable financial security in return for work in the "iron cage" that somehow gave "expression to the tremendous and purely psychological magic of 'freedom' ".[9] The settled security of a tenured life with kith and kin did not appeal even when in monetary terms it was superior.

With regard to marriage, the ideal of freedom applies, as we have noted, to the choice of a marriage partner. In general, interpersonal goals have superseded property goals in partner selection. The arranged marriage which often gave expression to those goals is now a rarity in modern society. The belief in the person as constituted by his freedom has gradually had the effect of stressing the importance of consent, of lifting restrictions on the marriage of certain classes of persons, and of at least tolerating marriages that violate other kinds of exogamous taboos. In a mobile industrial society, marriages that break down occupational, geographic, political, historically established, ethnic, religious, as well as class barriers are more likely, if as yet by no means without difficulty. A young couple today will in any event live in less dependency on their original group or groups, and even their kin, than heretofore. A pattern approaching that of an isolated conjugal or "nuclear" family seems to be appearing. In consequence the marital relationship itself is more significant and more onerous because more of the emotional well-being of the partners and children depends upon it.

The ideal of freedom as applied to the choice of marital partner is now less controverted than is its application in another direction: that of sexual pleasure. The separation of sexual intercourse from procreation which was made fully secure by the anovulant pill allows freedom for couples to love sexually without the inhibition that stems from the possibility of another, perhaps unduly burdensome, pregnancy. The development culminating in the discovery of the pill, has been seen in some theological quarters as profoundly threatening to that cluster of ideas which constitutes Western Christian sexual morality and in particular to those aspects of it which condemn contraception (and abortion) and which justify marital intercourse by a procreative purpose. This Christian position has been criticised for being oppressive of married life and unappreciative of the interpersonal dimensions and context for sexual intercourse. And many Christian theologians agree with this criticism.

There is concern in a wider theological circle about doctrines of sexual liberation which directly challenge the Christian moral ideal that limits sexual intercourse to a marital relationship which is monogamous, permanent, and responsible towards children born. The Christian churches, it is argued, have cultivated a distrust of sensual pleasure and this perhaps with the sinister purpose of controlling men and their institutions. The invitation is now that man through science should take control over himself and over all aspects of his nature, including his sexuality. Sexual mores are in this view solely and simply a private matter and civic legislation should reflect this as well. An extensive critique of Christian ideas has been developed along these lines and it behoves the churches and theology to come to grips with it.

II. The Modern Critique and the Specifications for a Model

The critical mood is in phase with a marked change in the ratio between expression and inhibition of sexuality in the public forum since Victorian times. If there is no more sexual activity than there ever was, there is certainly more discussion about it. This discussion is matched by a libidinisation of the mass media which often subvert sexuality to the market processes. The arts are also more erotically explicit than in recent centuries. The open discussion, the libidinisation, and the eroticism may be partly a function of the fact that there are now more young people in the world proportionate to the total population than at any previous recorded time. Moreover most of them will be in a position to marry and to marry early. In this they are unlike people of the last century in Western Europe among whom there was a high proportion of celibates and of late marriages. This was due partly to economic stringencies. An activity which involves directly a high proportion of the population so intensely and intimately will be widely discussed, will be the object of commercial interest and exploitation, and will stimulate the artistic imagination. This is quite apart from the perennial human interest in the play, the delight and the enigma of sexuality.

Most of the questioning of the social institutions and moral ideas that have for a long time surrounded marriage is taking place in the liberal sector of the white upper-middle class elites of such developed countries as Scandinavia, West Germany, Holland, certain parts of Belgium, England, the United States, Canada, Australia, and New Zealand.[10] The permanency of the marital relationship is questioned in theory and in practice; and so too is it exclusiveness. More radically it is questioned whether marriage should be formally and legally institutionalised at all, and if so whether it should be confined to a pair or might perhaps include several partners serially or simultaneously. Again, it is disputed whether homosexual couples might not marry. And so it goes.

The ideas, curiosities, and activities of this elite are influential because its members have access to the media of communication. Styles and fashions in mores travel all over the world from extremely tiny and concentrated centres of sophisticated living in the great cities of the industrial north. It may be that the exploration of theoretical possibilities which is at the heart of the scientific process (and, in the form of a restless curiosity in the mode of Don Juan, at the heart of modern culture)[11] has prompted the acting out of these possibilities in those parts of the world most influenced by science and technology. In these places modern industrialism has had most influence. This has involved both the destruction of the older extended family structure (and its restraints) and provided the affluence and the challenge to experiment (usually in the form of creation of "life styles").

Whatever the truth in these speculations and judgments regarding contemporary developments, we do know from the study of different societies and cultures by anthropologists that marriage is institutionalised in a great variety of ways. We know further from sociology that marriage is a different phenomenon among different people within our Western societies themselves. This would be the case for example between different classes of society. The knowledge of such differences has contributed significantly to that popular belief in the infinite malleability of man that is the correlative of those ideals of freedom that are central to the modern mind.

The social sciences were at first in the vision of Comte an integral part of that unlimited striving for human betterment without regard for human limits that was loosed on our civilisation by the French Revolution. This striving was fuelled by a moral passion for liberty, equality, and fraternity, and this passion was born of scepticism – though in an indirect fashion. The scepticism had been a widespread response to the Copernican revolution in physics. After Copernicus man was ousted from his central position in the universe and the existing theological cosmos was destroyed. Man now saw himself as but a "chance collocation of atoms, without purpose or meaning".[12] In such wise he was released from the Christian world, but retained nevertheless a Christian moral conscience. However, this conscience was directed not to man's individual salvation but to the betterment of human society instead.

These movements of thought reached their fullest expression in three figures of the nineteenth century. The destruction of the theological cosmos was proclaimed by Nietzsche; Marx expressed most profoundly the sense of moral indignation at the injustices of society; and Freud played the torch of scepticism on that most intimate citadel of all, the human psyche. The relentless critique of all three of these "masters of suspicion" has had a deep effect on our culture. They have expressed the trauma of our civilization. For this reason they cannot be ignored but they must be superseded. For in the end the scepticism undermines the morals as it has already the religion.[13]

In the area of sexuality no figure has been more significant than Freud in giving expression to the ideas that constitute the modern mind. In him there is a delicate equilibrium, or a subtle conflict which is not fully resolved, between a scepticism that would reduce human interaction to a physical model drawn from electromagnetics and a love of life that sees all forms of existence shaped by the force of *Eros*.[14] In his later works particularly, Freud conceived of man as in the hands of the mythic forces of *Eros* and *Thanatos*, and as regulated by *Ananke*, necessity. While this resort to the Greek roots of our culture saved Freud from a comprehensive nihilism, its effect was to re-inforce a passive view of man whose best thought might be to resign himself gracefully to his fate. This view is in any case already inherent in the *scientisme* that led Freud in his early work to speak of interactions as "mechanisms" and in the implication, never spelt out, that man is most himself when he is lying supine on a couch.[15]

New trends in the human sciences have moved away from images of man that regard him as the object of forces which if studied and codified as laws will render man manipulable and his behaviour predictable.[16] The freedom of man is now being taken extremely seriously. Far from being manipulative, no human science can even be "objectively" descriptive of human life, at least not according to Cartesian canons of objectivity. No observer can exclude his own subjectivity from the act of observing. We know by committing ourselves to what it is we want to know even though we have no clear apprehension of what that is. We believe or entrust ourselves in order to know. When the subject studied is man we entrust ourselves to a reality who is free, as we are free, and whose being is constituted on many interacting levels of existence. There is thus both an inviolable freedom and an excess of intelligibility about man. All conceptual models are inadequate but nevertheless relatively valid avenues to the truth about the kind of being man is and further what it is he ought to be doing on this earth in virtue of the truth about that being.

It is clear that the attempt to reach the truth about marriage must be set against the background of the truth about man. The institution, after all, serves man and not the reverse. The chosen model should reflect this basic perspective. While it is imperative to move beyond Freud, his extraordinary contribution to the study of man cannot be underestimated. He it was who opened up the area of sexuality to scientific inspection and there are signposts towards reconstruction in him which are valuable, in particular the stress on the centrality of love in human life. The model developed by Erik Erikson does see marriage in the perspective of a comprehensive anthropology which is open to the multi-dimensionality of man's existence and to his ethical concerns.[17] It is a Freudian model but goes beyond Freud. We must now turn to Freud and to the movement beyond him represented by Erikson for a model of human development that will enable us to situate the human reality of marriage correctly and to see it clearly in its fullness.

III. The Model and an Internal Criticism

Freud attempted to describe the vicissitudes of love in the growth and development of the person. To be sure his concern was with pathology rather than with normality, with sadism or masochism for example rather than with interdependent love. His concept of deviation, however, implies a norm from which a developmental process deviates. The movement in psychology to which Erikson belongs, ego-psychology, is concerned with making this normative development more manifest.

However, a base already exists in Freud. He had been trained as a physiologist in the era after Darwin. To sketch the growth and development of things according to the evolutionary pattern was the scientific task. Freud showed that sexuality develops in stages. These stages were understood in an analogy with physiological development *in utero*. Each organ has its own appointed time of emergence in the development of the foetus. If the proper rate or sequence of growth is disturbed for any reason, the result may be a *monstrum in excessu seu in defectu*. Growth is determined by the epigenetic principle. Somewhat generalised, this principle states that whatever grows has a ground plan. Out of this ground plan the various parts arise. Each part has its time of special ascendancy. At the end of the process all the parts will have arisen and will form a functional whole. Thus, in Freud's theory of sexuality the mouth is the centre of libidinal activity in the first years of life; the anus in the second and third years; and the phallus in the third to fifth years. Adult sexuality takes its special genital form in the period from the eleventh to the fourteenth year after a period of sexual latency. Genital sexuality organises the sexuality of the previous stages in a new *gestalt*, or overall pattern.[18]

In both Freud and Erikson the struggle for human growth and development is intimately linked with the institution of marriage, or else something very like it. And indeed it is sobering to reflect amidst the changes in our social life that our economic organisation imposes, our fantasy concocts, and our imagination envisages, that "the family, consisting of a more or less durable union, socially approved, of a man, a woman, and their children, is a universal phenomenon, present in each and every type of society".[19] It is through this institution primarily that the development of the young is ensured. This development is more protracted in humans than among other animals, and the nature and length of the rearing process in humans has a profound effect on the requirements for human mating. Without a stable institution to ensure this development, the species would die.

If Freud outlined the stages of *libidinal development*, Erikson was able to show how primitive *social relationships* were already implied in the process of human emergence at this organic level of man's existence. These social relationships are characterized successively as *trust*, *autonomy*, *initiative* and *industry*.

If the child develops psycho-sexually according to the oral, anal, phallic and genital schedule, and if, further, the child develops psycho-socially so that trust wins out over mistrust; autonomy over shame and doubt; initiative over guilt, and industry over inferiority, there is a sound basis for those strengths which enable people to survive with an active mastery of the environment, with a sound perception of the world and of themselves, and with a certain unity of personality. These strengths carry a person through the inevitable shocks of existence. No matter how successfully the development crises are negotiated there is always to a greater or less degree a new sense of estrangement from previous fields of emotional significance. These fields are in large part the creation of the parents at the early stages of life.[20] Growth in autonomy involves a succession of birth experiences in which former securities are set aside and the child more and more creates his own fields of action and feeling. He cannot however do this, and especially he cannot himself become a good parent, unless he has received love at the proper time and in the proper manner. However, there are some therapies, professional and otherwise, by which previous deficiencies and deprivations can be made up to some degree. Indeed the marital relationship itself often takes on the character of an informal therapy of this sort.

Before marriage and parenthood the crisis of adolescence has to be worked through. At this time in life the whole archaeology of person-hood – on the levels of organism, of society, and of responsible person – is thrown into disarray. Physiological change which involves body growth as rapid as that of early childhood with the addition of genital maturity lies at the base of the adolescent crisis. Traditional psycho-analysis saw here the time of re-awakening of the old oedipal "family romance". The problem of libidinal attachment to the parent of the opposite sex was solved in the old view by romantic attachment to a partner outside the family at adolescence. There is no denying the many important aspects of the adolescent crisis that involve sexuality but adolescent "falling in love" is "by no means entirely, or even primarily, a sexual matter – except where the mores demand it".[21] Rather, the adolescent is attempting to arrive at a clarification of his own identity by projecting it onto another and seeing it reflected back. Erikson goes on to say that "this is why so much young love is conversation".[22] Thus, only when the main work of adolescence is accomplished (that of achieving a consistent identity) does sexual love in a full sense become possible and so marriage.

Today, adolescence is an ever more marked and conscious period of the life-cycle. For reasons that form a complex interaction of economic and demographic factors adolescence has become almost a way of life between childhood and adulthood. The process of identity is in conse-quence often more protracted today than it was before. This process involves letting "oneself be identified as a circumscribed individual in relation to a predictable universe which transcends the circumstances of childhood".[23]

The adolescent peer group is now very significant in this largely unconscious process. This group confirms the person's continuity of meaning for others at the very time that his inner subjective continuity with the child that he once was is most in question. The inner confusion of adolescents is the reason that their groups have the exclusive (because insecure) quality of cliques. Typically, adolescents over-identify with the heroes of these cliques and with their ideals. Within the groups there is a testing, often to the point of perversity, of the members' capacity to pledge fidelity and in fact, the constellation of virtues most exemplified and prized by adolescents is that of truthfulness, sincerity, conviction, genuineness, authenticity, loyalty, fair-play, and devotion.

The adolescent however is rarely capable of ethical response in the strict sense because his fidelity, the cornerstone of his identity, is as yet too closely linked to and dependent upon affirming companions and confirming ideologies. In Erikson's view, the adult ideologies in the world and the identities that they confirm, do not normally represent an advance on the exclusive and totalistic quality of adolescent cliques. It seems to him that "each horde or tribe, class or nation, but then also every religious association has become *the* human species, considering all the others a freakish and gratuitous invention of some irrelevant deity".[24] The world has been divided into in-group and out-group. The evil in the world is projected onto the out-group. Members of this last group accept the evaluation of the dominant group and identify themselves in a negative fashion as "invisible", "nameless", or "faceless", as in short, a "nobody". What must be aimed at is the replacement of totalistic identities whether positive (but gained at the expense of an out-group) or openly negative, with the wholeness of a more inclusive identity. A more inclusive identity is "a development by which two groups who previously had come to depend on each other's negative identities (by living in a traditional situation of mutual enmity or in symbiotic accommodation to one-sided exploitation) join their identities in such a way that new potentials are activated in both".[25]

In the new industrial estate the identity conferred by occupation tends to solve pragmatically in the work situation the tensions created by ethnic, class or religious affiliation. This is still a far cry from an identity honed on the profound conviction of the dignity and respect that belong to every man irrespective of his origins or group. The divisions in the world, with their adolescent rather than adult or ethical quality, still provide the matrix within which marital choices are made. In spite of the changes wrought by industrialisation, most marital choices are still homogamous. In social terms, like marries like. A certain parity of wealth, age, religion, and social status normally provides the framework for love. On the other hand, there is diversity and complementarity on the level of psychological need within the homogamous situation.[26] It seems that it is an illusion to look with great expectation to the mobile industrial society to solve the intergroup tensions that make mixed marriages difficult. This is so because the existing groups are still quite resistant to dissolution, because the new groupings created by the criterion of merit exercise their own taboos, and because graduates from the ghettoes may be repressing rather than transcending their past in return for a commanding place in the rat-race. Men need to find new ways of living in their native communities so that they can at once be themselves and at the same time allow other contingent groups to be themselves. This cannot be done on the basis of absolute loyalty to one's group, but rather on the basis of a respect for the rights of every man because he is a man, and not simply because he is some favoured kind of man.[27]

A man or a woman who has emerged as an organism, as a social being, and finally as a responsible self who respects others, is the best candidate for marriage. The sixth stage of Erikson's life-cycle covers the period of courtship in which marital choices are made and it follows the history of the person in a marital relationship until early middle age. This period is marked in the first place by the consolidation of the identity achieved in adolescence and by engagement in productive work. A crucial aspect of this period is entry into caring and sharing relationships with a sexual partner and with friends. Failure to achieve intimacy in this way can result in a sense of isolation.

The key challenge to a couple entering marriage in psychological terms is to transfer "the experience of being cared for in a parental setting . . . to a new, and adult affiliation which is actively chosen and cultivated as a mutual concern".[28] The new affiliation is love. The partners confirm one another's identity precisely through the loss of self in sexual surrender to the other. The experience is one of losing oneself to find oneself.

Erikson delineates a utopia of marital relationship. Such a utopia involves: 1. mutuality of orgasm; 2. with a loved partner; 3. of the other sex; 4. with whom one is able and willing to share a mutual trust; 5. and with whom one is able and willing to regulate the cycles of *a*. work, *b*. procreation, *c*. recreation; 6. so as to secure to the offspring, too, all the stages of a satisfactory development.[29]

Marriage involves the creation of a joint life-style by two members of the opposite sex. Built into this relationship is a certain polarisation which is rooted, Erikson believes, in anatomy. His experiments convinced him that the sexes adhere to two differing but complementary principles of arranging objects in space and that these principles correspond closely to the basic construction of the male and female bodies. In accord with his general epigenetic principle in virtue of which the organic level is not repudiated but rather assumed into a higher and more differentiated level of being, Erikson believes that the difference in somatology has to be taken account of in psychology.[30] Practically speaking, this means that in marriage there will always be antagonisms. These antagonisms are inherent in the divided functions that are strongly suggested, when not imposed, by anatomy. However, this polarisation, and the distribution of labour which it entails, can and should be assumed within an overall pattern of love for one another and care for the young. The polarisation also makes for a mutual enhancement of experience. It is love, in mutual devotion, that works to subdue the inherent antagonisms and to enhance the experience of complementarity in marriage.

In most cases, middle age sees the marriage of a couple widen into a family formed by their children and themselves. This time of life has its own crisis to which Erikson gives the name "crises of generativity". What is asked of an individual at this time is the subordination of his personal needs and comforts to a concern for future generations, for the quality of life, and for the society in which his children will live. The institutions of education, art, and science are the special care of the middle aged. This stage of life is best characterised by a care that is a "widening concern for what has been generated by love, necessity, or accident".[31] This care "overcomes the ambivalence adhering to irreversible obligation".[32] If the quality of care is not exercised the person may "suffer the mental deformation of self-absorption, in which he becomes his own infant and pet".[33]

The qualities of fidelity, of love, and of care unfold in a certain development pattern. This pattern is dependent upon a satisfactory interaction with various significant individuals in a person's life and it requires for its maintenance an interdependent activation of respective strengths. All adult encounters should be characterised by a spirit of active choice, for only he who comes to another "in a (consciously and unconsciously) active and giving attitude, rather than a demanding and dependent one, will be able to make of that encounter what it can become".[34] Against the background of these considerations the work of love can be said to be the activation of the person loved in whatever strength is appropriate to his age, stage, and condition, just as the person who loves is thereby activated in the strength appropriate to his age, stage, and condition in life. A happy interchange of this kind, and no more crucially so than in the choice of a partner and life together with him or her, prepares a person for old age and death. Integrity is the stamp of the person who can sincerely look back on his life with satisfaction; despair is the fate of those who must look on their life's course with repugnance.

In some notable respects Erikson's scheme can be criticised from within the social sciences, especially by scientists with a strongly positivistic epistemology. Though his image of human development can be verified in some detail by empirical observation, it does have what Freud himself called a "mythological" aspect. For example, the scheme presupposes monogamy but there are societies that are polygamous. Again, the model presents marriage as a complex relationship over a span of many decades in which the needs and expectations of the partners change as well as their ability to fulfill those needs and expectations. The notes of this complex relationship are exclusivity, permanence and responsibility towards children. Yet, we have divorce, infidelity and irresponsibility. At what point, we may ask, does an empirically verifiable trend such as polygamy, divorce or adultery become as ethically valuable as any other empirically verifiable trend such as monogamy or permanence in the marital relationship? The question is irresolvable on the level of a mere cataloguing and comparison of behaviour. What is suggested here is that the scientist too makes an ethical choice. For his part Erikson believes that it is worthwhile to "recognise, even in glaring deviations, the order suggested by the way in which human beings strive to grow".[35] This he does in a manner that has as much intuition as rationality in it.[36] To read the suggestions of biology is as much art as it is science. There is some evidence here of that appreciation of form which characterised German medicine of the nineteenth century.[37] The preoccupation with morphologies came with a profound sense of the order according to which life should be lived.

IV The Model and Christian Theology

The dialogue between Christian theology and the human sciences is still young and it involves considerable methodological problems. For his part, Paul Tillich has linked psychoanalysis with existentialism, the mode of his own theology, in the common root of a protest against the "increasing power of the philosophy of consciousness in modern industrial society".[38] The victory of the intellectualist outlook which had been building up for centuries was complete in Descartes. Thereafter there were but sporadic protests on behalf of the voluntaristic and irrational in man by Pascal, Kierkegaard, Nietzsche, and a few others. All of these figures portrayed the existential self-estrangement of man. Freud is in this stream. He described scientifically man's attempts to love and the agonies and shortcomings that bedevil this central human venture. Erikson does not neglect the element of tragedy in human existence to which Freud was so deeply sensitive. He does however complement the tragic sense with a solid appreciation for those victories in love that make life possible at all. In Freud, in Erikson and in the psychoanalytic tradition as a whole there is a reminder for theologians of the primacy of love in the moral life of man. As the movement of protest emerges in Erikson we receive a clear picture of the necessity, the patterns, and the timing of love, as well as of the failure of love.

It is clear that Erikson's model is built around the conviction of the central place of love in its various forms in human life. Love is not a luxury; it is a necessity. There are certain irreducible minima which must be present if the complex interaction of organism, society, and the individual is to take place and if the crises of life are to be resolved on ever higher levels of differentiation. The achievement of trust in an infant is not merely a desirable goal but an event that must take place. The same can be said about the outcome of the other life-crises and about the achievement of various human strengths at strategic points on life's way. Relatively successful victories of love in various forms are necessary if man is to survive as man. Man is always, from first to last, in a nexus of inter-personal relationships and his responses are aroused, confirmed, and dependent upon that nexus.

What we have then is a phenomenology of love. This phenomenology is controlled by the image of embryonic growth. Each stage of life calls for a specific form of love. The child is at first dependent on the care of its parents and increasingly of the wider community. After achieving the necessary sense of self in adolescence the young person can pledge fidelity to friends and ultimately to a loved one in erotic companionship. Finally, in his turn, the person takes care both of those and of that for which he has made himself responsible. All love, as fidelity, as erotic love, and as care, should be marked by giving rather than demanding. This gift takes the form of an appropriate response to the specific needs of one's counterplayer according to his or her stage of life. We can perceive here a comprehensive and inter-locking picture of the traditional four loves – *storge* (care); *philia* (friendship); *eros* (love); and *agape* (generous and unconditional love) – at work at the various stages of life. Erikson makes clear the reciprocity of the love of parent for child, or friend for friend, and of spouse for spouse. All of these loves combine or fail to combine in the formation of human community or the lack of it.

In Erikson the pain of the world is the result of the breaching of necessary nexus of mutuality and care. It is the pain of mistrust, of shame, of doubt, of guilt, of isolation, of stagnation, or of despair. Growth is disrupted by the disruption of the relationships which define and support a man or woman at any given time in his life. If there is any key to Erikson's account of love it lies precisely in the concept of a "time-for-everything". The disruption he fears is that of the sequence of crises in the developmental cycle rather than the disruption caused by moving from place to place which is so common in modern society. Such is the essence of Erikson's views. We shall now see their import in specific ways for theology, and in particular, a theology of marriage.

In Erikson's view marriage is the institution more than any other by which the necessary nexus of love is maintained. Here the young are cared for, and deep friendship and sexual love are cultivated. The evaluation of the importance of marriage and the identification of its values is not new data for theology. The early schoolmen, on whom so much of the theology and canon law of marriage is based, acknowledged severally all of these aspects of marriage, as well as its central place in the maintenance of human community. Isidore of Seville regarded marriage as the foundation of the human environment in which children could grow up; Hugh of St Victor situated the essence of marriage in the interpersonal relationship of the partners of the marital community, with or without sexuality; and the School of Chartres regarded marriage primarily as a sexual community.[39]

What is new is that the old values are seen in the horizon of development. Marriage includes all three of these aspects, friendship, sexuality, and the care of children. However, at one time or another, care, friendship, or sexuality will predominate in a relationship without a loss of the profound connection that exists with the other two. This connection (or the lack of it) will only become apparent if one takes the relationship over the whole course of its unfolding. Marriage involves a complex interaction of all three aspects over a long period of time and must be dealt with as a dynamic reality. The theological search for definitions of marriage such as was conducted by the early schoolmen may have been inordinately prompted by jurisprudential problems connected with the exercise of authority over the institution. While such control can be and was a form of service, it carries with it the dangers of focusing pastoral and theological concern on the *act* of getting married rather than on the *process* of being married. To place marriage in the horizon of development has the effect of reminding the churches of their responsibilities to be concerned not simply with that irreducible legal minimum which provides protection from anarchy but more deeply with the phenomenon of love and failure to love between a man and woman over the whole course of their lives which is marriage.

The churches' commitment to the process of marriage is in virtue of the Christian commitment to all authentic human values. This commitment is all the greater the more critical the values in question are to the project of human existence. It is clear that marriage and its values are extremely critical to this project. With this in mind, the churches should gear their pastoral services to marriage and family life over all the stages of their unfolding. Help, support, and care can be offered in the shape of material provision, psychological services, parent and family discussion groups, and uniquely, in a family-orientated liturgical life. While other agencies in a modern society are also involved in the long-term education and support for marital partners, the churches, in the spirit of the good shepherd, can seek out the areas of service that have not yet been developed, and can also help where existing resources are meagre. Whatever power comes because of services so rendered is not for its own sake but for further service. The churches must continually ask themselves if there is truth in the accusation of sceptics that much of their involvement with marriage and family-life is but an arbitrary exercise in oppressive social control.

The case for the involvement of the churches in the support of inter-church marriages at the present time is especially strong in view of the implication of the churches in the divisions that helped towards creating the difficulty in the first place. Mindful of Erikson's remarks about the adolescent quality of many of men's groupings, the churches should examine themselves to see if they are supporting the egoism of groups or calling instead these groups to wider and more elevated forms of human brotherhood. Support for the inter-church marriage would be one form of this call to a wider human community based on respect for the person rather than on a grasping for the security of conformist in-groups.

Erikson's scheme shows very well and in detail how a man can fail in his attempts to love at any point in his development. This can be for reasons connected with the incapacities with which his early environment and native endowment have burdened him. Positive steps can be taken to structure the institution in such a way that foreseeable difficulties are obviated so far as possible. For example, adolescent marriages cannot be encouraged since that stability of identity that is necessary for married love has not yet been achieved in most cases. The extended nature of adolescence in today's society compounds the problem. Civil legislation has increased the age of consent over the past century beyond the levels set by canon law. Pastors can in an informal way discourage teenage marriages.

Apart from obviating preventable breakdown through legislation and counsel, there still is the problem of the subsequent breakdown of what once seemed to be, and may indeed have been, stable. The conditions of life today make for difficulties. This is both because the level of expectation has risen considerably due to romantic ideals consolidated through the media and because in fact so much more emotional support must come from a spouse than before. A marital breakdown is slow and painful. Those who are involved in it need love, compassion, and encouragement. Christians, who have been admonished not to cast the first stone, should ponder whether we have been vindictive towards those in difficulty or compassionate. Christians can have no truck with that naïve moralism that sees lapses in sexual matters as uniquely vicious. Erikson would encourage us about the ability of people to cope with difficulty if given the right kind of help. Ideally, this help should be made available before the breakdown is irreversible but this may not always be possible. Legislation should reflect a spirit of realism about the fact of breakdown when it occurs and encourage, as far as any legislation can, the picking up of the broken pieces. Christians should not turn their back on the painful process of separation and the difficulties in creating a new life while not neglecting the obligations in justice to children or the need to foster an environment of marital stability through legislation and other means.

In sum then, Erikson is telling theology that love is central to human life, that marriage is crucial towards maintaining love, that this married love takes various forms, that one form or another will be in play predominantly in a marriage at a given stage of the marriage, that marriage is for the mature, that difficulties and crises are not unlikely and that in consequence couples need support. The churches are committed to the living out and support of authentic human values. Crucial among these are those connected with marriage. This means a creative and intelligent support for the married over the whole life of a marriage.

V Christian Theology and the Model

Erikson's model makes clear the necessity, the centrality, and the ways of love. Christian theology cannot but approve of the way in which Erikson has put love at the centre of his account of human life. Theology will want to see however how the light of revelation illumines further the meaning of love, human development, and marriage, which Erikson has explored.

The exemplar and source of all human loves is God's love. Love in the image of God is unreserved; it loves the unloveable; it is faithful in the face of infidelity; and it searches out new ways to do good for the beloved. Erikson also commends a generosity and a non-demanding attitude in love. And indeed all the great religious traditions, East and West, commend that we do unto others as we would they would do unto us. The death of Jesus is in this tradition. It is an example and a reminder that the loving man will lay down his life for his friend. The love which Christians exercise finds its deepest patterns in the death and resurrection of Jesus. We die so that we may live. Even if this does not mean literal death for the sake of the beloved, it is clear from Erikson's developmental scheme that progress in life and love involves a kind of *ascesis*. We leave old securities aside so that we can progress to new and more differentiated stages along life's way. For a Christian, this ascetic path and the suffering it entails are given a deeper meaning.

This deeper meaning becomes clear in the light of the fundamental Christian belief that the saving deed of Jesus is not only crucial to the understanding of human life and love but also uniquely crucial to the conduct of human life and love. Through the death and resurrection of Jesus, and only through the power of these events, are we saved from that cycle of selfishness, of pride, and of concupiscence, which Freud described with a precise eye on the model of a closed electromagnetic system. The failures in love by and towards his patients had put them in the Kierkegaardian state of "shut-up-ness". Their actions no longer possessed the dynamism of life but were locked instead in perpetual cycles of self-punishment and/or punishment of others. It is by the power of God's gracious deed in Jesus that we can love unselfishly and so be truly free and freeing of others. We are given this power at baptism when we are immersed into the passion, death, and resurrection of Jesus. Through this act our suffering is linked to His, and our hopes for life and for love to his resurrection. There is no other nor more secure hope.

It is clear from Erikson that marriage is crucial to the maintenance of structures of love in human life. It is in fact the most fundamental school of love for almost everybody. We learn our lessons at the feet of our parents. Again, since the majority of people marry it is the more usual path through which they express their love. Given the fundamental and universal character of marriage in the maintenance and structuring of love in human life it is not surprising that all the Christian traditions recognise the holy character of marriage. In line with certain aspects of the biblical tradition they have recognised that in erotic love there is a special kind of losing of one's life in order to find it. The gift of self and the loss of self is the paradoxical condition of the finding of self in erotic communion with the beloved. This finding of self is concretised in offspring which are a deeply gratifying link with the future and offer a relative kind of immortality. The bible can find no more appropriate image of God's love than that of erotic love. The bible consistently refuses to mystify marriage beyond its human dimensions. Nevertheless, the mystery of God's love, symbolised by erotic love, acts in a reflex fashion to open up new dimensions of understanding of marriage as a whole and of erotic love especially. It vastly enlarges the horizons within which the human reality of marriage can be understood both in its ecstasy and in its failure, and points in between.

To mediate these dimensions of understanding involves the discussion of theological problems of great difficulty and persistence which can only be mentioned here. While the Protestant tradition, classically represented in Calvin, has held the institution of marriage in the highest esteem and understands keenly its place in human life, it has not singled out marriage for special treatment as a sacrament. This is the case because marriage was not seen to fulfill the definition of a sacrament as a divinely instituted sign given to confirm a promise, because of the historical problems surrounding the recognition of marriage as a sacrament by the church, because the sacramental nature of marriage was thought to be asserted for reasons connected with jurisdiction rather than with fidelity to the gospel, and, implicitly, because recognition of the sacramental nature of marriage seemed to mitigate the authenticity of the order of creation to which marriage indubitably belongs.

Whether the deepest meaning of the process of marriage is to be expressed by a church ceremony which gives voice to the Christological meaning of the fundamental mystery of marriage with reference to the sacrament of baptism, or whether it is recognised as a special sacrament in its own right, it is clear that Christians are challenged to manifest liturgically the deep link that exists between an institution so intimately connected with the maintenance of love in human life and the economy of salvation. The salvation which is given us in Jesus Christ must be brought into domestic life. Jesus is the example of how that life should be lived and the power by which such living is possible. Theological debate that is too closely tied to problems of group identity is not an authentic listening to the word of God but simply an ideological debate that happens to use theological terms. There is some danger of this occuring today with regard to marriage.

The understanding of the centrality, the meaning, and the possibility of love as presented us in the story of Jesus impells Christians to be on the side of the institution of marriage as Erikson is. We do this for reasons that Erikson does not explicitly acknowledge, but to which his scheme is eminently open. However, our reasons may lead us to be more critical than he apparently is of the social order within which marriage has to be lived today. Christ stands above all existing social orders and in virtue of our faith in him we always maintain a critical stance towards any existing arrangement of human affairs. The larger sociological milieu of modern industrial society undoubtedly places a strain on the achievement of friendship, fulfilling sexual expression, and proper care of children by a couple. We must not only be on the side of finding new ways of living married life so that it will better support all who are involved in it, but also criticise society where it is impeding true human growth and development.

The Christian institution of celibacy stands as a reminder too that love should be played out on wider horizons than simply that of the family. Christian celibates are more free to pursue adventurous forms of service and to criticise society. The freedom from domestic involvements is for service but it can symbolise too the call of all men to a state beyond marrying and giving in marriage. There is a certain stifling domesticity about Freudian models, perhaps springing from the social milieu of Freud's early patients in Vienna. They expressed the pain of the narrowness of *bourgeois* society. Man is destined for greater things. Again, models of development can miss entirely the mystery of human life if they are too rigidly employed. God's ways are not our ways and he writes straight with crooked lines. Yet we need to co-operate with his normal designs.

Notes

1. One typology of these relationships is provided by H. Richard Niebuhr in *Christ and Culture*. Harper, New York: (1956). The saving mystery is "against" or in contradiction to the human reality (as in monasticism); or it is "identified" with it (as in liberal Christianity). The saving mystery is "above" the human reality but fulfills it in hierarchical synthesis (Thomism); or they are in paradox, continual tension, or dialogue (Luther); or the saving mystery "transforms" the human reality (Augustine and Calvin).
2. The following writings were useful in providing background material for this section: George H. Joyce, *Christian Marriage: An Historical and Doctrinal Study*, Sheed and Ward (1948); Edward Schillebeeckx, *Marriage, Human Reality and Saving Mystery*, Sheed and Ward (1965); John T. Noonan, Jr. "Intellectual and Demographic History", *Daedalus* 97 (Spring 1968) pp. 463-485; John Meyendorff; *Marriage: An Orthodox Perspective*, St Vladimir's Seminary Press (1970); and Rudolf Ehrlich, "The Teaching of the Reformers on Marriage", *Biblical Theology* 24 (Jan., 1974) pp. 1-19.
3. Thomas F. O'Dea, "Thought in America", in *Thought* 56 (Fall, 1971) p. 330.
4. *United Nations Declaration of Human Rights*, Article 16.
5. I am indebted for this suggestion to John Bossy, "English Views of European History", *Encounter* 42 (May, 1974) p. 77.
6. Edward Shorter, "Industrial Society in Trouble: Some Recent Views", *The American Scholar*, 40 (Spring 1971) p. 330.
7. cf. "Changes in Family Patterns", in William J. Goode, *The Family*. Englewood Cliffs, New Jersey (1964) pp. 103-117.
8. Michael Polanyi, "On the Modern Mind", *Encounter* 24 (May 1965), p. 12.
9. as quoted and translated by Reinhard Bendix, *Max Weber: An Intellectual Portrait*, Doubleday, New York (1962) p. 22.
10. For this delineation of the areas of questioning I am indebted to Hermann Kahn, the futurologist, in an interview in *Single* 1 (August, 1973), p. 34.
11. The preoccupation with the romantic figures of Faust, Ahasverus ("The Wandering Jew"), "The Flying Dutchman", as well as Don Juan was a common and prophetic one in 19th century art and philosophy. Kierkegaard understood the implications of this theme very well. cf. *Either/Or*, Vol. 1: "The Immediate Stages of the Erotic".
12. Michael Polanyi, "On the Modern Mind", p. 12. I follow Polanyi's analysis here.
13. The moral nihilism that is the outcome of the fusion of scepticism and moral indignation reaches its peak in that type of modern revolutionary for whom "the degree of evil he is prepared to commit or condone in the name of humanity is the measure of his moral force. He gives effect to his immanent morality by his manifest immorality". Michael Polanyi, "The Two Cultures" in *Knowing and Being*, ed. by Marjorie Grene, The University Press, Chicago (1969), p. 44.

14. This is the conclusion of Paul Ricoeur in *Freud and Philosophy: An Essay on Interpretation*, Denis Savage, Yale University Press, New Haven and London (1970), p. 337.
15. This is the criticism of Erik H. Erikson in "Psychological Reality and Historical Actuality". *Insight and Responsibility*, Norton, New York (1964), p. 164.
16. These trends are conveniently summarised by Rollo May in "The Origins and Significance of the Existential Movement in Psychology", and "Contributions of Existential Psychology", *Existence: A New Dimension of Psychiatry and Psychology*, Basic Books, New York (1958), pp. 3-91.
17. Some recent writers on marriage who have theological interests have used Erikson extensively. Examples are Herbert Richardson, *Nun, Witch, Playmate: The Americanisation of Sex*, Harper and Row, New York (1971) and Jack Dominian, "The Cycle of Affirmation" in *The Tablet* (October 20 and 27 and November 3, 1973).
18. The theory of infantile sexuality is described in *Three Essays on the Theory of Sexuality*, trs. and ed. by James Strachey, Image Publishing Company (1940).
19. Claude Levi-Strauss, "The Family", in *Man, Culture and Society*, edited by H. L. Shapiro, Oxford University Press (1971), p. 334.
20. Erikson's account of the stages of life can be found in *Childhood and Society*, 2nd enlarged ed., Norton, New York (1963), pp. 48-108 and 247-74.
21. *Childhood and Society*, p. 262.
22. *Ibid.*
23. Erikson, "Identity and Uprootedness in Our Times", in *Insight and Responsibility*, p. 90.
24. Erikson, "Prologue", to *Identity, Youth and Crisis*, Norton, New York (1968), p. 41.
25. Erikson, "Race and the Wider Identity", *Identity, Youth and Crisis*, pp. 315-6.
26. Cf. Goode, *The Family*, p. 38.
27. Recent work in cognitive psychology corroborates Erikson's remarks on the character of adolescent moral thinking. For example, Lawrence Kohlberg's *Stages in the Development of Moral Thought and Action*, Holt, Rinehart and Winston, New York (1969), which is based on Jean Piaget's theories, indicates that adolescent moral thinking is "conventional" i.e. it is conformist and aims at maintaining family, group, or national norms as ultimate values in themselves. Hence, "my country, right or wrong". It would appear that many adults never go beyond this level of moral discourse.
28. Erikson, "Human Strength and the Cycle of Generations", in *Insight and Responsibility*, p. 128.
29. Erikson, *Childhood and Society*, p. 266.
30. Erikson is supported here by the women psychoanalysts Helene Deutsch and Karen Horney. Theirs is not quite a metaphysic of sexual polarity as expressed in the law of systole and diastole of Goethe. A metaphysics of sexual polarity is however argued in Jung

and from a Christian angle of vision by the psychiatrist Karl Stern in *The Flight from Woman*, The Noonday Press, New York (1965). An analogical point of view can be found in the works of the theologian Derrick Sherwin Bailey, notably in the chapter "Towards a Theology of Sex", in *The Man-Woman Relation in Christian Thought*, Longmans (1959), pp. 260-303. This kind of thinking is radically opposed by Simone de Beauvoir in *The Second Sex*, Alfred A. Knopf, New York (1953) and by recent writers on women's liberation. Erikson rejects the Freudian theory that would depict the fundamental emotional motif of women as an envious attachment to a putative missing penis. He does however indicate that in some suggestive ways anatomy is destiny and certainly rejects the opinion that if one views the sexes as convex-penetrating and concave-receiving, one is implying a kind of humiliation to the concave-receiving sex.

31. Erikson, "Human Strength and the Cycle of Generations", in *Insight and Responsibility*, p. 131.

32. Ibid.

33. Ibid, p. 130.

34. Erikson, "The Golden Rule in the Light of New Insight", in *Insight and Responsibility*, p. 231.

35. Erikson, *Gandhi's Truth: On the Origins of Militant Nonviolence*, W. W. Norton & Co., New York (1969), p. 35. Erikson gave some thought to the comparison between his stages of life and those of the Hindu tradition (apprenticeship; householdership; inner separation; and renunciation) but without great enlightenment. It is possible however to envisage within Erikson's basic scheme a stage in middle life where personal development might call for a radical change in the character of the marital relationship, if not its abandonment, for religious reasons. The concept of "ages of life" is a persistent one. For example, Philip Aries in his *Centuries of Childhood*, Penguin Books (1973) remarks that the conception occupied "a considerable place in the pseudo-scientific treatises of the Middle Ages. . . . A man's 'age' was a scientific category of the same order as weight or speed for our contemporaries" (p. 17).

36. Nevertheless, Erikson does have a considerable body of socio-scientific evidence to support the general lineaments of his model. With regard to polygamy, it has been argued that "if the sex ratio of a community were left undisturbed by such violent factors as war pursuits, hazardous hunting, and unnatural infanticide, and if an equality of opportunity of marriage existed for all, monogamy would be the obvious form of marriage most suited to the human family". Philip Ekka, "Anthropology and the Idea of a Universal Moral Law for Society" in *New Light on the Natural Law*, ed. Illtud Evans, Burns and Oates (1965), p. 113. Divorce is typically followed by re-marriage. The change desired is with regard to a partner not in the basic idea of the institution itself.

37. Cf. the illuminating account of 19th century German medicine by Karl Stern in *The Third Revolution*, Image Books, New York (1961), p. 30.

38. Paul Tillich, "The Theological Significance of Existentialism and Psychoanalysis". *Theology of Culture*, Oxford University Press (1964), p. 114.
39. Schillebeeckx, *op. cit.*, p. 290.

3. Marriage and Creative Freedom

Björn Björnsson

Theological discussion on the institution of marriage has to our mind often suffered from the fact that this institution has not been viewed sufficiently in its particular cultural and/or social setting. This becomes very clear when the attention is not so much focused on marriage as on the family. In this case, i.e. when the discussion centres on the family, it is seen as natural to refer to the existent social organisations of the family. This more open approach to questions relating to the family – while at the same time the social reality of marriage is being neglected – is all the more perplexing for the simple reason that no marriage exists without a family context.

The tendency to forget the social aspects of marriage would not be such a serious fault if it only made theological discussion to suffer. It is a serious fault, however, because it makes people suffer. The breakdown of marriages is a constant cause of human suffering and in these break-downs the discrepancy between an idea of marriage and its social reality plays a destructive part.

In view of this it is with some reluctance that we address ourselves to the question of the nature of marriage. The word "nature" encourages the mind to seek for what is natural and therefore inevitable and un-changeable irrespective of changing social realities. Linked with marriage, "nature" easily evolves into an idea which prescribes for marriage a certain character of timelessness and immutability.

All the same it may prove useful to ask the question about the nature of marriage, if for no other reason than to come a little closer to the realisation of what it is not.

Dr John Hayes, at the close of his discussion of the nature oi marriage, suggests that "with marriage, as elsewhere in theology, it is clear that we cannot answer the smaller questions without addressing the larger ones: e.g. how is the order of creation to be related to the order of redemption".

We would like in this short comment to take up Dr Hayes's sugges-tion as it is also our firm belief that no theological deliberation on the nature of marriage is valid or presentable without a primary reference to the nature of the relationship between creation and redemption. Our reading of this relationship will be decisive for our stand on social issues in general and on the institution of marriage in particular.

Martin Luther's approach to the relationship between creation and redemption is presented in his doctrine of the two kingdoms, and also, but more indirectly, in his teaching on law and gospel. This doctrine of two kingdoms, or two spheres of God's activity, has been notoriously influential in shaping Lutheran views on social concerns to the present day. It is a doctrine which has been much criticised, and it is a doctrine on the nature of which there is much debate among Lutheran scholars. In general terms this debate has focused on the question of the inter-relatedness of the two kingdoms, i.e. to what extent, if any, is it justifiable for the Church to intervene in secular matters. Luther himself was concerned to keep the boundary line clearly marked, to set apart the spiritual and the worldly spheres. This emphasis stands out, to take an example, in Luther's refutation of the sacramental nature of marriage and in his placing of this institution firmly within the worldly kingdom.

This is neither the time nor the place to enter into a detailed discussion on the doctrine of the two kingdoms. For our immediate purposes, however, it should be pointed out that this doctrine, besides offering an interpretation of the relationship between creation and redemption, gives a clue to our understanding of the relation between the righteousness of God, *iustitia christiana*, and civil righteousness, *iustitia civilis*. It is this latter relationship, between the two kinds of righteousness, which to our mind is the primary concern of Christian social ethics. Thus, if we accept the secular reality of marriage, the implications of this acceptance will only become clear when the relation of the secular, *iustitia civilis*, to the sacred, *iustitia christiana*, has been established. Now it is evident from numerous spokesmen of the Lutheran tradition that a rigid adherence to a two-kingdom doctrine leads to a position where *iustitia civilis* is understood to stand in no integral relation to *iustitia christiana*. Translated into Christian socio-ethical terms this means basically that the Christian faith leaves the social order untouched. There appears, in consequence, the familiar structural juxtaposition of two spheres, theologically grounded in personalistic piety, in a reading of the Credo which does not see the first article in any essential relationship with the second, and in a reading of eschatology which transcends history.

This position the present writer holds to be untenable. It is in sharp contrast to the New Testament witness to the relation of the Kingdom of God to the world. In particular there is revealed a wide discrepancy between the thinking in terms of two autonomous spheres on the one hand and the proclamation of Jesus Christ himself and of his disciples on the other, that to him, the Lord, all power has been given in heaven and on earth. (Mt 28:18; Eph 1:20 ff; Phil 2:9; Col 1:13ff). In obedience to this proclamation, led by the steps already taken by our Lord in incarnation, crucifixion and resurrection, we are directed to a formulation of the relationship between *iustitia civilis* and *iustitia christiana* which establishes an integral, organic, and therefore a dynamic relation between the two types of *iustitia*.

How does this formulation affect our understanding of the secular reality of the social orders? The answer to this question should bring us closer to the meaning of the nature of marriage.

The freedom in responsibility which is granted to us under the Lordship of Jesus Christ issues in a total concern for our brethren. It must now be seen as a part of this total concern that the social orders can no longer be regarded as absolutes, as ends in themselves because this by itself sets limits to God's involvement with man in the totality of his existence. That the orders have been affected by the Love of God explains how they have been affected. Freed as we are from investing the orders with ultimate meaning, the orders themselves become free for our living with them and our living in them, but also for our critical engagement with them. The relativity of the orders means that they have become relative to a purpose outside themselves, and this purpose we know to be the salvation of mankind through Jesus Christ. If we say therefore that the orders exist in order to serve man and not vice versa, this man is by no means any man, but real man, man as willed by God. In other words the telos of the social orders now stands revealed as that of helping man, any man, to be real man. Real man is the man who has been given freedom to live in responsibility to God and to his brethren.

This anthropological affirmation must now be established as the norm against which Christian social ethics views all social orders. A total concern for our brethren, that they may become and live as real men, cannot possibly be less concerned or not concerned at all about the social structure in and through which the brethren are called to live as real men. Rather, a continuous questioning of all social orders is bound to be involved in this total concern; which is but another way of expressing the integral relation of *iustitia christiana* to *iustitia civilis*. The orders are questioned as to whether they are functioning according to their telos, and whenever they are found to be at fault in this respect there can be no rest for an ultimate concern until it has tried its best to correct the fault. This may sound utopian, but it is not so when we realise that it is not the Kingdom of God that issues forth from the questioning, but simply *iustitia civilis*. The very fact of questioning points to the fact that there is something to be questioned, and the call for an unceasing questioning speaks for itself about the continuous questionable nature of historical existence. But the inbreaking of the new age into the old is also witnessed by the fact of questioning for, as we have seen, it is through the questioning that man in his world is called out of his self-contradiction and thus saved. Christian social ethics owes its existence, as it were, to this appearance in history of questioning, and it is no more optimistic nor pessimistic than is the questioning itself.

The engagement of the *iustitia christiana* with the social orders has been described as *"schöpferische Nachfolge"*, – "creative discipleship".[1] The coupling of these particular terms is significant. That the Christian socio-ethical concern is described as *Nachfolge* confirms that this concern is not a secondary aspect of the Christian faith but an integral part of it. That it is said to be a *schöpferische Nachfolge* points to the creative freedom which this concern has been given through its rooting in the New Creation.

How does this creative freedom operate? We have described it as a questioning of the social orders, but what more can we say about it?

Firstly, as a questioning of the social orders which is a function of the co-existence in time of the new and the old age, the creative freedom is realistic. As was explained above, its degree of optimism and pessimism is correlative to the fact of questioning itself. It is fully aware of the demonic structure of the world *extra Christum* (apart from Christ) and is constantly reminded of its own lapses into this structure and its need of the forgiveness of God. But insofar as it accepts this forgiveness, it exists within the boundaries of the New Creation from which it draws both its freedom and its creativity. By definition, therefore, as a creative freedom amidst the structures of the old it can never succumb to an attitude of defeatism towards the world. This unique mode of existing in the world without drawing one's criteria of existence from the world is the sort of realism we have in mind. It is accordingly quite clear that, for this point, Christian social ethics owes nothing to the non-theological disciplines, but everything to its confession of the Lordship of Jesus Christ. It is indeed a christological realism.

Secondly, questioning the social orders on the basis of its christological realism, the creative freedom operates with a norm. This norm is grounded in the Love of God for the world, that he "desires all men to be saved and come to the knowledge of the truth" (1 Tim 2:4). In the service of this Love the creative freedom is directed to measure all social orders against a norm which spells out the real humanity of man in terms of freedom to live in responsibility to God and to one's brethren. Once this norm has been established, the freedom given to Christian social ethics through the confession of the Lordship of Christ is set to apply its creativity to the engagement with the social orders. But it needs to be emphasised that this creative engagement is rooted in its unique sort of realism and knows therefore that man is not saved through his world. This knowledge, however, is precisely the salutary point. It opens the way for creativity without utopianism. The social orders are not requested to show forth the Kingdom of God, but a sound society, *iustitia civilis*.

Thirdly, grounded in the realism of the Love of God and guided by its norm, the creative freedom seeks to grow ever richer and richer in knowledge and insight of every kind, praying for the gift of true discrimination (Phil 1:9). At this stage the dialogue with non-theological disciplines is called for. The creative freedom has been freed from treating the social orders as absolutes, but at the same time it has been given freedom to treat them responsibly. It is in obedience to this responsibility that Christian social ethics seeks to "grow ever richer and richer in knowledge and insight of every kind", and this it does by listening carefully to what other disciplines have to say about its subject of special interest, man in society. The point here is that the questioning of the social order, integral to Christian social ethics, has a responsibility to be an objective questioning. There is a double objectivity involved, and too often we stress one to the detriment of the other. The questioning, in order to be true questioning in Christ, must be objective to its ground of being, but this objectivity does not absolve it from the duty to be equally objective at the other end. In fact refusal of objectivity at this end cancels out the objectivity at the first, just as refusing to go the second mile makes no good of the first. The call for objectivity at the social level, to go the second mile, has become all the more urgent because of the immense changes that industrialised societies have undergone during the last century and a half.

There can be no doubt that the task of "true discrimination", of "testing the spirits", has become vastly more difficult a task for Christian social ethics as the structure of society has grown more and more complex. The hard realities of a pluralistic, industrial society cannot be objectively questioned on the basis of an outdated social theory which places: "The rich man in his castle/The poor man at his gate". This indeed would be the only objective questioning if our confession of the Lordship of Jesus Christ led us to believe that: "He made them high and lowly/And ordered their estate". But this is the very opposite of our belief in the Lordship of Christ, because this belief always questions and therefore relativises every social structure, at any time. We are not burdened with sociological absolutes, not even with those which we inherited from our fathers, but we are privileged to share with our Lord an unconditional concern for our brethren who find themselves engulfed by a bewildering complexity of institutions, values, ideas, morals – a new society. The social sciences can help us to understand how this new society works, how the manifold systems of institutions intertwine, how pressures arise between conflicting interests, how social sanctions, direct and indirect, operate, etc. But, as we advance in knowledge and insight of every kind through the valuable instruction of the social sciences, our commitment is entirely to our brethren who are called to be real men in this society, free men in responsibility to God and to their fellows. Thus it is that our questioning in Christ goes from faith to faith, from one pole of objectivity to the other.

Finally, the creative freedom under the Lordship of Jesus Christ operates with socio-ethical maxims. It is inevitable that during the course of objective questioning, bearing in mind the double objectivity involved, this questioning will become more articulate and eventually take shape in distinctive questions. Thus we have seen the emergence of the fundamental norm about real humanity. But further questioning on the basis of this norm leads on to separate sub-questions which, although remaining but an expression of the basic norm, bring the questioning closer to the point in the specific areas to which these sub-questions apply. These sub-questions we identify as maxims. What is meant here can be clarified by taking as an example the social institution of marriage. In its engagement with this institution in the form of questioning, the basic norm about the real humanity of man issues in sub-questions which only apply to this particular social institution. One sub-question here is undoubtedly that of monogamy. Monogamy is a maxim which has become an inseparable part of the Christian socio-ethical questioning of the institution of marriage in any society.

We must say then that the maxims which Christian social ethics makes use of are inseparable from its act of questioning the social orders. Or better still, the maxims are functions of the act of questioning, they "issue forth" even as the *iustitia civilis* was said to issue forth through the encounter of *iustitia christiana* with the world. This will say that there is a correlation between the degree of ultimacy given to the act of questioning and the socio-ethical wisdom of Christian ethics. But there is more involved. As a result of the functional relationship between questioning and maxim, the maxims will not only differ from one social institution to another but from one social system to another. If this spells relativity for the maxims then well and good, because they are meant to be conditional, flexible, changeable. It is when they become unconditional, making total claims as absolutes, that they themselves inevitably will be questioned by our confession of the Lordship of Jesus Christ. The maxims bear witness to the christological realism, they do not purport to be pillars of the Kingdom of God, nor do they fit into the structure of *regnum diaboli*, but they are signs signalling the Love of God for the world as a world, as a creation. Maxims must accordingly be under constant revision in order to test their adequacy under different social conditions and from one generation to another. This revision is itself an inseparable part of objective questioning in its twofold objectivity.

After the relativity of the maxims has thus been emphatically underlined because of their penultimate status as *iustitia civilis*, another no less emphatic word must be said about their historical continuity. If we make a virtue of relativity for its own sake and not solely for the sake of the Kingdom, we fall into the paradoxical heresy of making relativity unconditional, thereby demonising it. Relativity itself has been demythologised, not by us, but by the Lordship of Jesus Christ who is the only demythologiser. There is nothing relative about the Love of God for the world, nor is there anything relative about the world as it rests in the evil. In spite of the most consistent transformation of social structures there is still the same family of man living upon the earth and under heaven. We would expect therefore that the universal questioning of man by God, going back to the first: "Where art thou, Adam?", had issued forth in certain universal sub-questions or maxims. And this indeed is so. Christian social ethics recognises for instance universal maxims in the Ten Commandments. It does not recognise them as spelling out a universal "natural law", because such a recognition relativises the Lordship of Jesus Christ. But it listens to the Commandments in the unique way of recognising them as being sub-questions to the fundamental question addressed to man in the "I am the Lord, your God . . .". The Ten Commandments are therefore inseparable from the objective questioning of man in his world to which Christian social ethics is committed through its confession of the Lordship of Christ. Other universal maxims are freedom, justice, equality, maxims which become demonic as soon as they are removed from their proper context as being sub-questions to the questioning of man by God in Jesus Christ. Monogamy is another universal maxim of this kind (cf. our example at the beginning of this discussion about the maxims).

In applying our discussion so far more directly to the particular topic of the nature of marriage we want to emphasise what was said earlier about the *telos* of the social orders as that of helping man, any man, to be real man. Marriage as a universal reality offers a unique opportunity for real humanity. And this it does increasingly because of the threat to humane living caused by the dehumanising elements of the advanced, technical society of the present day. Marriage has in this context been aptly described by Professor Roger Mehl as the reality of the "social-private" sector. Professor Mehl writes:

> Thus man has need of finding a place where he can show himself both as a being of communication, dialogue, and sharing and, at the same time, as a private being, that is, a being who is separate in regard to all his roles and social masks. His subjectivity must be able to manifest itself fully, without, however, degrading itself in individualistic egoism. His liberty must be able to manifest itself without any constraint other than that which comes from love. He has need of knowing in his life a sphere of existence that can be called the *social-private sphere*. . . .
> This place par excellence is the family and in the bosom of the family. More particularly still, it is the married couple, i.e. that private society, that non-public society, grounded in love, friendship, and companionship, where duality is shown in unity and unity in duality, where, finally, reciprocity of understanding is established as nowhere else.[2]

For marriage to play this important role for the protection of the person in an impersonal environment we must be ready and willing to accept its flexible nature, its sensitivity to rapidly changing social realities. Doctrinaire positions on behalf of the churches in a sphere of life which already is overcrowded with prejudices will hardly help a person to discover the opportunity for maturity and fulfilment which the encounter in marriage offers.

The acceptance of the flexible nature of marriage and in particular that the content of marriage is largely culturally determined, bears directly upon the complicated issue of mixed marriages. These marriages reflect by definition different cultural backgrounds. We are certainly wrong if we play down the importance of these differences. They can become destructive for a happy married life – and often are – but must it necessarily be so? The churches have a special responsibility here. They are questioned, each one of them, as to whether they are truthfully the instrument through which the ministry of reconciliation is carried out to the world and in the world. Reconciliation is a power stronger than any cultural difference. By its very logic it accepts that such differences exist, that they are real and will remain so, but reconciliation does not accept that, on the basis of these differences, walls of mutual suspicion, even hostility, are erected to keep people apart. A mixed marriage could, and should, provide an excellent ground for reconciliation, where love, as mutual concern for the individuality of the partners, unites instead of excludes different cultural traits and traditions. The churches are under an obligation to show forth that the walls have been broken, "that there is no such thing as Jew and Greek, slave and free man, male and female; for you are all one person in Christ Jesus". (Gal 3:28).

Notes

1. Ernst Wolf, "Schöpferische Nachfolge", in F. Karrenberg and W. Schweitzer (ed.), *Spannungsfelder der Evangelischen Soziallehre*, Hamburg (1960), p. 26 ff.
2. Roger Mehl, *Society and Love:* Ethical Problems of Family Life, Hodder and Stoughton (1965), p. 27.

This extract is reproduced by kind permission of Hodder and Stoughton Ltd.

4. Respecting the Unity: A Plea for Church Restraint

G. R. Dunstan

In a passionate soliloquy Dido Queen of Carthage asked herself two questions which a commentator does well to keep in mind. The first was *Quid loquor?*, "What am I saying?" What should I say in comment upon Dr Hayes's paper, more than, perhaps, to echo the words of the disciples, as reported by St Matthew, "If the case of the man be so with his wife, it were better not to marry"? But then I recall Dido's second question, *Aut ubi sum?*, "Where am I?"; and this brings me to my purpose, to our purpose here. The context, the subject, of our discussion is mixed marriages; it is in and for this context that I have to frame my commentary upon Dr Hayes.

Dr Hayes's learned paper analyses the state of marriage, in the language of anthropology, psychology and phenomenology, as a human institution, meeting personal and social human needs. The early chapters of Genesis tell much the same story, a little more simply perhaps. The woman is made from and for the man, to be an help meet for him, bone of his bones and flesh of his flesh; and they find satisfaction, joy, in one another, as we learn later from the Song of Songs:

Let my beloved come into his garden,
And eat his precious fruits.
I am come into my garden, my sister, my bride,
I have eaten my honeycomb with my honey;
Drink, yea, drink abundantly of love.

That sounds like a meeting of personal need, a man cleaving unto his wife and she unto him – which was the first commandment with promise. The second is to meet the social need – they are to be fruitful, and multiply, and replenish the earth, and subdue it, and exercise that divine, dangerous, power, *dominion*, together, over all the earth.

This is primal, primary, primitive. And the Bible asserts as a theological truth that it is so as God's ordinance, an expression of his word, his will. It follows, therefore, that what God has ordained the Church must respect; and particular churches must respect it, so that in their legislation for marriage, and for mixed marriages especially, they do not contravene the ordinance of God. This is my theme. Recalling where I am, I envisage what I am to say.

Let us not, however, over-simplify. The Bible values nature too highly to leave it alone; it quickens it with grace. So this human institu-

59

tion is laden with theology. The marriage of man with woman is made a sign of the marriage of Yahweh with the virgin daughter of Israel, of Christ with the Church his Bride; the wedding feast is a parable of the Kingdom and of the new creation wrought by the Lamb. Marriage is made a paradigm of the Covenant; and the essential ingredient of the Covenant is faithfulness, trust – which, it will be remembered, stands at the crown of Dr Hayes's psycho-social edifice as a *condition* of achieving personal identity. The theology of marriage, therefore, is a covenantal theology; since Vatican II the language of contract (a philological inheritance which at one time rather ousted theology from law) is being steadily replaced with the language of covenant, the language, incidentally, of the Anglican marriage rite since the Reformation. I do not seek, therefore, to subordinate ecclesiastical law to nature, but to theology, the theology of covenant which is central to the Jewish and Christian dispensation of the grace of God.

Neither do I wish to challenge the timeless and immutable. As the form, the social expression, of marriage has varied with time and place, so has the ecclesiastical provision for it. Dr Hayes has indicated how *late*, as time goes, came the Church's juridical and liturgical control of marriage. That story is told, in its bewildering variety of detail, by Fr Edward Schillebeeckx in *Marriage, Human Reality and Saving Mystery* (1965). Moreover, having established jurisdiction, the Church has variously decided what does and does not constitute valid marriage, changing the test or conditions of validity not once but many times; so that in truth it may be said that: "What God hath joined" came to mean: "What the Church permits or at least recognises God to have joined". It did this, of course, by adjusting the list of impediments, particularly the qualities and degrees of prohibited relationship – consanguinity, affinity, and even spiritual affinity, that complex of relationship set up between families by sponsorship or ministry at baptism and confirmation. In one epoch the degrees are extended; in another they are restricted; in a third they are cut off.[1] Marriage comes to be what the Church makes it to be. We today, in our responsible deliberations, are once more, perhaps, agents of change, seeking to conform the Church's law to the realities, as we see them, of marriage as God's ordinance for men and the sign of his covenant.

The perennial problem for the Church, therefore, is how to serve the theological ends of marriage without denying or encroaching upon the integrity and autonomy proper to its natural ends. Dr Hayes refers in passing to the suspicion entertained outside that the Church's "involvement with marriage and family life is but an arbitrary exercise in oppressive social control". Even within the Church we have to guard against the danger: it is all too easy for the logic of law to take over and lead us, from what look like the purest of motives, to encroach upon an area of natural autonomy. Dr Hayes, again, refers to the Reformation protest against this encroachment during the medieval ascendancy of the canon law – though I venture the opinion that he polarizes the issue rather too sharply. First, I think his statement of the tendency, fostered by "ideas about equality and the freedom of men under God", towards "marriage as a personal choice open to everyone" ignores the persist-

ence of serfdom, especially upon ecclesiastical estates, with the attend-
ant restriction upon and even denial of marriage to many. As late as in
the fifteenth century, ecclesiastical documents still referred to the union
of serfs as *contubernium*, the cohabitation of slaves – an attitude which
was exported with slavery into the plantations of America and the
West Indies, occasioning the gravest social harm. And the English
Reformation Settlement stands as a relevant exception to his statement
that the Reformers "firmly located marriage in the structure of Creation and under the authority of the civil magistrate", a fact which
invites further consideration.

The Anglican understanding of natural and sacramental marriage is
treated more fully in an appendix to this paper. It is enough to say here
that the liturgy and formularies of the Church of England, in this as in
so much else, were designed to avoid a choice between the rival systems
then being offered; rather to hold together the truths and strengths
which it perceived in each. As for jurisdiction over marriage, the
Church did not hand it over to "the State" for the simple reason that it
had no occasion to, and that "the State" as an entity distinct from the
Church did not then exist. Temporalty and spiritualty were but two
aspects of one realm. King Henry VIII had succeeded in bringing both
jurisdictions, that of the King's courts and that of the ecclesiastical
courts, under one fount of sovereignty, the Crown, which became the
final court of appeal in both. The canonical jurisdiction was not
abolished; it continued; and its exclusive authority over marriage and
matrimonial causes continued unchanged. By this means the canon law
of marriage became part, first of the Queen's ecclesiastical law, and
then, with the radical changes of the mid-nineteenth century, part of the
Law of England. The involvement of the Church *with* the State, not its
being set in conflict with the State, has continued in the subsequent
development of the relevant law down to the most recent enactment,
the Divorce Reform Act of 1969.[2] The meaning and value of Church
Establishment is here exemplified: the tension between marriage as a
natural state, for human and social good, and as a sacrament or sign in
the covenanted, redemptive order, is constantly expressed in legal and
political tension, not as between two antagonists, but as between
persons who, as temporal and spiritual persons, are fellow members o
one juridical society. This fact of English and Anglican life is of crucial
importance in the search towards a solution of some problems of interchurch marriage.

The law of England and the liturgy of the Church of England both
embody the theological truth that marriage is effected by the free consent of the parties themselves, provided that all else in the marriage is
according to law. The priest is a witness to that consent on behalf ot
Church and State. Not until Lord Hardwicke's Marriage Act of 1753
was the presence of the parochial incumbent or his deputy required *ad
validitatem*, and that for no theological reason, but to lessen the risk and
evil of clandestinity. The absence of theological significance from the
provision is established by subsequent legislation which empowers other
witnesses, including civil registrars, to fulfil the requirement of the law.
For Roman Catholics the Council of Trent, in its *Tametsi* decree,

anticipated Lord Hardwicke by two centuries, and for precisely the same reason: to guard against clandestinity. The decree was not promulgated in Britain until it was made universally binding by *Ne temere* in 1907 – the date at which the problem of contracting an Anglican/ Roman Catholic marriage, as we have it now, really begins. In origin the "canonical form" required by *Tametsi* – that the marriage of a Roman Catholic, in order to be valid, must be celebrated before the duly authorised Roman Catholic priest – was disciplinary in intent and without doctrinal significance. Unfortunately it has now acquired an essentially irrelevant doctrinal significance because of the place held by the Roman Catholic Church and its priesthood in Roman Catholic ecclesiology as developed since the Council of Trent. It is only as progress is made in ecumenical agreement on ecclesiology and ministry that an escape from this *impasse* becomes possible.

Has it yet become possible? Even though the Statement on Ministry and Ordination agreed upon by the Anglican/Roman Catholic Commission at Canterbury in September 1973 awaits ratification in some form by the authorities of both Churches, it points to a theological convergence of significance and promise.[3] And even though there are disputed points of interpretation at critical places in the document,[4] on the nature of ministerial priesthood, these do not *substantially* affect the question of canonical form, since the essential function of the minister at a marriage is not priestly in the sacramental sense: the ministers of the sacrament are the parties to the marriage. The purposes of the requirement of the canonical form are disciplinary and pastoral – to prevent clandestinity, and other evasions of the law, and to assure adequate pastoral preparation for the married life. Given, therefore, a growing theological accord, and given with it an increasing mutual confidence between the churches and their respective ministries, it would appear to be possible to escape the *impasse:* an authoritative declaration by the Roman Catholic authority that the Tridentine requirements of canonical form would be met by the ministrations of the clergy of designated churches would obviate the need for the dispensations already selectively given. The third, and published, Report of the Anglican/Roman Catholic Commission on Mixed Marriages records a recommendation to this effect: that "on condition that joint pastoral preparation has been given, and freedom to marry established to the satisfaction of the bishop of the Roman Catholic party and of the competent Anglican authority, the marriage may validly and lawfully take place before the duly authorised minister of the Church of either party".[5] Such a provision would remove the suggestion of unseemly competition between churches which can so easily bring discredit where mixed marriage is in contemplation; it would also respect the secular, social interest in marriage, by permitting the parties to follow the customs of the community to which they belong, which, in Britain at any rate, generally indicate marriage in the church or locality of the bride.

Much greater difficulty attends the promise concerning the baptism and up-bringing of the children required of the Roman Catholic partner as a condition of the granting of dispensation for entering into a mixed marriage. The existing Roman Catholic legislation, that of the *motu proprio* of Pope Paul VI published on 30 April 1970, contains the following (Norm 4):

> To obtain from the local Ordinary dispensation from an impediment, the Catholic party shall declare that he is ready to remove dangers of falling away from the faith. He is also gravely bound to make a sincere promise to do all in his power to have all children baptised and brought up in the Catholic Church.

To a member of another church, sympathetic as he is with the positive concern of the Roman Catholic Church for the fidelity of its members and for the proper religious and spiritual nurture of their children, this requirement is objectionable on two major grounds. The first is important, though it is not to be pursued far in this present context. It is that the Apostolic Letter assumes without argument that the obligation to give the children of Christian parents a *Christian* upbringing is necessarily and exclusively equated with the obligation to give them a *Roman Catholic* up-bringing. "This obligation is already there from the law of God", says the Directory of the Episcopal Conference of England and Wales. Such a statement presupposes acceptance of an ecclesiology which identifies the Church of Christ exclusively with the Church in communion with and accepting the plenitude of jurisdiction of the See of Rome. Non-Roman Catholics cannot admit this identification. They resent the imputation that a Christian up-bringing, after baptism, in the faith and communion of their own Church is not a Christian up-bringing recognised by the Church of Rome as fulfilling "the obligation already there from the law of God". God has not "legislated" for the Church of Rome, but for all mankind gathered into the Church of Christ. But this objection, I repeat, need not be pursued further now. Behind it is a question of ecclesiology which the theologians of both churches must resolve as a condition of further progress.

More material to the present discussion is the second objection. It is that the Roman Catholic Church requires a unilateral promise from one partner to a marriage concerning matters of deep spiritual import which ought, on theological grounds, to be determined within the unity of the marriage itself. The Church of Rome, in imposing this requirement, violates a theology of marriage which it shares with other churches: it fails to respect that ordained unity which is primary to marriage in both its natural and its sacramental, or covenantal, aspects.

The Second Vatican Council, in the Pastoral Constitution on the Church in the Modern World, encouraged the spouses in marriage to "experience the meaning of their oneness and attain to it with growing perfection day by day". The pastoral, legislative and, indeed, liturgical provisions of the Church should further this process in every good way. In particular, spouses should be encouraged to deliberate and to decide together the questions of the utmost importance in their married life. Foremost among these are decisions concerning their children: the responsibility is inescapably theirs for decisions concerning their conception, baptism, nurture and Christian education; and we should look for and foster the emergence of a "conjugal conscience", a union in moral decision, concerning them. Considered with this theological, psychological and social truth in view, the requirement of a promise from one spouse in a matter to which the other cannot, *ex hypothesi*, be a party, must seem to be an unwarranted intrusion.

Is there another way by which the Roman Catholic Church could satisfy itself that its duty has been done, *pro viribus*, to secure the maintenance of its faith? In my personal view there is. The Catholic party could be relieved of the responsibility of giving a promise; the parish priest, who is more directly and properly *subjectum iuris*, could be required to satisfy the bishop that *he* has, *pro viribus*, reminded the Catholic partner and, where there is consent, the non-Catholic partner also, of the expectations of the Roman Catholic Church concerning the Christian up-bringing of the children; and no more could, or should, be required of him or of them. The effective decisions must be their own, taken within the emerging unity of their marriage.

A change of this sort, required by our theology of marriage and by the respect due to the unity of it, would go far to remove a source of bitterness and resentment against the Roman Catholic Church – against the *whole* Church, which is brought into discredit when ecclesiastical division thrusts itself into an occasion of family unity. A change of form, however, is not enough: the change must come from a new conviction, and a new respect for the "conjugal conscience" of the married pair. Already, in fact, a certificate from the priest is, in some episcopal jurisdictions, required in addition to the promise. The Scottish Episcopal Conference, for instance, issues a green form to accompany its Directory on Mixed Marriages; the form is to be completed and signed by the priest who forwards the application for a mixed marriage to his bishop. One part of the certificate states that

> The non-Catholic party
> has agreed not to oppose   *delete the lines*
> in my judgment will not oppose   *which do not apply*
> in my judgment will oppose
> the practice of religion by the Catholic or the Catholic baptism and up-bringing of the children who may be born of the marriage.

The priest is to certify whether he recommends or does not recommend the granting of a dispensation, for reasons to be stated by him on the back of the form. He is required to ensure "that the pre-nuptial instructions for mixed marriages, as prescribed by diocesan regulations, are given by himself or by another and that neither party excludes the ends and essential properties of marriage". Everyone who reads *Humanae Vitae* knows that one way to "exclude the ends and essential properties of marriage" is to practise contraception. The formal inclusion of the phrase, first in the *motu proprio* and then in the form of the priest's certificate, inevitably invites the suspicion that a priest's decision whether to recommend the granting of the dispensation or not may well be influenced by what the non-Roman Catholic partner says, or even does not say, in the pastoral interviews concerning these matters, integral to the married life, and properly the concern of the spouses alone, to be decided in their joint conscience – informed, of course, by the moral teaching of the Christian Church in its diverse forms. It is intolerable to an observer nurtured in the traditions of the common law that a man should be judged, in a way adverse to his interests, by his silence. A new trust is required, an increased reliance on moral persuasion, and less on law. Unless our ecumenical conversations are engendering this trust – trust, not only between churches and their clergy, but trust also in our people – they are somehow conducted amiss; and the Church will continue as an instrument of division even where in the order of nature there is the strongest impulse to union.

There is one further matter in which the churches continue to be at variance, where closer consideration might well enable them to recognise that they seek a similar end but by different means, by different forms of words. This is in their response to defective marital situations, particularly where marriages have "broken down" and a new marriage is in contemplation.[6] On the first-order principle of marriage, that it is of its nature an exclusive and life-long commitment, there is no dispute. On the acceptance of a principle of nullity – that some unions, purporting to have been a marriage, have never in fact been a marriage – there is no dispute. On the need of second-order rules, to guide the Church and to govern its faithful when, through sin or error or weakness, the first-order principle is no longer being observed and cannot be, there is no dispute: such second-order rules stand in the New Testament, in the so-called Matthaean exception, in the so-called Pauline privilege, and elsewhere, alongside of Our Lord's re-assertion of the first-order principle in the language of the Genesis ordinance. Simply stated, the disputes begin when the non-Roman churches develop their second-order provision for defective situations in the language of divorce and liberty to remarry, while the Roman Catholic Church develops its provision by extensions of the principle of nullity and by such dispensations as that given by the Holy See *in favorem fidei*. This assertion can be made – and here it is made – without the imputation of bad faith on either side. It is the duty of the Church, in fulfilment of its pastoral task, to make such second-order rules and to administer them – recognising their secondary and contingent character, and claiming nothing for them of the absolute and immutable character pertaining to the first-order principles given us by God and confirmed by his Son. Resentment grows only when one church claims, in fact, that its second-order rules are no more than means of recognising that the first-order principles have never in fact been broken – that the marriage in question has never been, despite human indication and evidence to the contrary – so that what in a non-Roman church is accepted as a permission to re-marry is in the Roman Catholic Church offered as marriage for the first time.

Progress will be possible only when there is a general, and concerted, re-examination of the whole procedure, in a new freedom to recognise the reality behind formulae and words, and a new freedom to admit that often our ecclesiastical provisions are only approximations to the good, the true, the divinely ordained; the absolute is often beyond our reach – we deceive ourselves if we pretend to dispense it. But the world is not deceived.

It may appear that this paper is more provocative than it was intended to be. It tends to put one side of the case, leaving out much that could be said on the other. But since 1968 I have been engaged in putting both sides in the Reports of the Anglican/Roman Catholic Commission on Mixed Marriages – and the final Report of that body is still to come. Meanwhile our public, if we have one, must be rather bored with waiting for a practical outcome to our discussions. A little provocation, therefore, may occasion no harm. It may appear also that the onus of defence or of change has been chiefly put upon the Roman Catholic Church. That is, in a sense, inevitable, since it is that Church which relies most heavily on the arm of law to signal its moral convictions and pastoral aims. But if any church is accused of overstepping the bounds which nature, society and a theology of matrimonial unity prescribe, all churches are, in some degree. Too often the marriages of church-going people are over-clericalised: the unity of the rite is fragmented, the primacy of the lay covenant made between the man and the woman before God and the congregation is obscured, by a sequence of clerical voices breaking the service into apportioned pieces. The soldiers were more seemly, before the seamless robe. It is one thing to invite a priest to participate who has, perhaps, cared for one spouse or other from baptism until now; it is quite another to intrude ministers from this church or that in order to "represent" the churches involved in a mixed marriage. One of the reasons commonly relied upon to justify dispensation from the canonical form is a "close relationship of the non-Catholic party to a minister or officer of another denomination" – a new form of benefit of clergy, the *privilegium cleri*, which cries out injustice in this essentially lay and universal sacrament. All churches have to learn a new sensitivity; to leave their heavy shoes on the threshold of mystery, the mystery of the marriage of a man with a woman which is wrapped in the mystery of the marriage of Christ with the Church. We look for a new St Bernard to give us a new commentary on the Song of Songs.

Notes

1. The Pontifical Commission for the Reform of the Canon Law proposes the abolition of the impediment of spiritual affinity. *Communicationes*, III. 1 (1971) p. 75.
2. See *Putting Asunder: The Report of a Group appointed by the Archbishop of Canterbury*, SPCK (1966); *Theology* LXXIV (Jan. 1971) pp. 1-4; (March 1971) p. 123 ff., The Bishop of Exeter, *"Putting Asunder and the Divorce Reform Act"* (July 1971) pp. 289-91.
3. *Ministry and Ordination*, SPCK (1973).
4. See *Theology*, LXXVII (Feb. 1974) p. 57 ff.
5. *Theology*, LXXVI (Apr. 1973) p. 197.
6. The most effective counter to this variance would be a common commitment, not simply to joint or complementary pastoral care in the parochial setting, but also to systematic research grounded upon

therapeutic service in a Christian Institute like the Marital Research Unit established by Dr Jack Dominian in association with the Central Middlesex Hospital, London.

Appendix: Natural and Sacramental Marriage

The Anglican Understanding

I Method

A proper judgment upon the Anglican understanding of marriage will be formed less from speculative writing than from the formularies of the Church itself. The liturgy of marriage contains our formal doctrine.

The Anglican understanding of marriage, in this formal sense, does not differ markedly in the Anglican Communion from that enshrined in the Book of Common Prayer of the Church of England. Differences are of emphasis only, not of substance. Roman Catholics (and members of other churches) who would understand Anglican doctrine might well study it in the Form of Solemnisation of Marriage in the Prayer Book of 1662, comparing that, if they will, with the version of 1928, where changes of style were embodied, but none of substance. In this paper I select only elements related to natural and sacramental marriage.

The opening address by the Priest to the Congregation describes Holy Matrimony as

1. "an honourable estate,
2. instituted in the time of man's innocency.
3. signifying unto us the mystical Union that is betwixt Christ and his Church;
4. which holy estate Christ adorned and beautified with his presence, and first miracle that he wrought in Cana of Galilee,
5. and is commended of St Paul in holy writ to be honourable among all men, and therefore...."

In these words, and in others in the rite itself where the substance of each clause is embodied in the prayers and recited in passages of Scripture, lies the fullness of our subject. In particular, it lies in a conjunction of clauses 1, 2 and 3.

II Marriage in the Created Order

Clauses 1 and 2 reflect our understanding of marriage as partaking of "the order of nature", of God's natural creation. They reflect the Genesis myth, to which Jesus appealed, and on which he based his own teaching, with the words "from the beginning of creation" (Mark 10:6). The words "honourable" and "innocency" point to marriage as part of God's *primal* ordinance or gift for man, as something essentially or in itself good, and not as a remedial consequence of the Fall. The remedial function, man being fallen, is asserted later, in the second of the "causes for which Matrimony was ordained":

6. Secondly, it was ordained for a remedy against sin, and to avoid fornication; that such persons as have not the gift of continency might marry and keep themselves undefiled members of Christ's body.

But as a natural ordinance, marriage is part of pure creation; its soteriological function is secondary. The same primary emphasis on the order of creation is found in the prayers: the old nuptial benediction from the Sacramentaries, for instance, went into the 1549 Book in two parts, of which this is the first:

7. O God, who by thy mighty power hast made all things of nothing; who also (after other things set in order) didst appoint, that out of man (created after thine own image and similitude) woman should take her beginning: and knitting them together didst teach that it should never be lawful to put asunder those whom thou by Matrimony hadst made one . . .

The final blessing of bride and bridegroom before the Mass or Sermon also began:

8. Almighty God, who at the beginning did create our first parents Adam and Eve, and did sanctify and join them together in marriage: . . .

This location of marriage in the order of Creation would seem formally to exclude it from the category of sacraments "as generally necessary for salvation" as defined in the Catechism (also in the Book of Common Prayer) and in the Thirty-Nine Articles.

The *Catechism* has an appendix on the sacraments, added to the 1549/1552 book in 1604, but based on Nowell's Catechism of 1570, and it begins thus:

9. *Q*. How many Sacraments hath Christ ordained in his Church?
   A. Two only, as generally necessary to salvation, that is to say Baptism, and the supper of the Lord.

In answer to the next question, "What meanest thou by this word, Sacrament?", there follows

10. *A*. I mean an outward and visible sign of an inward and spiritual grace, given unto us,
11.   ordained by Christ himself,
12.   as a means whereby we receive the same, and a pledge to assure us thereof.

The catechising which follows covers only Baptism and the Holy Communion.

As a natural ordinance, therefore, grounded in the Creation, marriage would appear to be excluded from this definition and enumeration of the sacraments; first, by its being ordained, *not* "by Christ himself" (11), but in Creation; and secondly by the rooting of the sacraments in the dispensation of "salvation" (9), in the order of redemption.

Article XXV of the xxxix Articles of 1562 is consistent with this:

13. There are two Sacraments ordained of Christ our Lord in the Gospel, that is to say, Baptism and the Supper of the Lord.
14. Those five commonly called Sacraments, that is to say, . . . Matrimony, . . . are not to be counted for Sacraments of the Gospel, being . . . partly . . . states of life allowed in the Scriptures;
15. but yet have not like nature of Sacraments with Baptism and the Lord's Supper, for that they have not any visible sign or ceremony ordained by God.

It is chiefly on this relation of the "two" to the "five" that differences of emphasis lie within the Anglican Communion. My personal interest is two-fold: it is, first, to do justice to the texts themselves which, fairly interpreted, I believe, can only yield an intention at that time to restrict the Sacraments to two: it is, secondly, by further exegesis of the Liturgy, to show how it contains within itself a theology which fully justifies the limited use of a sacramental terminology for marriage by those who wish to use it – *limited*, because when the full technicalities of formal analysis of a sacrament are applied to marriage, language is inevitably stretched and the exercise reveals itself as artificial. In my own view, the extension of the language is unnecessary: the language of *covenant*, employed extensively in the liturgy, gives us all the theology we need to meet the requirements sought in the language of sacramentality. It is my further belief that this language of *covenant* provides a meeting-point with the conciliar documents of Vatican II (e.g. *Gaudium et Spes*, n. 48) and with the relevant parts of the *Lex Ecclesiae Fundamentalis* founded upon them.

III Marriage in the Sacramental Order

My route to this is in clause 3 of the priest's opening address, with its implicit reference to St Paul's writing in Ephesians 5:25-32, a passage quoted in full later in the homily to be read by the priest "if there be no sermon", and woven also into the major prayer of nuptial benediction. After the opening section quoted at 7 above, the prayer continues:

16. O God who hast consecrated the State of Matrimony to such an excellent Mystery, that in it is signified, and represented the spiritual Marriage and unity betwixt Christ and his Church; look mercifully upon these thy servants, that both this man may love his wife according to thy word, (as Christ did love his Spouse the Church, who gave himself for it, loving and cherishing it even as his his own flesh) and also that this woman may be loving and amiable, faithful and obedient to her husband, . . .

The link between this passage in Ephesians and sacramentality is in the word "mystery", translated in the Vulgate by *sacramentum*. Ephesians 5: 32: *to mustérion touto mega estin;* Vulg: *sacramentum hoc magnum est*. The transition of *sacramentum* appears to have been from the (early) "preliminary engagement entered into by an enlisting soldier" to the (very frequent and classical) equivalence of *iusiurandum*, "the military oath of allegiance", to the (mostly post-Augustan) general notion of "an oath, solemn obligation or undertaking" – the usage which it constantly carried in the administrative Latin of the medieval Church. (In this sense "sacrament" is applied to marriage in the only instance known to the writer in Reformation Anglican formularies: it occurs in the Elizabethan homily "Of Swearing" in a context which leaves no doubt that the binding power of an oath was the meaning assumed.)[1] Thence, in the developing ecclesiastical Latin, it came to include "something to be kept sacred", and so to a "secret", a "mystery", the "type" conveyed in mysterious teaching, the Gospel revelation, a "bond" (Cyprian, *de unitate*), the sign of the cross; and then to "sacrament" in the developed sense – *signa, cum ad res divinas pertinent, sacramenta appellantur* (Aug., *Ep.* 138). After this its history becomes part of the history of sacramental terminology and theology in general, the elaboration and definition of which by the end of the fifteenth century caused the Reformers to react against it in ways indicated above.

The two ingredients of *sacramentum* relevant to our purposes are (a) the shewing or disclosure of a mystery as the saving act of God himself, in *mustērion* in Ephesians 5 – the "mystery" of the abiding covenant of Christ with his Church; and (b) the notion of a bond created by an oath derived from the *sacramentum* tradition in Latin use. My belief is that the Liturgy of the Book of Common Prayer, and hence the Anglican doctrine of marriage, enshrines both: (a) the "saving act" of God, inherent in the Ephesians pattern, whereby marriage, originating in the order of creation, is taken also into the order of salvation or redemption by incorporation into the concept of the body of Christ, the Church bound by Christ to himself in an everlasting covenant; and (b) the affirmation of the necessary bond, created by an oath, in the language of "vow and covenant" in which the marriage bond is described. This is apparent in the prayer said immediately after the giving and receiving of the ring (and adapted from the Sarum blessing of the ring):

17. . . . so these persons may surely perform and keep the vow and covenant betwixt them made . . .

The prayers and homilies, in fact, reflect the two poles within which I have set this exposition of doctrine – the grounding back in creation, with reference to God as "the creator and preserver of all mankind", and the pointing forward to the attainment of everlasting life, by the faithful keeping of themselves as "undefiled members of Christ's body" by the living faithfully within the vow and covenant made between them. The function of grace and of the Holy Spirit in this is frequently asserted. The Homily on The State of Matrimony, published in 1562 (and another of the Church's formularies, though a lesser one), speaks of marriage that

18. It is instituted of God, to the intent that man and woman should live lawfully in a perpetual friendly fellowship, . . .

It speaks of

19. this godly knot once begun between you.

It urges that

20. married persons must apply their minds in most earnest wise to concord, and must crave continually of God the help of his Holy Spirit, so to rule their hearts and to knit their minds together, that they be not dissevered by any division or discord.

IV The Permanence of the Marriage Bond

The practice of the Church of England agrees with its formularies in attaching the mark of permanence (as well as of exclusiveness) to "natural" marriage, marriage in the order of creation, as well as to "sacramental" marriage, that is marriage in the order of redemption. In this it accords with the word of Jesus in Mark 10:6, "From the beginning . . .", reflected in the reference to Adam and Eve in the blessing, quoted at no. 8. It follows necessarily that the Church of England accepts as valid and binding any marriage, even of the unbaptised, regularly contracted by the free exchange of consent before the civil registrar. The "covenant" interpretation of marriage, following St Paul, grounds marriage in the covenant relation of God with Israel and of Christ with the Church: husbands are called upon to exhibit towards their wives the faithfulness of God in his covenant with Israel, and of Christ in his new covenant with the Church. Marriage is thus a "sign" to the world, in terms which the world can see and understand, of the "mystery" (*sacramentum*) of that invisible divine covenant, revealed in Christ. And as the Reformers spoke of sacraments as *signa exhibitiva*, signs exhibiting or making apparent the invisible Christ, a more than exemplary significance may be read into the reference to "Christ's presence and first miracle (*sēmeion*, 'sign') that he wrought in Cana of Galilee", in the priest's opening address to the congregation. The "sacramental" balance of the Church's doctrine is thus, I believe, obliquely maintained. The abandonment of the marriage covenant is thus an abandonment of witness to the divine covenant, a form of apostasy from Christ.

The coinherence of the two covenants is demonstrated in the rubric, dating from 1662,

21. *It is convenient that new married persons should receive the Holy Communion at the time of their marriage, or at the first opportunity after their marriage.*

The original form of the rubric in 1549 was:

22. *The new married persons (the same day of their Marriage) must receive the Holy Communion.*

In 1601 the vicar of Pocklington, Yorks., was censured at a Visitation for omitting the Communion service at a wedding.

It should be added that, in the 1928 Revision of the Prayer Book, references to Adam and Eve, and to other Old Testament characters and precedents, were removed, partly because the Church, still in retreat before the critics of Genesis as being unhistorical and unscientific, had not yet formulated an adequate valuation and interpretation of "myth" with which to defend the Genesis stories; and partly from a desire to reduce what was felt to be verbosity in the prayer. These verbal reductions are not of such significance as to undermine the theology of creation on which the whole service rests: and in any case the 1928 Book is not a formulary of the Church, despite its extensive and, in some respects, well-deserved popularity.

Note

1 "By holy promises with calling the Name of God to witness we be made lively members of Christ, when we profess his religion, receiving the Sacrament of Baptism. By like holy promise the sacrament of matrimony knitteth man and wife in perpetual love, that they desire not to be separated for any displeasure or adversity that shall happen. By lawful oaths which kings, princes, judges, and magistrates do swear common laws are kept inviolate. . . . Therefore lawful swearing cannot be evil, which bringeth unto us so many godly, good, and necessary commodities." From the SPCK edition of *Homilies and Canons* (1864), p. 74. The distinction between upper case for the Sacrament of Baptism, and lower case for the sacrament of matrimony is in the printed text, and, if original, would imply the distinction between the two "sacraments of the Gospel" and the other five which the English Reformers insisted on.

Interchurch Marriage

1. The Ecclesiological Problems of Interchurch Marriage

Alasdair Heron

I Introduction

This title may be found surprising by many people who are involved, directly or indirectly, in interchurch marriage. It is indeed open to predictable criticism from at least two angles, and it is worth noting what such criticism might be. First, the subject may well seem to be abstract, and quite irrelevant to the many practical and pastoral issues which the reality of interchurch marriage raises. Are not other topics – the Christian understanding of marriage, the churches' responsibility for pastoral care, their laws and practice in dealing with interchurch marriage – at once more down to earth and more important than ecclesiology, the doctrine of the Church itself? Indeed, by speaking of "ecclesiological problems" do we not immediately risk the characteristic theological leap into ethereal regions where the real human questions are disposed of simply by being left far behind? Second, it might be argued – especially, though not necessarily only by non-Roman Catholics – that the very term "ecclesiological *problems*" in the plural misleadingly diverts attention from *the* ecclesiological problem which lies, quite simply, in the self-understanding of the Roman Catholic church and finds expression in that church's legislation on interchurch marriage. Both criticisms must be taken seriously, and by taking account of them now I hope to clarify the scope and purpose of this discussion.

1 The suggestion that ecclesiology is abstract and irrelevant may serve to remind us that interchurch marriage is indeed an actual human reality. The temptation to avoid that reality and the concrete problems which it poses by taking refuge in any kind of theological abstraction must be strenuously resisted. It is little comfort to a Christian profoundly distressed – and many are – by the treatment he is receiving from his own or his marriage partner's church to be told that the reasons lie in unresolved theological difficulties about which he knows little and cares less – not, let it be stressed, because he is necessarily a careless or uncommitted Christian or church member, but simply because the difficulties form no part of his own existential horizon. He is right not to be comforted. What is at stake is his own life and marriage, the identity and integrity of his family, the upbringing of his children. If we may believe on good authority that the Sabbath was

made for man, not man for the Sabbath, we must surely also be prepared to recognise that marriage, even interchurch marriage, is an end which theology and law must serve, not ignore or distort. Even if we must deal in theological theory, we cannot be content with mere theorising away from the reality.

This said, however, we must add that ecclesiology is not in fact ultimately abstract or merely theoretical, but extremely concrete. It deals with the way in which the Church understands its own identity, and so also the identity, rights and obligations of its members. As such, it has the most practical implications, because it underlies the way in which the Church – or any particular church – actually behaves. Questions of the nature of marriage, of pastoral care, or of church law and practice in regard to interchurch marriage cannot in the long run be separated from ecclesiology itself. Indeed, a failure to take account of the ecclesiological issues can only have the effect of confusing those other questions, by leaving out of account their implications and the varying presuppositions with which different traditions tend to approach them. To turn to ecclesiology is not to escape from more practical matters, but to attempt to find the wider frame of reference within which they are located. So long as this is borne in mind, the suggested criticism need not trouble us; but it is as well to remember the criticism itself as a warning against any deviation from our course.

2 The alternative suggestion that there is really only one ecclesiological problem is equally important. It stresses rightly that the major storm-centre in current discussion is the practice of the Roman Catholic Church. No other major Church in the Western tradition lays down comparable conditions before permitting an interchurch marriage, or reinforces such conditions with comparable sanctions. And it is no mere coincidence that the Roman Catholic Church also subscribes to an ecclesiology unique in the West, seeing itself alone as fully authentic and all churches not in communion with itself as at best defective (though of course in varying degrees). This ecclesiology is the chief foundation of Roman Catholic interchurch marriage legislation; and other churches, not themselves having such legislation, find themselves in the position of having to react to Roman Catholic practice and the underlying claims of the Roman Catholic Church. It is scarcely surprising that there is a widespread impression that the problem, the whole problem, lies in the Roman Catholic approach.

This impression is, nevertheless, misleading. Roman Catholic ecclesiology and legislation are a very large part of the problem, but not the whole of it. It would be more accurate to say that the past and current practice of the Roman Catholic Church represents an attempt to come to terms with interchurch marriage as perceived from a Roman Catholic perspective. That this attempt only succeeds in intensifying the problems as they are perceived from non-Roman Catholic standpoints should not prevent us from recognising that there are deeper underlying issues involved in interchurch marriage itself. It is because of those issues that the Roman Catholic Church has taken up its present posture, and they should not be lost sight of in any attack – however justified – on the Roman Catholic attempt to deal with them.

Fundamentally, they arise from the fact of division in the Church; they then take on a particular shape and colouring according as that division itself is understood and assessed from different ecclesiological bases.

For this reason, while we shall have to touch on Roman Catholic ecclesiology and its implications for the evaluation of interchurch marriage, it will be as well not to begin there. Instead, we shall attempt to cast our net more widely in order to view the issues from as many angles as possible within the limited space available. A distinction may be made between (a) the fundamental problem of interchurch marriage in the context of interchurch division, (b) the ways in which that problem is seen from different ecclesiological starting-points, and (c) the way in which it can be seen from the perspective opened up by the reality of interchurch marriage itself. We shall briefly discuss each of these in turn, for all in one way or another have to do with ecclesiology, but all set in a slightly different light. In the nature of the case, not one of these viewpoints is adequate to reveal the whole problematic; but the attempt to pay at least some attention to each will help to clarify the different aspects of the question.

II The Fundamental Ecclesiological Problem

The root cause of the various difficulties and problems associated with interchurch marriage does not lie simply in the attitudes of separated churches to each other. Much less does it lie in the temerity of those who, while belonging to one church, marry a member of another. Certainly a good deal of discussion of the subject does appear to begin with one or the other of these diagnoses. This is understandable; but such discussion is not and cannot be radical enough. The foundation of the whole problem is the distinct existence of separated churches. Were there no division between the churches, there would be no such thing as interchurch marriage; because there are divisions, and because these divisions pose serious questions about the nature and identity of the Church itself, interchurch marriage can not only take place, but become a source of difficulty and tension.

Given, however, that the reality of interchurch separation underlies the problem of interchurch marriage, we may go on to ask how exactly interchurch marriage itself comes to be a problem. The answer can be stated in simple enough terms, even if the initial simple statement needs to be followed (as simple statements usually do!) by a certain amount of rather more complicated clarification. In interchurch marriage two principles which normally combine to support each other come into conflict; those of church membership and loyalty on the one hand, and family membership and loyalty on the other.

In the usual run of things (even if this is now in many places less usual than it used to be) Christians have tended to marry members of their own church. Their marriage and family have thus belonged without question in that church; the smaller community of the family has found its natural place within the wider community of the congregation and the church as a whole. In theory at least, this common church affiliation is a source of strength for the marriage and family, and the coherence of the family contributes in turn to the stability and continuance of the church. Thus the two principles of membership and loyalty are in a manner concentric; there is no *prima facie* conflict between them.

In the interchurch marriage by contrast, these principles become eccentric to each other, and a *prima facie* conflict appears. The unity of the family is no longer supported by a single church affiliation, nor does it contribute to the stability of a single church. A kind of incoherence replaces a kind of coherence; a threat of division replaces a potential source of unity within the family; a threat of alienation replaces a potential source of cohesion within the church. The stronger the loyalties are to the church on the one hand and the marriage partner on the other, the greater these threats will appear. What under other circumstances would naturally have tended to strengthen church and marriage now tends to set them against each other. (This is not to say that in particular cases the tension cannot be resolved, or that it must necessarily have destructive rather than constructive consequences. It is to say that the interchurch marriage by its very nature is set in a different force-field from the marriage between members of the same church.)

This incoherence of principles can, however, be evaluated in more than one way, depending on how the nature of church and family membership respectively is understood. The church, and so also church membership, can be pictured in largely institutional terms, and contrasted with the more individual, personal and spontaneous sphere of life represented by marriage and family. Alternatively, the church can be seen as a wider human community as compared with the smaller community of the couple and their children. Each of these models casts some light on the incoherence which interchurch marriage involves, though neither is adequate either on its own or in combination with the other to discover the particular poignancy of the situation.

Where the church is seen primarily as an institution and contrasted with the sphere of personal freedom and choice in which marriage and family are located, the tensions of the interchurch marriage will be interpreted as being between the claims of the institution, expressed largely in juridical terms, and the rights of the individual to a degree of freedom and responsibility in the choice of a marriage partner and in decisions about his own and his family's religious life. Interchurch marriage is indeed very often spoken of as if it were to be seen chiefly, even exclusively, in this horizon. A good deal is said on the one hand of the obligations of church membership, and on the other of the rights of the individual person or family; and it is widely felt, for obvious reasons, that these are somehow in conflict. Both the juridical approach of the Roman Catholic Church to the subject, with its characteristic emphasis on the responsibilities of Roman Catholics, and the equally characteristic insistence of Protestant churches on the rights in conscience of non-Roman Catholics tend to set the issue in the institution-individual horizon. This tendency is only reinforced by the – often puzzled and almost inarticulate – feeling of interchurch couples that their own rights and dignity have been violated by the churches' treatment of them. Nevertheless, although the tensions clearly do in part flow from the institution-individual dialectic, they cannot properly be grasped if they are seen only in these terms. Churches are indeed institutions; but they are not merely juridical entities making juridical claims on their members. They are also communities bound together by personal, social, and above all religious and spiritual ties. Conversely, marriage and family themselves have institutional character. They are not only a sphere of free personal choice, though allowing for a much greater range of such choice than can a larger community such as a church. To see the tension between church membership and family membership purely as the tension between institution and individual is to overlook the essential nature of both church and marriage, and to squeeze the interchurch marriage into an inadequate frame of reference.

If on the other hand the church is understood primarily as a community, and contrasted with the smaller, nuclear community of the family, a rather different picture of the tensions of interchurch marriage can be developed. Both communities have a religious identity, but also a social and cultural one; and the problem with interchurch marriage is that the two community identities cut across each other. To this extent it can be seen as comparable to other types of intermarriage across religious, social, cultural or racial divides. Marriage is after all a common phenomenon, and it is a universal human characteristic to belong to wider communities and yet on occasion to marry outside of hem. This recognition makes it possible to regard interchurch marriage as one type of intermarriage, and to interpret both its difficulties and its potential in the light of comparisons drawn from other types. Such an approach, in a broad sociological or anthropological horizon, can be extremely illuminating – above all in helping to show that what are often thought to be simply religious or even Christian principles of loyalty and church membership are in fact human, even all too human principles of allegiance to one's own group – and as a result liberating. The general "intermarriage" model is, however, no more adequate than the "institution-individual" one. If the latter is too narrow, the former is too wide to make clear the particular nature of interchurch marriage. Useful and even necessary though each is in a partial way as highlighting aspects of the situation, some more adequate conception of the matter is needed.

This more adequate conception can only be found if it is remembered that interchurch marriage is by definition Christian marriage, and that Christian marriage and the Christian family are not only *within* but actually *of* the Church itself. The Church is a community, and marriage and the family constitute a cell of that community. As such, while not in themselves a distinct or complete *ecclesia*, they have a kind of ecclesial character. This fundamental perception of Christian marriage is expressed in certain traditions in what may loosely be called the "sacramental" understanding of marriage, by which Christian marriage is marked off from other marriages; but those other traditions which do not follow that approach, and tend rather to emphasise the "humanness" of marriage in general, including Christian marriage, still generally see the Christian marriage and family as forming in principle a constituent cell of the Church, itself the whole family of God. Whether the Christian marriage is regarded as different in *kind*, or rather as bearing a particular *meaning* is of secondary significance compared with the primary conviction that it is Christian and as such belongs radically within the Church as a part of the Church, as a place in which the life of the Church is lived. The concept of the Church in the fullest sense includes the family and its relationships; the life of the Christian husband or wife, parent or child in his or her family is a part of his or her life as a member of the Church.

From this it follows that the inherent problematic of the interchurch marriage as seen from a Christian viewpoint must be understood in terms of the nature both of interchurch division and of Christian marriage as something which is of the Church itself. In it, allegiance to the marriage partner and to the family as a cell of the Church as represented by the particular church to which both partners belong is replaced by a divided allegiance to two distinct churches and to the marriage and family in which these churches impinge on each other. Were there no division between the churches, then allegiance to the Church would not have come to be mediated through allegiance to a particular church as opposed to other churches. So long, however, as marriage is limited to members of the same church, the inherent difficulties of such mediation remain concealed. Once the question of interchurch marriage arises, they break out of this concealment. Instead of the straightforward belonging of a single family within a single church, and so uninterruptedly within the Church, there are now three different communities, each of which in some way has to do with the Church, yet none of which is fully able to include the others: the two churches and the interchurch marriage. Thus the identity or adequacy of each of these three communities in its relation to the Church is thrown into question; and none of them can easily press its own claims without in some measure denying those of the others, or at best allowing them only a relative validity. This is the fundamental ecclesiological problem of interchurch marriage: Church and marriage, which in principle belong together, have fallen out of phase with each other because of the division between the churches; and thus the identity of the churches and the marriage alike is threatened.

From this radical ecclesiological incoherence flow the other problems of interchurch marriage. These can however be seen in very different ways from different standpoints within the overall fragmentation of the situation. (Such variation of standpoint is itself the best proof of that fragmentation: wherever a structured whole has fallen apart, a unified overall view is no longer possible, and one must do what one can with the partial and broken perceptions afforded by varying one-sided, selective and mutually inconsistent perspectives.) This is the prime reason for the numerous and persistent problems of communication on the subject between church and church, or between church and interchurch family. The horizons, the questions, the problems vary according to where one stands and how one assesses the position; and what from one point of view appears self-evident can from another seem utterly wrong. Yet because the overall unity which would reconcile these conflicting standpoints and perceptions has been lost, the only way in which we can sketch out the different dimensions of the problem is to take the most important of the varying standpoints in turn. Each supplies a kind of window into the total situation; and while the views from the different windows cannot but conflict to some extent with each other, the attempt to do some kind of justice to them may serve then to indicate the way in which at least a partial reconciliation, some softening of the edges of the conflict, may be achieved.

Essentially, there are two such perspectives: that of the church, one of whose members is marrying a member of another church; and that of the interchurch marriage itself. After all that has been said, it is clear that the contrast here cannot simply be characterised as being between an external and an internal approach to the marriage: it can as properly be understood as being between an internal and an external approach to the church. In fact, it is better not to see the contrast in those terms at all, but rather to recognise it as reflecting two different approaches to a single broken situation. The third and fourth sections of this paper are therefore concerned with these two approaches.

Within the first of these perspectives, however, further distinctions must be made. The approach of any particular church to an interchurch marriage will vary greatly according to that church's general understanding of the nature of interchurch division and its particular evaluation of the other church which is also involved. It will also vary according to the church's general approach to marriage: in particular the responsibility which the Roman Catholic Church feels itself to have for the marriages of its members is a factor which cannot be left out of account, for it too has ecclesiological implications. Further, in any particular case there is the problem that *another* church and *its* attitudes and claims are always also involved: the resultant antinomies are central to the ecclesiological problematic of interchurch marriage. The third section will touch on those three specific areas.

III From the Standpoint of the Churches

1 Attitudes to Interchurch Division and to Other Churches

The attitude of any church to interchurch marriage is inevitably coloured more by its assessment of the other church than by any other single factor. This is not because the nature of marriage as marriage is not taken seriously: rather the reverse is the case. It is precisely because marriage is taken seriously as a cohesive reality with which the church has to do that interchurch marriage raises difficulties. These difficulties increase in direct proportion to the extent to which the ecclesial status of the other church and the Christian standing of its members are seen as problematic. It is not a question here simply of whether that other church is viewed with friendliness or hostility, important though that *also* is. It is, much more radically, a question of how far that other church is felt to be authentic as a church, of how far membership of it is felt to be proper membership of the Church. Here

there is a whole range of possible positions, from total and unconditional acceptance, through varying degrees of substantial or partial
recognition, to utter and complete rejection.

We might attempt here to construct a kind of scale of degrees of
recognition, and to plot on it the attitudes of particular churches to
others. Any such attempt would however be extremely difficult to carry
through with even a reasonable degree of accuracy and fairness. Positions can change and do change; official positions may be and often are
largely theoretical, and much less significant in practice than unofficial
and informal ones; and in numerous instances there may well be no
explicit official position at all, but a whole variety of unofficial attitudes.
Anything so ambitious as an attempt to give an exhaustive classifica-
tion of the ways in which even the four major churches in Ireland –
Roman Catholic, Anglican, Methodist and Presbyterian – regard each
other would be likely to meet with protest from all kinds of quarters as
misrepresentation. On the other hand, there is a danger even greater
than that of possible misrepresentation of the views of this or that
church or of groups within it. That is the even greater distortion
involved in the refusal to recognise that the various churches do tend to
have rather varying opinions of each other's authenticity. It is too easy
to assume that the churches have a fine democratic approach to each
other, or that because they somehow ought to have such an approach,
no attention should be paid to their disagreements in their mutual
evaluations. Such assumptions only serve to confuse the debate, to
remove it a stage further from reality.

Thus while we shall not undertake a comprehensive survey of
attitudes, it is as well to remind ourselves of the kind of approach which
tends to be characteristic of the main Churches in Ireland. The Roman
Catholic Church, first of all, still finds it impossible today as in the past
to extend full and complete recognition to any Church not in communion with itself and not recognising the authority of the Papacy.
Only the Roman Catholic Church can claim the uniqueness, completeness and comprehensiveness which go to make up "catholicity".
Other churches are not, however, all seen in exactly the same light.
The Eastern, Eastern Orthodox and Old Catholic Churches are recognised as possessing valid orders and valid sacraments, and thus as being
very substantially if not fully authentic.[1] Other churches than the
Orthodox have traditionally been relegated to a virtually non-ecclesial
status and treated as heretical or schismatic. Since Vatican II, however, some fuller theoretical recognition has been offered to them, and
the existence of authentic elements of the Church outside the boundaries of the Roman Catholic communion has been officially admitted.[2]
These elements, and in particular the baptism of non-Roman
Catholics, are, however, seen as belonging in principle to the Roman
Catholic Church, and as possessing an inherent dynamic towards
reunion with it through which they will be rescued from their present
fragmentariness, and restored to the fullness in which they properly
belong.[3] All the main non-Roman Catholic traditions have in the
years since Vatican II been treated with a new openness reflecting this
shift in attitude, so that while a formal statement of the attitude of

Rome to Methodists or Anglicans or Presbyterians – or Lutherans or Baptists or Pentecostals . . . – has not been made, we may properly assume that they are all included in the more generous horizon introduced by the Council. In particular, while an official definition of the standing of the Anglican churches in Roman Catholic eyes has not been given, the particularly intensive dialogue between Rome and Canterbury, and the recent emphasis on the special relationship between them, would seem to indicate some informal recognition by Rome of a special Anglican status, superior (if one may use the term) to that of other non-Roman Catholic and non-Orthodox Churches.[4]

On the Protestant side (if one may use the term "Protestant" in the loose sense, common in Ireland, to include Anglicans as well as Methodists and Presbyterians, and so merely as a convenient label) there is one fundamental difference from the Roman Catholic approach. At least in theory, none of these churches regards itself as the only and exclusively authentic church, or makes recognition of its own exclusive claims and communion with itself an absolute pre-requisite for the admission of the full authenticity of another church.[5] Rather, each sees itself as a part or branch of the Church, and is prepared in principle to recognise other churches as parts or branches of it as well.[6] This recognition is then advanced or withheld according as certain marks of the Church are perceived to be present or absent. These marks are in general defined in terms of adherence to Scripture and particular doctrinal standards and the right administration of the two dominical sacraments of Baptism and the Eucharist, together with some form of church order and discipline. In the official Anglican position, this last criterion is formulated more narrowly than by Methodism or Presbyterianism: the appropriate form of church order must include the historic episcopate. To these marks a further general principle should be added, although it is really only an implication of them. A church which by and large meets the criteria of authenticity, but which also subscribes to other doctrines which are not acceptable – so for example the Marian dogmas, or the dogma of papal infallibility – may be regarded as impaired in its authenticity by such subscription. Thus these Protestant churches all have greater or less reservations about the full authenticity of the Roman Catholic Church, though not denying that authenticity altogether. They can and do also vary in their attitudes to each other: in principle at least, it is easier for a Methodist or Presbyterian church to admit the full authenticity of an Anglican church than *vice versa*.

Thus in the case of Roman Catholic/Protestant interchurch marriages, the churches on both sides are most likely to offer only partial recognition to each other. Further, this recognition will rest on a different basis in each case. The other churches can recognise in the Roman Catholic authentic elements of the Church of which they regard themselves as being a (probably more authentic) part. Rome on the other hand can recognise in them authentic elements of the Church which Rome itself represents in its fullness. This asymmetry of attitudes must not be lost out of sight, as it affects the *kind* of partial recognition extended in each instance. It should perhaps also be remarked in passing that both the Roman Catholic and Protestant churches would agree in totally rejecting the ecclesial status of various other bodies – the Mormons, or the Jehovah's Witnesses, for example. To extend partial recognition across the divide opened by the Reformation is not necessarily to open the floodgates! We must therefore ask after the implications of such partial recognition for the evaluation of an interchurch marriage. Before doing so, however, it will be worth pausing to consider the limiting cases where there is either full recognition of the other church or total rejection of it.

Where the other church is fully recognised, and regarded accordingly as virtually equivalent in ecclesial status, an interchurch marriage raises relatively few problems, and those in general more pastoral and practical than ecclesiological. This is quite simply because the church membership – and so by implication the Christian status – of the two partners is regarded as comparable, as equally privileged. A certain anomaly remains in the division of the marriage between two churches; but it is not perceived as a partnership of unequals. Thus a marriage with a member of the other church is not seen as a threat to one's faith; the prospect that one's children will be brought up in the other church does not appear to involve the loss of their Christian birthright; the possibility that one might even go over to the other church for the sake of marriage and family unity does not raise the grim spectre of apostasy. Of course, decisions on all kinds of questions still have to be made, and there may be various difficult choices on matters of church membership and the upbringing of the children. But these do not raise basic theological difficulties. On the other side of the coin, the possibility of some kind of dual loyalty, or even dual membership, can at least be contemplated; and any problems which prevent its realisation are likely to be of a technical and institutional rather than a radical theological or ecclesiological nature.

Where on the other hand the authenticity of the other church is totally rejected, so that the marriage is not strictly speaking "interchurch" from the point of view of the church with whose attitude we are concerned, the reverse is the case in every respect. The marriage is a partnership between unequals, because there is no common ground of faith and Christian status and equivalent church membership. The marriage is seen as a threat to one's faith; the prospect that one's children will be brought up in the other church as the loss of their heritage and of their proper Christian home; the possible going over of oneself to the other church as apostasy. There can of course be no question at all of dual loyalties or membership; for the common basis on which such duality might have been built is lacking. Thus the best solution of the problems of such marriage is likely to be seen in its prevention; or, if that is not feasible, in hedging it around with such safeguards as may be devised to guarantee the continuing loyalty of one's own members and, if possible, the upbringing of their children within their own church and not in the alien body. To these may also be added the hope that the partner from the other church may be persuaded to come over, and so establish the marriage on a unified basis of church membership.

It is less easy to give even a broad indication of the kind of attitude likely to develop where the other church is neither fully accepted as equivalent nor utterly rejected as a non-church. All that can be said is that one may reasonably expect the attitude to lie somewhere between the extremes just indicated, and to approximate to the one or the other according as the ecclesial status of the other church and the Christian status of its members are positively or negatively evaluated. When one comes to the specific question of Roman Catholic/Protestant interchurch marriage as it is manifested in Ireland, it seems not unreasonable to say that on both sides of the divide, the general evaluation tends to the negative rather than the positive, and that as a result the approach to interchurch marriage is designed first of all to discourage, and, failing that, to ensure or at least encourage (a) the continuing allegiance of one's own members, (b) the upbringing of their children in their church, and (c) the conversion of the marriage partner, though as a rule little emphasis is placed on the last of these. The clearest example of this is of course the Roman Catholic position; but parallels, albeit less juridically and less absolutely formulated, can be found in at least some of the Protestant churches as well. [7] Even when due allowance has been made for the important fact that, as we have already noticed, the Protestant churches are in part in reaction against Roman Catholic treatment of the matter, it still remains clear that there is a similar unhappiness about Roman Catholic/Protestant marriages on the Protestant side as well. The greatest difference lies in the way in which the Roman Catholic and Protestant churches *handle* marriage in general and interchurch marriage in particular: to this we shall turn in our next section.

The asymmetry of attitudes already mentioned must not, however, be forgotten. Even although Roman Catholic/Protestant interchurch marriages are approached with similar reservations by the churches on both sides, the ecclesiological basis for such reservations is different. While the difference does not radically affect the attitude, it is of great potential significance for any move towards resolution of the problems. If a church subscribes to the kind of ecclesiology characteristic of the Protestant churches, it can then in principle accept another church – albeit with reservations – as a potential equal partner in dealing with the common problem of interchurch marriage between their members. The question then becomes whether such a Protestant church can, or under what conditions it could, accept the Roman Catholic Church as such a partner. If on the other hand a church holds to the kind of ecclesiology typical of the Roman Catholic Church, such acceptance is in principle difficult to contemplate. This at least is the contrast between the two sides as it appears on the theoretical level. In practice, matters are not so clear cut. The Roman Catholic Church has in fact shown a new readiness in recent years to take other churches more seriously even in the matter of interchurch marriage, thus extending a kind of *de facto* if not *de iure* recognition to them. This of course raises the question of whether such *de facto* recognition does not of itself challenge the traditional Roman ecclesiology, with which it is only with some difficulty reconcilable. These and similar questions will occupy us again later.

2 The Authority of the Church over Marriage

The ecclesiological divergence between the Roman Catholic and Protestant churches is to some extent reflected and paralleled in the equally important contrasts between their approaches to marriage in general and the regulation of interchurch marriage in particular. Here it must serve our purpose merely to note certain major points of difference.

a. In the eyes of the Roman Catholic Church it is still as in the past a requirement of divine law[8] that Roman Catholics should both remain Roman Catholics and, even if married to a non-Roman Catholic, do all in their power to bring up their children as Roman Catholics too. This is of divine law because the Roman Catholic Church is the only authentic church. The Protestant churches on the other hand (i) do not in general find the concept of divine law very helpful, and (ii) do not in any case hold that it is required by God that a Methodist, or Anglican, or Presbyterian should remain so and do all that he can to ensure that his children become even as he is. (This may well be regarded as desirable, even highly desirable: but there is a certain unwillingness in the Churches of the Reformation to identify what is desirable with the will of God). It is not my concern here to take sides; indeed, the taking of sides in this matter usually leads to some kind of uncomprehending caricature of the other's position, as when Roman Catholics simply conclude that Protestants are endemically casual and lacking in respect for authority, or Protestants that Roman Catholics are naïvely arrogant and unthinking in their assumptions of superiority. Both positions in fact fairly reflect the underlying ecclesiology, to which we have already given enough attention, and even though both are capable of grotesque distortion, our concern is not with the distortions but with the straightforward attitudes themselves.

b. In order to preserve this divine law from possible violation, the Roman Catholic Church lays down a series of protective provisions. First of all, it forbids marriages between Roman Catholics and non-Roman Catholics, whether baptised Christians or not. This prohibition is not however absolute. It is canonically formulated, secondly, in the *impediments* of "disparity of cult" (where the partner is not a baptised Christian) and "mixed religion" (where he or she is a baptised member of another church). Thirdly, it is laid down that if a Roman Catholic fails to obtain a *dispensation* from the relevant impediment, the marriage is automatically *invalid* (i.e. non-existent) in the former case, and *illicit* (i.e. genuine but irregular) in the latter.[9] Fourthly, certain *cautiones*,[10] or conditions, must be satisfied before either of these dispensations can be granted: these are formulated primarily in the *promises* which must be made, and which are designed to ensure that the requirements of divine law will be met. There is of course no parallel to these provisions in the law or practice of the Protestant churches: not subscribing to these "impediments", they do not give dispensations from them, and accordingly do not lay down conditions for the granting of such dispensations. Nor, more importantly still, do they regard marriages contracted under conditions other than those they might desire as illicit or invalid.[11]

It is worth pointing out that the force of the legislation specifically directed towards mixed marriages by the Roman Catholic Church makes a clear distinction between marriages involving non-Christians and marriages with non-Roman Catholic Christians.[12] In the latter case, failure to obtain the dispensation merely makes the marriage illicit, not invalid. Thus an interchurch marriage by a Roman Catholic who fails to observe his own church's requirements should in principle still be recognised as a marriage, albeit an irregular one. In fact, however, this is not the case in most instances because of other Roman Catholic legislation which has to do with marriage in general, not specifically with mixed or interchurch marriage. This brings us to our third point of contrast between the Roman Catholic and Protestant Churches: the question of the *canonical form*.

c. Under present legislation, a Roman Catholic must normally be married before the appropriate Roman Catholic priest and two witnesses – what is known as the *canonical form* – or obtain a dispensation permitting him to be married in some other form. Failure to conform to this requirement renders the marriage invalid. This applies regardless of whether the other partner to the marriage is Roman Catholic or not, Christian or not. (The only significant exception is where the non-Roman Catholic partner is an Eastern Christian:[13] then, failure to observe the canonical form, or to obtain a dispensation from it, merely makes the marriage illicit, not invalid.) It is this provision which ultimately underpins the specifically mixed and interchurch marriage legislation, and makes the latter even more rigid than it would otherwise be. A Roman Catholic who – for whatever reason – fails to obtain a dispensation from the impediment of mixed religion, and whose marriage in virtue of that failure would be *illicit but not invalid* in the eyes of the Roman Catholic church, is automatically debarred from marrying according to the canonical form, or from obtaining a dispensation therefrom, so that his marriage ends up by being *invalid as well as illicit*. As the relevant legislation here has to do more with marriage in general than with interchurch or mixed marriage, and as it reflects a peculiarity of the Roman Catholic position over against the Orthodox on the one hand and the Reformation traditions on the other, it may be as well to digress briefly and sketch how it has come about.

In the early church there appears to have been no idea that marriage, even between Christians, *needed* to be celebrated in the presence of the Church to be valid. As the Church became established, however, the practice developed of having a church ceremony. From this there emerged in the Eastern Orthodox tradition the doctrine that the actual celebrant of the marriage was the priest, that *he* "marries" the couple, and that without his participation there is no marriage at all. The Western Church, however, rejected this doctrine, holding to the principle that the couple themselves are the ministers of the marriage to each other, and that the role of the priest is merely that of witness – a role which is not essential to the validity of the marriage itself. This contrast between East and West emerges as early as 866 in the *Responsio ad Bulgaros* of Pope Nicholas I, and remains to the present day. The Western doctrine led, however, to further complications and caused enormous problems for Church and society alike in the Middle Ages. Because marriage was regarded essentially as a matter for the couple themselves, in the celebration of which neither the secular nor the religious authorities absolutely *had* to be involved, so-called "clandestine marriages" became frequent, and led, human nature being what it is, to numerous abuses. Many attempts were made to discourage the practice – particularly by excommunicating those who engaged in such marriages – but with little success. The one obvious solution would have been to adopt the position of the Orthodox Church, and to declare that a priest must marry the couple; but this was felt to be theologically impossible, both because it would involve a departure from the established teaching of the West on the nature of marriage, and because it would represent a radical alteration in the form of administration of what was now coming to be universally regarded as a sacrament – an alteration so radical as to be beyond the power or authority of the Church.

Only after the Reformation, at the Council of Trent, did the Roman Catholic Church finally find a way of grasping this nettle. After much debate and heart-searching, in which it was again made clear that the Eastern Orthodox solution was not acceptable, a somewhat roundabout method of coping with the problem was devised. The Decree *Tametsi*, approved in the 24th Session of the Council on 11 November 1563, laid it down that those who did not contract marriage in the presence of the appropriate priest and two or three witnesses were incapable of contracting it at all, and that all such marriages were accordingly null and void. Thus the failure to observe the canonical form was made an impediment, preventing the marriage from occurring. The presence of the priest and witnesses, while still not being essential to the marriage itself, was made a necessary *precondition* of the marriage, which was then established, as in the past, by the free exchange of consent of the partners.

Tametsi was of course a piece of Roman Catholic legislation. The churches of the Reformation, already separated from Rome, did not appropriate it, and still hold to the principle that a marriage is contracted by the partners and, other things being equal, is valid whether or not the ministrations of the Church are involved. But even in the Roman Catholic Church, the provisions of *Tametsi* did not immediately come into universal effect. The Council decided that these should only begin to apply thirty days after the Decree had been published in any particular place or area; and in many parts of the world it was either never published at all, or else only many years or even centuries after Trent. The requirement to observe the canonical form thus existed in some places but not in others. To complicate matters further, special legislation was on occasion passed to exempt interchurch marriages from *Tametsi* even in areas where it had been published: the most important of these was the Declaration *Matrimonia quae in locis* issued by Pope Benedict XIV in 1741, and also known as the *Benedictina*. This exempted Protestant marriages and interchurch marriages in the Netherlands from the need to observe the canonical form for validity, and its provisions were subsequently extended to certain other countries as well. The resultant unevenness in law and practice lasted until the present century, and was only removed partially by the Decree *Ne Temere* of 1907, and completely by the *Codex Iuris Canonici*, which came into effect in 1918. *Ne Temere* imposed on all Roman Catholics everywhere except in Germany and Hungary the obligation to observe the canonical form, whether or not they were marrying another Roman Catholic; and the exception of Germany and Hungary was then removed by the *Codex*. This remains the position to the present day, with the exception already mentioned of interchurch marriages between Roman Catholics and Eastern Christians.

The most serious point of contrast here between the Roman Catholic and Protestant churches is not simply that the latter do not possess legislation comparable to that of the former. It is that they in general have very serious theological reservations about the right of any church to use the threat of invalidity in this fashion. And in this there is no doubt that they have the tradition of both the early Church, and, more importantly perhaps, the medieval Western Church on their side. Further when it is noticed that the conditions which *Tametsi* was intended to meet no longer obtain in any modern state which insists on the official and public registration of marriages, and that the demand for observance of the canonical form in the context of interchurch marriage makes Roman Catholic interchurch marriage legislation effectively much harsher and more rigid than it would otherwise be even within its own terms, not to mention the fact that such earlier legislation as the *Benedictina* actually tended to *exempt* interchurch marriages from the provisions of *Tametsi*, it is understandable that the development of the more rigid law and practice signalled by *Ne Temere* and the *Codex* is very much under fire from the Protestant side, however logical or even necessary it may appear from a Roman Catholic point of view. Of course, other churches are not primarily concerned with the claims or practice of the Roman Catholic Church where it is legislating simply for its own members, and specifying conditions under which it is prepared to recognise their marriages as valid or invalid, even if they regard such claims and practice as highly questionable. But in the case of an interchurch marriage, these become a matter for their concern as well, as they impinge directly on their own people. It is for this reason that *Ne Temere* has in countries such as Ireland taken on a powerful symbolic value, and is frequently misunderstood as if it had been primarily concerned with mixed and interchurch marriages, or as if it had for the first time introduced the canonical form, the impediment of mixed religion, and the promises. In fact it did not; but it did represent the beginning of a massively consistent application of legislation which had grown up over centuries but had never before been so firmly and widely applied.

d. Underlying these divergences between the Roman Catholic and Protestant traditions is, as has already been hinted, a conviction on the part of the Roman Catholic Church that it has a particular responsibility for and authority over Christian marriage in its theological and juridical aspects. Only because of this conviction, whose roots lie at least as far back as the developments of the Middle Ages by which marriage came to be regarded as one of the seven sacraments, and marriage cases to be treated as lying within the scope of ecclesiastical rather than secular or civil courts, can the Roman Catholic Church lay down juridical norms, failure to meet which entitles it to dismiss a marriage as invalid. The Protestant churches, while certainly recognising the possibility that a "marriage" may be invalid – for example in a case of consanguinity or bigamy – do not in general feel that it lies within the competence of the Church to lay down such narrow conditions as the Roman Catholic Church has done, or to treat a marriage as invalid because of the infringement of merely ecclesiastical regulations, however well-intentioned.

There is thus a fundamental divergence of approaches to the question of what the Church can or cannot, may or may not do in dealing with marriage in general and interchurch marriage in particular. In the Roman Catholic view, the Church is entitled, conceivably even in conscience compelled, to impose restrictions on interchurch marriages, and to hold out the ultimate threat of invalidity to re-inforce them. From a Protestant standpoint, the Church is not really entitled to behave in this way, however much it might wish to, because it simply does not have that kind of authority. The ecclesiological asymmetry already discussed is reflected here in the asymmetry of approaches to marriage and interchurch marriage discipline, and leads to the most serious tensions in practice in the matter of interchurch marriage.

3 The Inadequacy of Unilateralism

Thus far we have considered the approaches of the Roman Catholic and Protestant churches to interchurch marriage involving their members, and have seen how those approaches both resemble and diverge from each other. Now, however, we must go a stage further and take account of the fact that no approach from the side of only one of the churches involved can ever adequately grasp the problems of any interchurch marriage. Simply because there is always another church implicated, and because its standpoint will as a rule differ from and in various respects contradict that of the first church, pure unilateralism can never formulate the difficulties or advance satisfactory solutions for them. Even a kind of mutual unilateralism, where each church advances its own hopes, fears and claims in opposition to those of the other, can serve only to consolidate within the marriage the boundaries between the churches, to intensify within the marriage the strains of interchurch division. The best result of such a meeting can only be some more or less unsatisfactory compromise; the worst, the destruction either of the marriage or of the church loyalty of one or both marriage partners.

The inherent tendency of a unilateral approach is, in brief, to treat the other church as part of the problem, rather than as a potential partner bearing responsibility for the situation. It matters little whether the problem is seen as lying in its very existence (as in the case of the traditional Roman Catholic approach to the Protestant churches) or in its particular claims and legislation (as in the case of the usual Protestant attitude to Roman Catholic treatment of interchurch marriage). Either way, the other church is regarded as the difficulty, the anomaly, the obstacle; one's own existence and claims are not perceived as problematic. The fact that in the eyes of the other church these may be very problematic indeed is perceived simply as a further justification for a defensive unilateralism, a withdrawal into isolation where the problems can be assessed and dealt with exclusively in terms of one's own horizon, without interference from outside. This can have the further effect that the other church is in practice treated as even less of a church than it is in theory believed to be: the emphasis comes to lie on opposition and rejection rather than on what the churches actually have in common. Similarly the Christian faith and church loyalty of the marriage partner from the other church tend to be valued and appreciated only to the extent that they conform or can be made to conform to those of one's own members. Thus even partial recognition of the other church comes in practice to approximate to rejection of its authenticity, because it is the differences and disagreements which occupy the forefront of attention.

It cannot be denied that such unilateralism has in the past characterised the approaches of the churches to Roman Catholic/Protestant marriage, and to a large extent does so still. The years since Vatican II have, however, brought a new element into the situation. Alongside the older unilateralism, and in very manifest tension with it, there has been developing a search for ways of sharing responsibility in a bilateral or multilateral way. The Council, in its *Votum* on Mixed Marriage during its third session in November 1964, explicitly recognised that the legislation of the *Codex Iuris Canonici* needed to be modified and brought into line with the spirit of the *Decree on Ecumenism* and the *Declaration on Religious Liberty;* and subsequent legislation in the *Instructio Matrimonii Sacramentum* (1966) and the papal *Motu Proprio Matrimonia Mixta* (1970) has brought a significant relaxation of discipline in the treatment of mixed marriages, though without altering the underlying principles of Roman Catholic ecclesiology.[14] The Roman Catholic Church is now also involved in more than one international commission on mixed marriage with representatives of other communions; at national level, joint statements and recommendations on pastoral care of interchurch marriages have appeared in various countries; and at local level in many places Roman Catholic clergy have set out to do as the Pope required in *Matrimonia Mixta* by establishing "relationships of sincere openness and enlightened confidence with ministers of other religious communities" in order "to aid the married couple to foster the unity of their conjugal and family life, a unity which, in the case of Christians, is based on their baptism too."[15]

On these developments, a few final comments may be in order. First it is clear that an improvement in the treatment of interchurch marriages on a local, national or international scale depends above all on the attitude and practice of the Roman Catholic authorities. Only where they are prepared to initiate steps or at least to respond positively to overtures from other churches or the couples themselves can the situation be changed, simply because it is the legislation and requirements of the Roman Catholic Church which most concretely bring the difficulties of mixed marriage to the forefront of attention and set up limits and hurdles which must be negotiated. With the best will in the world, no other church on its own, and no combination of other churches, can alter the position as far as interchurch marriages involving a Roman Catholic are concerned.

Second, however, the relaxation of discipline which has already been brought about demonstrates the possibility, even from the Roman Catholic standpoint, and even with all the Roman Catholic Church's reservations about other churches, of taking these other churches seriously as partners who *also* have genuine concerns and responsibilities for the marriages of their members. This *de facto* if not *de iure* recognition, and the spirit of openness and confidence which it presupposes, supplies the only adequate basis for constructive co-operation between the churches. It does not imply that all kinds of disagreement have been removed. It does take the degree of partial recognition which is already extended to those other churches as the foundation for a positive rather than a purely negative attitude. It points to the possibility of a kind of respect even in disagreement, of a constructive concentration on what is shared, not merely as a lowest common denominator, but rather as a basis for future growth in understanding.

Third, and closely related to the preceding remark, it is significant that the changes brought about first by the *Instructio Matrimonii Sacramentum* in 1966 and then by the *Motu Proprio Matrimonia Mixta* in 1970 have been in the area of discipline and practice rather than in that of the fundamental ecclesiological principles to which Rome still subscribes. This can be and has been made a stick with which to beat Rome;[16] and from the standpoint of the other churches, the beating is doubtless still merited. Nevertheless, the situation can also be viewed in a positive light. The recent legislation has shown once and for all that the monolithic combination of ecclesiological principle and extremely rigid practice classically represented by the *Codex Iuris Canonici* is not the only option open to the Roman Catholic Church, that indeed this particular option has been tried and found wanting. Insofar as the application of the principles has been somewhat softened, they have themselves been made less threatening to other churches and less damaging to ecumenical relations, while the general loosening which has taken place holds out hope of further development of a positive kind. Nor is this all. Practice does not derive deductively from principle in every case: it happens as often that principle emerges from practice. And when change is to take place, it usually comes more easily in the first instance in the area of practice, not that of principle. If through experimentation it is discovered that a new form of practice, which at least hints at some shift in principles, is both viable and constructive, some re-appraisal and re-formulation of the principles themselves may eventually be expected to follow. To this extent, the recent relaxation of interchurch marriage discipline by the Roman Catholic Church must be welcomed not only as a partial improvement in the present state of the situation, not only as a hint that still further improvements may eventually be hoped for, but also as a sign that Rome itself is moving in the only feasible way towards an ecclesiological stance more acceptable to the other churches.

Finally, all the developments of the last few years, partial, uneven and ragged though they be, hint at a wider ecumenical horizon in which interchurch division itself may yet be transcended in a deeper unity of which the interchurch marriage itself is a fragmentary sign. There is still a lengthy and difficult road ahead, and the shape of the destination is still altogether unclear; but a beginning has been made. Everything depends, now and in the future, on the spirit in which the churches encounter each other. We have the choice on all sides between opening and closing, between confidence which goes out to meet the other and defensiveness which retreats into isolation. Only one of these ways is adequate – and it is not the way of unilateralism.

IV From the Standpoint of the Interchurch Marriage

If the natural tendency of a church viewing interchurch marriage is to regard the other church as the problem, the natural tendency when the matter is seen from the perspective of the marriage itself is to see the division between the two churches as the problem. It is a problem not primarily because of the disagreements and conflicts between the churches *in themselves*, but because these disagreements and conflicts introduce a source of disunity and tension *into the marriage*. This perspective is as valid as the other, and must be taken equally seriously. The interchurch marriage is in principle a fully authentic Christian marriage, and deserves to be treated as such; and when it is so treated, it is the separate existence of *both* churches (not only of one of them!) which comes to appear the cause of the difficulties, by throwing the unity and cohesiveness of that Christian marriage into question, by threatening it in its very centre.

Before we go on to consider this aspect in more detail, it is worth reminding ourselves of the obvious but often forgotten fact that every marriage is to some extent "mixed". It is established between two individuals of different sex, from different families, commonly from different places and varying backgrounds, with their own individual attitudes, interests, values, opinions and beliefs. A certain diversity and complementarity is built-in in every marriage, and its success is largely determined by the extent to which this diversity becomes a source of growth and strength rather than of fragmentation and conflict. It cannot be assumed *a priori* that any particular divergence is of necessity going to weaken the marriage rather than strengthen it; nor of course can it be assumed *a priori* that in the event of any such difference, the opinions or beliefs of one partner must of right become dominant. In the instance of Roman Catholic/Protestant marriages, it cannot properly be supposed either that they are doomed to failure, or that the Church membership and loyalty of one partner – whether Roman Catholic or Protestant – must retreat before the claims of the other. However desirable this may appear from the standpoint of one or other of the churches, it is hardly compatible with an open and unprejudiced, which is to say an objective and realistic approach to any particular couple in their own individual circumstance. What is a reasonable and suitable recipe in one case can become a prescription for disaster in another unless each is judged on its own merits.

The question is thus in any marriage not whether there are differences, even major differences, between the partners, but how those that are present may best be coped with constructively by and for this particular couple. Where the partners belong to two different churches, there are broadly three options open to them. They can settle for a common indifference to church membership; they can agree that for all practical purposes, the membership of one partner will become normative for the family as a whole; or they can attempt to preserve both allegiances and to integrate them somehow into the life of the family. The first two of these alternatives in effect cut the Gordian knot: they resolve the problem of the family's interchurch status by setting it aside. The majority of such families most probably do in fact choose one of those ways, or else settle for the third only in the weak sense that each partner goes his or her own ecclesiastical way, settling the question of the upbringing of the children either through indifference or by handing over the children to one partner and his or her church – variants, in effect, of the first two "solutions".[17] There is however a minority, and there are signs that it is growing, who wish to take the way of integration in a more full-blooded sense. It is with them that the problems and possibilities of an authentic interchurch marriage really emerge in the attempt to weave some kind of double church loyalty into the fabric of the marriage and family.

It would scarcely be possible here to discuss the presuppositions and implications of this attempt in any detail, or to consider at length all the various means by which it can be realised. Many of these are discussed elsewhere in this consultation; in addition I would refer particularly to two recent documents: *The Joint Pastoral Care of Interchurch Marriages in England, Wales and Scotland*, which approaches the topic from the point of view of the churches and their pastoral responsibility, and *Two-Church Families*, written by partners in interchurch marriages themselves.[18] It may however be in place in the limited space remaining to consider what general principles underlie the attempt at interchurch integration within a single family, and to indicate some practical steps towards which it would seem to point.

The first and most radical implication – though one which is usually overlooked, perhaps because of the difficulty of taking adequate theological account of it – is that there is a kind of *de facto* setting of the churches on an equal footing in relation to the marriage. This is not to say that the respective church loyalties and commitments of the partners are necessarily precisely equivalent: such things cannot be mathematically measured. Nor is it to say that there may not be in practice a leaning in the direction of one of the churches rather than the other, especially once questions of the baptism and upbringing of the children arise. It is to say that the attempt to take seriously the church allegiance of both partners within the marriage in principle rules out any absolute or unconditional assumptions about the superiority of one church over the other. Insofar as each partner holds to his or her own church membership in preference to substituting for it membership of the other's church, he or she is of course making a personal choice as to the preferability of this church over that. But this is immediately balanced by the other partner's choice. So far as the interpersonal dynamic of the marriage itself is concerned, the churches are on a level with each other. Each is recognised as having a stake in the marriage; neither is allowed to claim exclusive rights. What is desirable when the matter is approached from the standpoint of the churches, the replacement of unilateralism with a respect-ful bilateralism, is demanded, is in fact built into the structure of the interchurch marriage itself. If it is not then actually realised in the marriage, that can only be because the implications of that structure have become obscured or actually suppressed.

It must be stressed that what is involved in this relativisation of the churches within the marriage is not to be confused with, and need not necessarily lead to, indifference to the churches on the part of the partners. Rather it is a question of a Christian unit, the marriage and family, which by its nature has an orientation towards the wider community of the Church, and which expresses that orientation through a certain allegiance to two churches. That this church allegiance is thus relativised is not the fault of the marriage, but of the interchurch division. Of course the position is anomalous; but so is the separation of the Churches from each other. Insofar as the interchurch marriage transcends the division between the churches, it does so by pointing to and reflecting a unity which is deeper than that division. This is by no means incompatible with genuine and deep loyalty to the churches themselves, even if at the same time it serves to challenge the churches in their division. Seen in this light, the interchurch marriage can come to take on positive meaning and significance as a sign of the presence of the Church among the churches; and, given that meaning, it can begin to be a place where the churches meet, not merely in opposition and separation, but in the movement of growth towards each other: a growth which begins with the couple, but because of their church loyalties and membership also involves, even on a tiny scale, the churches themselves.

If an interchurch marriage is to develop in this way, and so become what it is by its nature, then clearly the very serious questions on which the churches involved diverge must also somehow be taken account of. This demands on the part of the couple themselves first of all a fundamental willingness to respect, even in disagreement, a preparedness to let certain things be, both in points of doctrine and in matters of religious practice. If the spirit of sincere openness and enlightened confidence is needed by pastors dealing with interchurch marriage, it is even more necessary for the couple. Toleration of this kind is, let it be said again, not the same as mere indifference: it presupposes both a degree of commitment to one's own position and willingness to accept and respect the different views of the other. Second, and growing out of this toleration, is the endeavour to understand sympathetically what seems at first sight merely alien, incomprehensible or wrong-headed, to discover how the other perceives matters from his or her own religious and Christian viewpoint. This can then lead in the third place to the unexpected discovery of affinity even in what had at first seemed simply difference, to the recognition of one's own faith, in however altered expression, in the forms and practices familiar to the other. Where these stages are traversed – and similar stages must be traversed in the most various fields of life, and certainly in the most various aspects of marriage: they belong to the growth of human maturity as well as of ecumenical understanding – such common ground as may have been present to begin with is extended and cultivated and made fruitful. No doubt in many cases various differences and disagreements, some of them serious, will still remain; but these can be robbed of much of their sting as the partners grow in understanding of each other, and of their different traditions. It is not utopian to believe that in such a case, a certain awareness of affinity to the other's church may develop even in one who remains loyal to his or her own, a certain feeling of belonging in the other Christian community as well. Such a feeling of affinity – which of course is only likely to develop if the churches involved also play their part in welcoming and supporting the interchurch couple – can in turn transform the anguished and painful decisions which past years have seen on such questions as the baptism of the children. He who has come to have some genuine appreciation of or even affection for his partner's church is much more likely to approve the upbringing of his children in it – the more so if his partner and his children are in the way of discovering the same kind of affinity for his church as well.

These reflections on the principles governing the attempt to build on the interchurch dimension of marriage already suggest several general practical conclusions. There must be a sympathetic and open treatment of the couple by the clergy of both churches. There must be an atmosphere of welcome in the congregations themselves. There must be opportunity for the gathering of information on the other church, and for participation in worship and other activities. Where these are lacking – and all too often they are more conspicuous by their absence than their presence – then even the best-intentioned interchurch couple are likely to become first frustrated and finally bitter. But so much is already obvious. There are more radical and theologically more difficult issues to which we must now briefly turn: those of church membership, of admission to the Eucharist and of Baptism. In speaking of those it will be advisable to deal first with the interchurch marriage partners themselves, then to turn to the question of their children.

Assuming that the partners have discovered or are in process of discovering some significant affinity to each other's churches flowing out of their shared Christian life, then the question of eucharistic sharing must eventually arise. Whether and in what form this can be made possible depends on so many variable factors that it is difficult to make general and comprehensive statements on the subject. The alternatives are numerous: occasional restricted eucharistic hospitality for particular individuals, as has for example been on occasion extended by Roman Catholic bishops under certain circumstances in some countries to the non-Roman Catholic husbands and wives of Roman Catholics;[19] more general admission of such couples to the eucharistic celebration in each other's church on a regular basis; eucharistic sharing in the context of a wider arrangement for intercommunion between two churches; the development of full communion between the churches;

the practice of what is loosely called "open communion" in, for example, the Methodist and Presbyterian traditions;[20] nor, finally, can one ignore the fact that ministers and priests have on occasion been known deliberately to admit to the Eucharist members of other churches whom, strictly speaking, the regulations of their own church would have excluded, and that other clergy again, while not deliberately seeking to do so, would as a matter of principle receive to the Table any persons coming for communion even if they knew them to be so excluded. What can be said is, first, that there is evidence of an increasing desire among many interchurch couples to be able to share in the Eucharist in each other's churches; second, that the steps taken, for example, by the Bishop of Strasbourg demonstrate that even the Roman Catholic Church, which in general of all the western churches sees the greatest theological (and juridical?) objections to the admission of members of other churches to the sacrament, can in fact nevertheless move in that direction; and third, that such moves (and not only by the Roman Catholic Church) would seem to represent a more adequate theological response to the situation of the interchurch couple than the alternative of continuing to exclude one partner from the Eucharist.

Certainly a move towards the admission of members of other churches to communion together with their husbands or wives (and the corollary of permitting one's own members to communicate in the church of their partner) must have some adequate theological basis if it is not to appear merely as a purely pragmatic – and perhaps dangerous – accommodation to the situation. But surely such a basis is in fact present? It is to be found, first of all – and this is in effect the whole burden of this paper – in the shared Christian community established by the interchurch marriage. But at an even more radical level, it is established by the fact that both partners are baptised and have in common the sacrament of initiation into the faith and into the Church. Baptism is not a denominational matter, and in spite of all divergences in practice and some variations in emphasis and interpretation, its fundamental meaning and significance are not at issue in the ecumenical debate. Nor do the different churches (with the exception of the Baptist) regard their own baptism as somehow different from or superior to that administered in other communions. Rather, the main Christian traditions can agree in using the formula of Vatican II in *Unitatis Redintegratio*, par.3: those "who believe in Christ and have been properly baptised are brought into a certain, though imperfect, communion with" all the baptised, and so even with those churches to which they do not belong. It can of course be held that the degree of communion between members of separated churches is *so* imperfect that the Eucharist, the seal of unity, cannot be shared by them. But might it not be better to hold – without entering the debate as to whether intercommunion is the destination of the move towards unity or a means towards it – that the Eucharist is always *both* seal of unity already achieved *and* promise of unity not yet attained; and that at least in the case of those who are joined not only by baptism but also by marriage both the achievement and the promise are sufficiently present to justify the celebration of the feast?

Before we turn to consider the position of the children, the question of church membership must be touched on, albeit in a thoroughly tentative way. We may at least ask whether it is possible, or conceivable, or desirable that some means could be found by which interchurch couples were recognised, while remaining members in the ordinary sense of their own churches, as having some kind of special relationship with the church of their partners. So far as I am aware, there is no model in the ecclesiastical sphere which is immediately helpful. Two situations do, however, come to mind. The first is when a member of one church, while living away from home and cut off from that church, is accepted as a kind of temporary visitor in another – a stranger within the gates, as it were. This happens frequently, if informally; but of course it is not a precise parallel. The second case is where – as now happens quite frequently – the possibility of formal "dual membership" of two communions simultaneously is mooted, usually in the context of a joint parish which is somehow integrated into the structures of two churches, and recognised and ministered to by both. This again is not a direct parallel. Nevertheless, these examples hint at the possibility of some kind of officially recognised "double belonging". Parallels can be found in other spheres, as that of citizenship; while the concept of a secondary, associate membership is equally common in all sorts of societies and institutions. Certainly there does seem to be something rather strange about the idea that a person could be a member of one church and yet formally associated with another, for church membership is as a rule exclusive. But need it be so exclusive as it has up to the present been? Does that exclusiveness not in part rest on an identification of a particular church with *the* Church, so that the membership of *the* Church, which is by its nature exclusive, is translated immediately into membership of *a* church, implying simultaneously non-membership of other churches? And is such identification not at least open to question? Does the general ecumenical situation, in which already at least some members of different churches find themselves aware of a sense of belonging *also* to and with their fellows in other communions, to say nothing of the particular case of the interchurch marriage, not at least suggest that some further structures of personal association with different churches might be desirable? The thought seems worthy of consideration.

The question of church membership and the associated subject of baptism take on a fresh urgency when we come to the position of the children of the interchurch marriage. In the case of the parents, whether or not some sense of dual belonging, if not of dual membership is developed, the interchurchness of the family is established by the fact that each individually belongs to and remains in his or her own church. But the child is a single individual, not two people. Assuming that he is baptised into the Church, and that this in turn involves his formal location within an actual church community, there are in principle three possibilities. Either he "belongs" to one of the churches, and has no real ties, except incidentally through one parent, to the other; or he "belongs" primarily to one church but is recognised as being linked specifically to the other as well – here, the concept of associate membership, if it could be worked out, would apply to him in the same way as to his parents; or he "belongs" equally to both churches. Some kind of decision about these possibilities has to be made, and it will as a rule demand attention at the point of the child's baptism, and again when the question of confirmation and admission to communion arises. The general practice in the past, and indeed up to the present, has been to place the child within one of the churches only – normally, in the case of Roman Catholic/Protestant marriages, in the Roman Catholic, if only because of previous Roman Catholic legislation – and it is only recently that the possibility of some other arrangement has come to be sought by some interchurch families, if not by the churches themselves. Yet when one begins with the interchurch family itself, and perceives the situation and the issues from that starting-point, it is less than obvious that the alternatives are or should be impossible or undesirable, however difficult or unwelcome they may appear from the official perspective of the particular churches. Why should not the child of such a marriage be recognised as linked to *both* churches, either primarily to one and secondarily to the other, or even in some sense of belonging fully with each communion? The only insuperable barrier would appear to be a conviction on the part of this church or that that membership of itself, in the fullest sense, must automatically *exclude* membership of the other. But is this conviction, though generally held, in fact valid in any final or absolute sense? One may at least wonder; one may at least repeat in relation to the children the question already raised in regard to their parents.

It is such considerations as these that are leading a small but growing number of interchurch couples to look for some way of locating their children in the Church through baptism without at the same time determining that they shall belong to *this church rather than that*. From this flow the devices mentioned elsewhere in the papers of this Consultation – postponement of baptism, or baptism with registration in both churches, or even in neither. There is a certain understandable uneasiness in the churches about such devices: they seem to come dangerously close to relegating the children to a kind of interchurch Limbo, in which they really belong neither here nor there. This uneasiness on the part of the churches is only likely to be strengthened by the kind of argument which is sometimes advanced by couples in this position: we prefer, they say, that our children should grow up knowing both churches and eventually make their own free decision whether they shall belong to the one or the other. This sort of argument, though sincerely offered, resembles rather too closely that of parents who refuse to give their children a religious upbringing at all on the ground that when they are grown up they will then be properly placed to decide freely and objectively whether they will choose this or that religious allegiance or settle for indifference – a position which tends to be unaware of its own bias towards indifferentism, and in any case ignores the existential conditionedness of all human choices by reason of its commitment to a utopian ideal of objectivity. But unless or until some means is found of reducing the present implicit pressure on parents to decide at the point of baptism which church their children shall belong to, some way of developing an authentic sense that their children belong in and to both churches, more and more interchurch parents are likely in the future to feel that a refusal to commit their children to either is the only honest option open to them.

Certainly it would be wrong to make these questions seem simpler or easier to answer than they actually are. They hint at territory which is still largely uncharted, and it is not possible to foresee all the consequences which might flow from the development of dual membership. No doubt it might well be that moves in this direction would have negative consequences as well as positive ones. In particular, by removing the pressures presently operative in interchurch marriages, they could have the effect of making the slide into indifferentism on the part of couples who are already less than fully committed even easier than at present. Nevertheless, it can fairly be pointed out that a more rigid and conservative treatment of interchurch marriage has not always been markedly successful in preserving the allegiance of such couples, and that in any case the legislation and practice of the churches must make room for the fullest possible development of the life and allegiance of the committed rather than limit itself to hedging around the weaknesses of the uncommitted. The interchurch marriage, if it is to be adequately and positively assisted, must be seen in a constructive and favourable light in order to bring out its potential.

Clearly, however, this can only be achieved if the reality of the interchurch marriage as a Christian marriage, as a cell of the Church, is taken seriously by all involved – both by the partners and by their churches. This in turn demands from the churches not only respect from each other, but also a particular respect for the couple who wish to take this way forward. The prerequisite for such respect is the recognition by the churches that they are themselves in their division the real problem of interchurch marriage, that such a marriage is a challenge to them in their divided existence, and that the challenge is justified. Only a certain radical humility on the part of the churches, a willingness to admit that a unilateral and defensive concentration on their own claims serves merely to intensify the difficulties, can lead to a better future for the interchurch family and indeed for the churches themselves.

Notes

1. It is at least in part for this reason that the Roman Catholic regulations for marriages between a Roman Catholic and an Eastern Christian are less rigid than where the non-Roman Catholic is a member of a western church. In the former case, as established by the Decree *Crescens Matrimoniorum* published on 22 February 1967 by the Congregation for the Eastern Churches, the canonical form (see below) is required for a marriage to be licit, but not for absolute validity. This effectively removes the ultimate sanction from the interchurch marriage legislation: a Roman Catholic can marry an Eastern Christian without dispensation from the impediment of

mixed religion and without observing the canonical form, and his marriage is recognised by the Roman Catholic Church as valid, though irregular. No doubt one important factor underlying this permission, apart from the greater degree of recognition extended by Rome to the Orthodox churches, is the fact that in general an Orthodox must marry before his own (Orthodox) priest for the marriage to be recognised by his church, and that there is no regular Orthodox machinery for circumventing this requirement. Paradoxically, however, *Crescens Matrimoniorum* does not limit this relaxation to cases where the Eastern Christian is Orthodox: it also covers the other eastern churches who, by their rejection of Chalcedon, are strictly rather less "orthodox" than the churches of the Reformation!

2. Vatican II, *Lumen Gentium*, par. 8; *Unitatis Redintegratio*, par. 3; W. M. Abbott ed., *The Documents of Vatican II*, Geoffrey Chapman (London, 1965), p. 23; 345-6.

3. Ibidem.

4. While at present the Roman Catholic regulations treat all the other western churches alike, and make no special provision for Anglicans marrying Roman Catholics, the possibility of some more differentiated treatment of particular non-Roman communions is at least hinted at in the papal *Motu Proprio Matrimonia Mixta* of 1970 when it notes that canonical discipline "must be adapted to the various cases . . . according to the distinct circumstances of the married couple and the differing degrees of their ecclesiastical communion". The suggestion has more than once been made from the Anglican side that an Anglican marriage celebration might be recognized by Rome as fulfilling the requirement to observe the canonical form – see for example the *Third Anglican-Roman Catholic Report on Mixed Marriages*, par. 10: the document is published, among other places, in *The Furrow*, 24 (1973), pp. 313-17 – but so far without favourable response from the Roman Catholic Church.

5. The question is sometimes raised in all sincerity by Roman Catholics whether the attitude of Protestant churches towards Rome is *really* so very much different from the Roman Catholic attitude to them. The fact that demonstrably equivalent hard-line positions are adopted officially and unofficially on both sides might seem to suggest the contrary. Nevertheless, the difference should not be overlooked. The problem currently facing the Roman Catholic Church is that of developing a new openness of approach which is not merely a reflection of the ecclesiological principles to which it has held in recent centuries, but to a considerable extent cuts across them. That facing the Protestant churches is more one of establishing a practical approach which will reflect the ecclesiological principles to which, in theory at least, they have always been committed, while often straying far from them in practice. Obviously the problems, and their manifestations, are very similar; but they are not quite the same: the movement in each case is in an opposite direction.

6. To avoid misunderstanding, let it be said that to talk of other churches as branches of the Church does not necessarily involve the celebrated branch theory developed in Anglo-Catholicism. According to that theory, the churches possessing the historic episcopate in apostolic succession – i.e. the Roman Catholic, Orthodox, Anglican and Old Catholic communions – are all branches of the one Church, the trunk being the original undivided apostolic Church of the early centuries which figures so largely in Anglican ecclesiology. This theory offers one way of thinking of churches as branches; but the term can be and often is used in a much looser sense by and of churches which this model would exclude.

7. Most strikingly in The Code: *The Book of the Constitution and Government of the Presbyterian Church in Ireland*, par. 260: "It is recommended that a minister do not join in marriage a member of the Church with a member of the Roman Catholic Church, nor with a person professing anti-Christian views, until in each case profession of adherence to the Presbyterian faith is made, after careful instruction has been given . . ."; cf. also the brief summary of the results of a survey of the attitudes of Presbyterian ministers to mixed marriage in the *Annual Reports to the General Assembly of the Presbyterian Church in Ireland*, 1970, pp. 151-2. We may also mention the current refusal of some Church of Ireland clergy to assist at an Anglican/Roman Catholic wedding if any promise about the upbringing of the children has been given by the Roman Catholic fiancé(e).

8. An explicit appeal to divine law in this connexion only appears in official Roman Catholic documents within the last 200 years, and seems first to have been employed in a papal statement in Pius VIII's letter *Litteris altero* of 25 March 1830 (quoted by L. Örsy, "Documenta Selecta de Educatione Religiosa Prolis ex Matrimonio Mixto Natae", *Periodica*, 53 [1964], pp. 267-284. Since then, it has become standard. In any case, however, the introduction of the – somewhat problematic – concept of *ius divinum* served merely to formulate even more sharply than before the already firmly-anchored conviction that a member of the Church must preserve his faith and hand it on to his children intact. This conviction found juridical expression as early as the Council of Chalcedon, which in its 14th Canon laid down that the children of marriages between catholics and heretics must be baptised in the Catholic Church, or, if already baptised, must at least be brought up in it. Earlier still, other councils legislated more generally to forbid such unions: the first record we have is the 16th and 17th Canons of the Synod of Elvira (c. 300). Further back, there lie the prohibitions of mixed marriage in the Old Testament (e.g. Deut. 7:3-4, which speaks of the danger to the allegiance of the person so marrying, and Mal. 2:15, which specifically mentions the danger to his children) and the Pauline(?) fragment in II Cor. 6:14ff. The drawing of any direct line from these biblical and patristic instances to contemporary Roman Catholic legislation is of course a dubious undertaking: it is by no means clear that the situations are parallel. Nevertheless, they

may serve to illustrate each other, if only by showing what long (and often tangled) roots underly contemporary positions.

9. This distinction is based explicitly on the baptism common to the Roman Catholic and the non-Roman Catholic Christian: it was theologically formulated in these terms by Thomas Aquinas, *Summa Theologiae* Supp. q. 59, art. 1, ad 5, and then became accepted officially.

10. Information on the history of the *cautiones* is given by A. J. Connick, "Canonical Doctrine concerning Mixed Marriages – Before Trent and during the Seventeenth and Early Eighteenth Centuries", in *The Jurist*, 20 (1960) pp. 295-326; 398-418. On the particular question of the upbringing of the children, see L. Örsy, art cit., pp. 267-84.

11. This point is perhaps too easily overlooked by those who make the well-intentioned suggestion that the problems of interchurch marriage could be shifted if the Protestant churches were to demand of their own members the same kind of promises which are required of Roman Catholics. The aim of this would be to put each partner in the same kind of situation, thus forcing the couple to come to some kind of responsible compromise on their own. But while this may have something to be said for it as a pragmatic solution, it is open to two objections. First of all, as indicated above, the Protestant churches do not normally exercise the sanctions which are necessary to support such demands, nor in general do they feel that they ought to do so. Secondly, to attempt to undermine the pressure exerted by one church by imposing a balancing pressure from the other side in order that the pressures should be cancelled out is, to say the least, a roundabout way of going about things. Particularly as this kind of suggestion tends to come from Roman Catholics, it seems fair to ask whether they would not be better employed in advocating change within their own church than in recommending other churches to take the path which they are implicitly rejecting; for their presupposition is clearly that pressure of this kind should *not* be imposed. Certainly stranger things have happened, and sometimes one can only write straight with very crooked lines indeed; but one may be sceptical about this particular twist!

12. The distinction is re-emphasised by the Pope in *Matrimonia Mixta*: "Neither in doctrine nor in law does the Church place on the same level a marriage between a Catholic and a baptised non-Catholic, and one between a Catholic and an unbaptised person." The Protestant churches, however, while welcoming this reiteration, are equally entitled to point out that *in practice* the insistence in both cases on the requirement of canonical form, or a dispensation from it, makes the distinction purely nominal and does place them on the same level.

13. Cf. note (1) above. One other exception should be mentioned for the sake of completeness: the canonical form is not required for validity in cases of danger of death, or where a priest is not available and is not likely to be available for a further month: there, a marriage before witnesses alone is valid (Canon 1098 of the *Codex Juris Canonici*).

14. It must, however, be said that the extent of the relaxation varies very greatly from one country to another, and even in some countries (such as Ireland) from one diocese to another. In the *Motu Proprio* of 1970, the Pope required national episcopal conferences to lay down conditions under which dispensations from the impediments and the canonical form would be granted uniformly throughout their territory (Norms 7 and 9 of *Matrimonia Mixta*). Various episcopal directories have since been published, and a number are analysed and compared in *One in Christ*, 7 (1971), pp. 216-35. From this comparison it is clear that there is a very wide variation both in the spirit in which the question is approached by different episcopal conferences, and in the extent to which their new regulations simplify procedure and make matters easier for the interchurch couple. It is a matter for particular regret that the Irish bishops in their brief comment on the *Motu Proprio* (published in *The Furrow*, November 1970) have not only taken up a stance more markedly conservative than almost all the other European hierarchies, but have also found it impossible to do what the Pope required in laying down uniform norms for their whole country. This leaves both non-Roman Catholic clergy and the interchurch couples in a cloud of often poisonous uncertainty as to the position affecting themselves – a situation hardly improved by numerous reports that certain bishops persist in refusing to grant dispensations for mixed marriages *at all*. It is to be hoped that the current round of interchurch conversations will lead to an improvement in the position: for the initial discussion see the papers read at Dundalk, 26 September 1973, and published in *The Furrow*, 25, 1 (1974), especially pp. 19-20; 27; 29-33; 37-9; 39-43.

15. The most useful single source in English for information on all the developments mentioned in this paragraph is the journal *One in Christ*, which regularly devotes considerable space to documentation and comment on mixed marriage questions.

16. See for example the detailed and penetrating criticism by Rudolf Ehrlich, "Motu Proprio Matrimonia Mixta: the Development of Roman Catholic Legislation with regard to Mixed Marriages (1918-1970)", *The Reformed World*, 21 (1971) pp. 265-74.

17. The compromise which was widely, if unofficially, practised in the days before *Ne Temere* and the *Codex*, whereby boys were brought up in the church of the father, girls in that of the mother, or else the children were assigned alternately to the different churches regardless of sex, is also really another variant of the cutting of the knot. It does indeed preserve and continue among the children the allegiances of their parents, but it does not integrate the interchurch dimension within the life of the family: rather, it consolidates interchurch division there. While it is certainly a better solution than indifference, and arguably preferable to the handing over of all children to one church alone, it remains more a *modus vivendi* than a constructive overcoming of difficulties.

18. *The Joint Pastoral Care of Interchurch Marriages in England, Wales and Scotland.* Recommendations by the Joint Working Group of the

British Council of Churches and the Roman Catholic Church in England, Wales and Scotland, available as a pamphlet from the British Council of Churches, and also published in *One in Christ*, 7 (1971), pp. 235-54; and *Two-Church Families*, published by the Association of Interchurch Families, Lincoln (1973).

19. See in particular the directive of the Bishop of Strasbourg, mentioned in the paper by Professors Lienhard and Hoffmann on the pastoral care of mixed marriages in France.

20. The Methodist tradition is to welcome to participation in the Holy Communion "all who love the Lord Jesus Christ": this does not necessarily presuppose, though it would normally suggest, formal church membership. The usual Presbyterian formula invites to the celebration "members of any branch of Christ's Church", which does in fact presuppose communicant membership. The term "open communion" is often used to cover both approaches, though of course neither stands for a complete "openness" to all comers. They are "open", rather, by contrast with the more restricted traditions of such churches as the Orthodox, Roman Catholic and Anglican – though the Anglican churches have in the past practised a greater degree of "openness" than these others, and in recent years have become more "open" still in the extension of eucharistic hospitality to members of other churches.

2. The Ecclesiological Significance of Interchurch Marriage

Geoffrey Wainwright

All consideration of the ecclesiological significance of interchurch marriage must begin with frank recognition of the two present realities implied in the very phrase "interchurch marriage": first, there exists an institutional division of the Christian people into separated ecclesial communities each of which claims to embody in some sense and degree "the Church"; second, some Christians do in fact marry in good conscience across the boundaries of those separated ecclesial communities. My aim here is to show briefly how the second fact may help in the solution of theoretical and practical problems of ecclesiology posed by the first – or (to put the matter more simply) to show how mixed marriages may further church unity. There is no thought of belittling the difficulties which ecclesiastical disunity causes for the partners in a mixed marriage, nor those which mixed marriages cause for the respective ecclesiastical authorities. But my emphasis will fall on the creative value of serious Christian marriages between partners of different denominations; as promises of the future, such marriages have a part to play in the work of Christian unity. I stress that I shall be thinking all the while of marriages where both partners are committed Christians.

Concrete institutional disunity weakens or annuls many of the splendid statements that may properly be made about the Church when the latter is viewed in an ideal, metaphysical or eschatological light. Where there is a discrepancy between the Church as it is in history and the Church as it is meant to be in the purposes of God, then our ecclesiological statements and our ecclesiastical practices must become such as best allow the gap to be closed through the historical Church's nearer approximation to its divine vocation. The factual existence of mixed marriages ought so to stimulate the separated churches' reflection and practice in interdenominational matters that a closer approach is made to the note of unity which ideally, metaphysically and eschatologically characterises the Church. Interchurch marriage provides an occasion for elaborating an *in via* ecclesiology suited to the Christian people on the road to unity.

In such an ecclesiology, serious Christian married life between partners of different denominations may be seen – because Christian marriage constitutes a "domestic church" – as an instance of church unity already achieved at the level of everyday personal existence.[1] Bed and board are shared: this existential reality of the couple gives the denominational churches the opportunity to develop a corresponding practice in their rites and disciplines which will widen and deepen the existential unity of Christendom. In the one direction, the existential reality of the united couple must be allowed to stimulate the wider ritual and canonical practice of the partners' churches in such a way that some benefits of the couple's achieved unity may be spread more broadly in both denominations. In the other direction, the ritual and canonical practice of the denominations should be so arranged as to give the couple support from both denominational communities – protecting and deepening the couple's unity. In all this, it is the ritual and the canonical which are rightly serving the existential, and not the other way round. The sabbath was made for man, and not man for the sabbath!

Let us see how this could work out at the most significant point of eucharistic communion. In my view, the church of each partner should – openly and regularly – admit the other partner in a mixed marriage to communion. From pastoral experience, I can testify that this may achieve two happy results: first, the existential unity of the couple is protected and deepened through their eating and drinking together at the Lord's Table, with the eucharistic meal thus both resuming and informing every meal they share at their own home table (the element of protection is important in face of the tensions that may from time to time threaten the harmony of a couple from any source); and second, the joint communion of the couple makes an exemplary witness of Christian unity to at least the local denominational communities which see marriage partners of separate churches united at the ritually central point of the holy eucharist. Such a practice is most easily achieved where the denominations of the two partners in any case accord a high degree of recognition to each other as ecclesial communities and to each other's eucharist. But I am convinced it could also work in the case of Catholic-Protestant couples.

Objections can of course be made, as they are to any kind of inter-communion. But it seems to me that the arguments advanced in favour of practising creative intercommunion in the case of sustained ecumenical encounter and collaboration become, in the case of a mixed marriage, so overwhelming as to swallow up all objections. It may be objected, first, that eucharistic communion must express an already existing unity before it may produce the fruit of greater unity (*significat et efficit unitatem ecclesiasticam*). The reply is that by their baptism and by their prayers and daily life together (which marks an existential "improvement" of their baptismal unity), the partners of an inter-church marriage are already sufficiently united for their joint communion at the eucharist to be expressive of an existing unity that is far from negligible. Their joint communion at the eucharist ought then to be allowed in order to increase and deepen that unity.

It may be objected, second, that joint communion at the eucharist is impossible because there is not full unity in faith and truth between the partners of an interchurch marriage – and each partner's church may argue that such a unity will occur only when the other partner makes undivided submission to its own authority (and the marriage thereby ceases to be "mixed"!). The reply is that while such a demand for immediate total surrender is consistent with a Cyprianic or at least an Augustinian view of Christian unity (according to which the signs of Christianity are invalid or at least unfruitful in a "schismatic" community), it goes against the perspective prevailing in modern ecclesiologies worked out on the basis of ecumenical experience. Because schism is no longer regarded as a simple matter with all the right on one side and all the wrong on the other, modern ecclesiologies rightly recognise the real existence of varying degrees of Christian faith and truth in ecclesial communities other than one's own. In the case of a mixed marriage, each partner brings at least the measure of faith and truth which is his in virtue of his membership of his own denomination. But more than that: by his willingness to marry a partner whose total being is "qualified" through membership of the other denomination, each partner has in some sort "accepted" as at least "possible" the beliefs and practices "embodied" in the other partner – at least in so far as he sees himself in conscience as not infringing the apostolic injunction not to be mismated with an unbeliever (2 Cor. 6:14-7:1). (My use of inverted commas in the last sentence shows that formulation is not easy here: a lived reality is struggling to find theological expression.) If a Catholic finds his Protestant partner (and thereby the partner's ecclesial community) sufficiently "catholic" for himself to be in communion with them, and if a Protestant finds his Catholic partner (and thereby the partner's ecclesial community) sufficiently "reformed" for himself to be in communion with them, then the respective ecclesiastical authorities have the strongest basis possible – short of an individual transfer of denominational allegiance – for recognising "the true faith" in the marriage partner belonging to the other denomination. Insofar as that partner is still considered to fall short in faith and truth, love should be allowed to fill the gap.[2]

It may be objected, third, that the view I am advocating is tantamount to indifferentism. The reply is that indifferentism is a loaded word inappropriate to a case in which *both* sides (rather than *neither* side) are being taken seriously in their ecclesial claims.

Joint communion at the eucharist of both churches: this would express, protect and deepen the unity already existing between the partners of an interchurch marriage; it would also make an exemplary witness within both ecclesial communities to the greater unity of the Church which is being sought by both denominations. Such a witness, focused in the eucharist, could also be applied in the area of ecclesiastical government. The "other" partner in a mixed marriage could be invited – insofar as he has the necessary gifts and graces and is willing to submit to the discipline of the inviting denomination – to play his part in the courts of his spouse's church (leaders' meeting, presbyteral council etc.).

The reciprocity of the proposed arrangement – each partner being "received" by the other partner's church – should prevent my proposals from being dismissed on grounds of the disloyal pursuit of

Christian unity through individual (semi-)conversions from one denomination to another.

Some, however, may label my proposals as a kind of "dual membership" and dismiss them as an anomaly. Admittedly, "dual membership" *is* an anomaly. But this minor anomaly arises only on account of a prior and greater anomaly: that of ecclesiastical disunity. Ecclesiastical disunity is the major anomaly: and within a situation of major anomaly, the choice between alternative minor anomalies (for the inability of husband and wife to be in communion at the one eucharistic table is no less a "minor" anomaly than is dual membership) should fall in favour of the practice that will best help in the righting of the major anomaly; and the creative power of joint communion will, I have argued, precisely help in the achievement of ecclesiastical unity.

If such a positive significance is to be attributed to interchurch marriage, then the churches ought also to apply themselves to elaborating appropriate rituals for the celebration of interchurch marriages. Because Christian weddings are normally celebrated in a liturgical context (indeed the Roman Catholic Church requires the presence of a priest for the marriage to be licit), the churches have a golden opportunity for working *together* to produce wedding rites that will not only meet the normal requirements of each church as to form in its own marriage law but will also bring out the special character of the interchurch marriage and the hopes that are being invested in it by both ecclesial communities.[3] Such wedding services – under the joint presidency of ministers of the two denominations – could contain a ceremony for admitting each marriage partner to the continuing eucharistic communion of the other's denomination. That same ceremony of eucharistic admission could also be used in the case of couples who had not been able to begin their married life under these arrangements but who now wished to take up the opportunity.

The kind of "dual membership" I have been proposing would alos alleviate the problems of the ecclesiastical upbringing of the children of mixed marriages. In the case of a mixed marriage involving a Roman Catholic partner, the unilateral promise by the Catholic partner "to do all in his power to have all the children baptised and brought up in the Catholic Church"[4] could be replaced by a reciprocal and joint undertaking to encourage the children in a sympathetic participation in the life of *both* ecclesial communities (just as the parents themselves are trying to achieve such a participation). Upon reaching a suitable maturity, the child – if he chose to exercise the Christian faith – might himself opt for one church or the other, or he might exercise his own kind of "dual membership". As long as the child remained under the tutelage of his parents, *final* responsibility for decision (where options are called for) concerning his religious upbringing should, I think we must say for the present, rest with the *husband* in the interchurch marriage. This is certainly in accordance with the biblical view that "the husband is the head of the wife" (Eph. 5:23). Now the biblical view of the subordination of women to men is grounded at the level of creation: 1 Cor. 11:8f. And while it may be true, as Julian Huxley has insisted, that human evolution is now essentially a psychosocial or cultural rather than a biological matter, there is as yet no culture in which male supremacy in or out of marriage has disappeared. Therefore the final authority remains, at this stage in the process of creation, with the husband . . . who will, however, remember that his authority must now be exercised according to the example of Christ's sacrificial love: Eph. 5:25.[5] It may happen that Christian marriages, under the influence of such principles as the Pauline "In Christ there is neither male nor female", will eventually help to prepare a culture in which male supremacy in marriage is overcome – though it must be observed that the seeds of silent revolution contained in the Pauline "In Christ there is neither slave nor free" took a very long time before beginning to bear cultural fruit (and Paul himself seems to have had no vision of the end of slavery as a social institution, though the relations between Christian masters and Christian slaves were now qualified in several ways through being "in the Lord"). On the other hand, some may argue that the husband's supremacy over the wife has been permanently fixed through the Scriptural establishment of Christ's supremacy over the Church as the model for Christian marriage (Eph. 5:22-24). But all this, though not without relevance to the subject of interchurch marriage, is something of another story; and to relate it all to the movement for "women's liberation" now taking place in some areas of some societies would take us even further afield.

What may we conclude regarding our main subject? The experience and imagery of marriage has an honourable place in Biblical tradition: it was, for instance, through his marital experience that Hosea was taught God's love for Israel, and in the New Testament the wedding is a favourite image of the messianic Kingdom. Could the experience of interchurch marriage in our time become the creative image of the future great Church? If it is properly related to the central sign of the eucharist along the lines I have suggested, I believe it could.

Finally, let me declare that I write as the husband in an interchurch marriage.

Notes

1. Clement of Alexandria applies to couple and child the word of the Lord in Matt. 18:20; "Where two or three are gathered in my name, there am I in the midst of them" (*Strom.* III, 10; PG 8, 1169). John Chrysostom says "The home is a little Church" (*In Ep. ad Eph.*, hom. *XX; PG 62, 143*). See P. Evdokimov, *Sacrement de l'amour*, Epi, Paris (1962) pp. 163f., 168f.
2. For a developed argument in favour of the primacy of love over truth (as the truth is imperfectly seen) in the un-ideal circumstances of a Christian disunity needing to be surmounted, see my *Eucharist and Eschatology*, Epworth Press (1971), pp. 143f.
3. A start has been made in Switzerland and in Germany. In German-speaking Switzerland, the use of a service-book entitled *Oekumenische Trauung* (1973) is officially permitted by the Roman Catholic, Protestant and Old Catholic Churches. In Germany, the Roman Catholic archdiocese of Freiburg and the Protestant Church in

Baden published in 1974 a common order of service under the title *Gemeinsame kirchliche Trauung* (Formular C), and its use has been approved by the Old Catholic Church and by the Moravian and Methodist regional authorities.

4. Paul VI's Motu proprio, *Matrimonia Mixta,* 1970.

5. Various social factors may have to be taken into account by the husband, e.g. the existence of a matrilineal family system (in parts of Africa) or the custom of the mother playing a major role in the concrete religious upbringing of the children (in many parts of the world).

3. Interchurch Marriage in the Service of the Kingdom

Gabriel Daly

"His conscience had been taken out, and the Church put in its place".[1] Thus Benjamin Jowett about John Henry Newman. As a judgment on Newman, of all people, it was outrageously unjust; but the Master of Balliol was writing to Margot Tennant, and aging dons may be allowed their aphorisms when writing to attractive and witty young women. For all its inapplicability to Newman, the remark reflects an age-old antithesis between Protestantism and Roman Catholicism. Roman Catholic theology has developed an ecclesiology so strong and pervasive that many Protestants instinctively feel that legitimate Christian freedom is thereby stifled. Protestant theology places so high an evaluation on the individual conscience that many Roman Catholics instinctively feel that the claims of divinely-sanctioned authority in the Church are thereby set aside. The Roman Catholic Church tradition-ally claims to possess the fullness of revealed truth and invokes the con-cept of divine law to forbid any derogation from full mental adherence to its doctrines and unfeigned obedience to its hierarchically-graded authority. This attitude may be construed as arrogant by Protestants, and as seriously unnuanced by many contemporary Roman Catholic theologians, but it is the ecclesiological foundation for the Roman law on mixed marriages. Paul VI's *Motu Proprio Matrimonia Mixta* (1970) is in many respects a deliberately eirenic document which tempers the insensitive requirements and wording of previous legislation, but it is adamant on the one issue which Protestants regard as cardinal. Norm 4 states bluntly that the Roman Catholic party in a mixed marriage is "gravely bound to make a sincere promise to do all in his power to have all the children baptised and brought up in the Catholic Church". This rebarbative injunction is controlled by the ecclesiological pre-suppositions mentioned above. I make this stark observation from the outset in the hope that we shall not spend too much time in approaching the problem merely at the level of church law and administration. Ecclesiology may seem rather remote from the existential concerns of a couple contemplating or living an interchurch marriage, but it is the area in which the only real, as distinct from verbal, progress will be made.

It is a tragic fact that it should be marriage and the family which give constant and abrasive prominence to an ecclesiological question of great complexity and sensitivity and one demanding patient theological analysis. Every interchurch marriage involving a Roman Catholic appears to Protestants as an act of ecclesiastical imperialism, of spiritual annexation. The Roman Catholic reply, even when stated in conciliatory language, is in effect: "Here I stand, I cannot do otherwise". The theological task facing all of us who want to break out of this impasse without hurt to conscience and conviction must be to examine that "ich kann nicht anders" with a view to discovering whether the theological position which inspires it is as intractable as we have until recently taken it to be. It cannot be said too often that progress towards Christian unity comes not from negotiation over convictions, but from the joint examination of common problems. There is a species of ecumenical tact which recognises that many of the problems in dispute between separated churches are also to some extent in dispute within the individual churches themselves. Any informed Protestant observer knows that contemporary Roman Catholic ecclesiology is undergoing a critical upheaval which for many conservative Roman Catholics is little short of traumatic. Protestants who recognise that this is so, and that it is material to the problem of mixed marriages, can make an invaluable contribution to the eventual resolution of that problem. Roman Catholics, especially in Ireland, can be in no doubt that their Church's legislation on mixed marriages is regarded by Protestants as a major obstacle to good interchurch relations.

One must hope that the Dundalk interchurch meetings will point the way towards a solution. It would do a great deal for national morale in these troubled times if Irish theologians could give a lead to the rest of Christendom at least in this one eminently practical area of ecumenical concern. Given the present situation in Ireland, and the world-wide notoriety it has received, nothing could be more certain than that an initiative from this country would be accorded close and sympathetic examination both in Rome and in Geneva. We are renowned for our conservatism, – a fact which could be turned to considerable advantage if our church officers were to put forward a truly creative piece of theological thinking. None of our Irish churches is going to be charged with irresponsible radicalism. It is surely time we recognised that to be an Irish Christian it is not strictly necessary to be a theological helot.

For this reason I make the plea that we tackle the problem at its deepest level. Simply to suggest that legislation be changed would be to fail in this respect. It must be our aim to do more than treat symptoms: we must address ourselves to the underlying causes of the symptoms. It is not enough to recommend that canon law should leave it to the consciences of the interchurch couple to decide where and by whom they shall be married and in what Christian tradition they shall bring up their children. This would be merely to reverse Jowett's stricture and thus place an intolerable burden on many couples. Change in legislation must be supported by a renewed ecclesiology together with a catechetical and pastoral programme which reflects that renewal.

Such observations fall primarily within the province of theologians, and the non-theologian may experience understandable impatience with the *longueurs* and technicalities of theological debate. From a purely academic standpoint the debate over Church authority can all too easily be protracted into inconclusive, albeit courteous, exchanges of conflicting points of emphasis. Nevertheless theological investigation, discussion and debate are necessary, though unfortunately they generate a tempo of their own which rarely aspires to *andante* and never to *con brio*. However, a little existential impatience would not come amiss in these days when ecumenism itself shows signs of sclerosis and weariness of spirit. Interchurch couples with the energy, dedication and determination to inject personal concern into academic impersonalism could be a significant influence in the movement towards unity.

Dr Heron justly remarks that interchurch couples often feel "that their own rights and dignity have been violated by the churches' treatment of them". He points out that an interchurch marriage creates an association of three different communities, and that because of the division between the churches, church and marriage have fallen out of phase. His metaphor puts one in mind of an analogy from another area of Christian theology. One might say that an interchurch marriage inherits an original ecclesiastical sin which encumbers the couple with a divided situation that they themselves did nothing to bring about. The immediate problem, then, is how to give that divided situation a redemptive dimension. Let us see what happens if we try to make a theological virtue out of a fallen ecclesial state. In what follows I wish to pass beyond the specific problem which results from present Roman Catholic legislation and look at the question in a wider context.

Most Christian theologians today accept the thesis that the Church exists to serve the Kingdom of God. On the whole, traditional Roman Catholic theology has emphasised the points of unity between Church and Kingdom, while most Protestant, and much recent Roman Catholic, theology has sought to distinguish the two without divorcing them. In the context of a divided ecclesial situation there is a good deal to be said for greater concentration upon the Kingdom as a focal point of theory and practice. In seeking to promote the aims of the Kingdom, divided churches can grow closer together. Ecumenical ecclesiology is of its nature provisional and temporary. If concentration upon the claims of the Kingdom helps to give ecclesiology a goal, then that of itself is a persuasive argument in favour of such concentration, especially if it helps to give ecclesiology an impetus towards re-definition of aim.

The three communities mentioned by Dr Heron as resulting from an interchurch marriage can find a point of cohesion in their common, though sinful, service of the aims of the Kingdom. The family, of its nature a more personal and immediately real entity than either church, has a better potential than they for reflecting the personal and existential characteristics of the Kingdom as portrayed in the New Testament. The interchurch family can become as powerful an agent of the Kingdom as any single-church family. Indeed, on the analogy of what psychologists call compensation, the interchurch family has all the possibilities of becoming a more effective witness to some values than many single-church families. Furthermore, it can carry out the prophetic role of constantly recalling the churches to the personal consequences of their divisions, thereby infusing a note of urgency and pastoral concern into their ecumenical deliberations.

Theologically, then, the interchurch family may be said to begin its life as the inheritor of a pathological situation not of its own making. This situation, however, offers all the possibilities of full fidelity to the Kingdom and to the teaching of Christ, even while it mirrors in microcosm the macrocosmic separateness of two Christian churches. Fidelity to the Kingdom will inspire the couple to work for unity while suffering the effects of disunity. They will seek to light a candle rather than curse the dark. They will set out to allow the grace of God to heal at a familial level the divided heritage which their respective churches have bequeathed to them. Since we are speaking of a consciously *Christian* marriage and family, we are by that fact speaking of a situation in which *eros* and *agape* can be therapeutic, and this healing will be ecclesial too, if the couple choose to make it so.

One of the stock arguments against mixed marriages is that disparity in doctrine simply lays yet another burden on a way of life which already has enough. This is certainly a factor which any thoughtful couple will have pondered before marrying. I envisage here the case where they have decided to accept the challenge, not merely as husband and wife, but as Christians seeking unity. As such they will accept their inherited division as an ascesis necessary to the progress of the Kingdom preached by Christ. They will accept ecclesial separation as part of their share in the cross of Christ and they will find in it not an additional burden and strain upon their marriage but the possibility of transforming a potential hazard into an apostolic and personal enrichment.

The quest for Christian unity needs, perhaps, to be sited more consciously in the context of Christian asceticism. Even though official deliberations will normally take place in the civilized surroundings of the conference-room, Christians are committed by the Gospel to doing their basic thinking in the shadow of the cross. Interchurch couples, who are forced by daily circumstances to make difficult decisions of conscience without the relief of procrastination, can be a powerful inspiration to the rest of us who are free to choose our ecumenical occasions and to modulate the sense of urgency we bring to them. An interchurch couple intent on integrating their marriage into the movement for Christian unity will find in practice that they are thrown into the van of the movement. They will have to make difficult decisions about worship and the education of their children. They will discover that much of their childrens' religious education will have to take place in the home, since neither a normal denominational school nor an interdenominational school employing a lowest-common denominator religious syllabus will meet their needs. Not only will the couple have to shoulder all the frustrations which normally beset the ecumenically committed members of any church, they will probably have to expose themselves and their children to misunderstanding, suspicion and disapproval, especially if they live in a local community lacking the vision of, and will towards, Christian unity. Their churchly practices will inevitably appear "advanced" (to use the mildest term) to the "normal" (to use the kindest term) members of their respective churches. They will have the right to demand that the argument from precedent shall not be invoked against them in their more adventurous initiatives. Commandos should not be restricted to the strategy and tactics of conventional troops.

It will be objected that in all this I am envisaging a couple with considerable religious sophistication. I do not deny this. Paradigmatic cases must have a special excellence about them. We might, however, do well to reflect that the number of such cases could be increased by better catechesis and more extensive training, especially of the clergy, in pastoral ecumenics. Interchurch families deserve, and have a right to expect, all the moral, theological and spiritual support that the rest of us can give them. They are, after all, giving witness to the truth that conscience and church membership are not exclusive alternatives but partners existentially estranged by an original ecclesial sin and kept out of phase to some extent at least by institutional inertia.

Note

1. *The Autobiography of Margot Asquith*, Penguin Books (London, 1936) I, p. 107.

Pastoral Approaches to Interchurch Marriage

1. Positions and Trends in Britain

John Coventry

I General Position (mainly England and Wales)

It is difficult to generalise about a country (three countries!) in which ecumenical development has gone at different paces, and in which the denominational map varies, from region to region. The writer has only direct experience of England, where the main partner in dialogue for Roman Catholics is the Church of England. In Wales it is the Free Churches. In Scotland it is the (Presbyterian) Church of Scotland: there people are more traditional and church-going; more conscious of being Protestant or Catholic; more entrenched in traditional positions; less cosmopolitan and less influenced by what is happening in the rest of the world. In England people are more aware of being either Christians or nothing (apart from other main religions). In England, if some very rough figures may be hazarded as an indication, something like 70% of Roman Catholic marriages are mixed, and of these mixed marriages up to 90% are with those who have no particular religious conviction. It is therefore understandable in this situation that pastors should feel very specially concerned about the continuing religious practice of Christian partners, and about the religious upbringing of the children.

It has been found useful, even necessary, in this country to use the term "interchurch marriage" for the family sincerely committed to two different churches,[1] as the more general term "mixed marriages" also covers Christian marriages in which one partner (or both) is only nominally a member of any church, as well as marriages between Christians and non-Christians. Interchurch marriages may be quantitatively or proportionally few, but they are coming more and more to be seen as qualitatively of great importance – because of their own needs, because the way they are handled easily affects the relationship between churches, and because of the witness for unity they can give in their immediate surroundings.

It is fairly clear that the promise about the children is still rather variously interpreted by Roman Catholic priests. In contrast to what is clearly indicated in some episcopal directories from the continent and elsewhere, most priests north of the border, and many south of it, still have the conviction that they should not or cannot apply for (or, in the case of bishops, grant) a dispensation for the Roman Catholic partner to marry, unless they are morally certain that the children will be baptised and brought up as Roman Catholics. This may be partly an attitude carried over from the period 1966 to 1970 when, under the rulings of the interim papal Instruction *Matrimonii Sacramentum*, a bishop could only give the dispensation to marry himself when he had such moral certainty, and had otherwise to send the case to Rome. The attitude may also be due to the fact that the *Directory Concerning Mixed Marriages* of the English and Welsh bishops, issued to clergy with the English text of *Matrimonia Mixta* in 1970, does not give any clear guidance on the point.[2] Indeed, this *Directory*, in commenting on Norm 4 of the papal *motu proprio*, has the following:

> It is perhaps the most noteworthy innovation in this document that no declaration or promise is required of the non-Catholic. This opens the difficult question as to what is to be done if it appears that the non-Catholic is determined to prevail upon the Catholic to abandon the faith, or is determined that some at least of the children shall be baptised and brought up outside the Catholic Church. This problem is acute when the non-Catholic adopts this attitude from conscientious conviction.

> In such a situation *it is not enough for the Bishop to know* that the Catholic has declared his readiness to preserve his faith and has promised to do his best to ensure the Catholic baptism and upbringing of any child of the marriage (author's italics).

> Information regarding the strength of faith and religious practice of the Catholic, together with an account of the outlook of the non-Catholic, will also be required before a decision can be made.

In the first place, the passage only treats the, surely rare, case where the non-Catholic is determined to override the conscience of the Catholic (the opposite has been far more commonly experienced), and not the many cases in which the non-Catholic is neither so "determined" nor simply prepared to be, as it were, dictated to by Catholic conviction. Secondly, the italicised phrase could be understood to mean that, for his pastoral care of marriage, "it is not enough for the bishop to know" the bare facts; or it could be understood to say that, for the bishop to grant the dispensation, it is not enough for him to know that the Catholic has done all that the papal norms require of him. And, thirdly, the passage leaves in a very unhappy obscurity the question whether information about the non-Catholic's attitude, obtained in the course of a personal and pastoral discussion between the priest and the couple, should be "used against them" in deciding whether to grant the dispensation: the papal norms only require that the non-Catholic should be informed, not that his attitude should be known. Hence one is left with the impression on reading the passage that this *Directory* requires more than other episcopal directories do, or than *Matrimonia Mixta* itself, which does not require that the non-Catholic's disposition should be examined as a condition for granting the dispensation, though obviously this would come up in the course of trying to give pastoral guidance to the couple.

These and similar questions are under discussion by the Anglican/ Roman-Catholic joint commission (England), which is in process of issuing an agreed joint statement for the guidance of those of their churches intending to marry.

Dispensations from canonical form, to allow the marriage to take place in the church and according to the rite of a committed non-Catholic partner (usually the bride), began tentatively in England and Wales in 1966 in cases where the non-Catholic bride was closely related to a minister of her church. It was, however, soon realised that a class distinction had inadvertently been introduced – those related to ordained ministers are middle class – and since 1970 such dispensations have become increasingly common, irrespective of reasons of kinship. It has been seen that the improving of relationships between the churches itself provides a serious ground for granting such dispensations.

As far as the writer knows, there have as yet been no cases of admission by bishops of the non-Catholic partner to Holy Communion in the Catholic Church. But, in the light of the Unity Secretariat's Instruction of June 1972, of directions that are known to have been given in some dioceses abroad, and of deepening realization of the needs of the true interchurch family, the Ecumenical Commission of England and Wales has proposed the matter for discussion by the hierarchy, and it is under urgent consideration. The same Commission has also fully discussed the possibilities of the ecumenical celebration of baptism for interchurch families, and has drawn up a full statement of the theological arguments and the practical possibilities for discussion at diocesan level. There have been a few cases of baptism by a Catholic priest in an Anglican church, but the request for a general policy from the bishops has led to a temporary recession rather than to advance. It has been one of those matters in which it has proved unwise to ask for collegial decision, and would have been better to encourage quiet if uneven growth.

II Association of Interchurch Families

Some eight years ago a small group of interchurch couples was formed in an informal way in Sheffield by the Revd. Martin and Ruth Reardon, an Anglican priest married to a Roman Catholic. This small beginning has led to a growing "movement", now flourishing in various parts of England and going by the name of the Association of Interchurch Families. Since 1968 it has held an annual week-end meeting at the Dominican conference centre, Spode House, in the midlands; and it has organised itself into four main regions in which meetings are held from time to time. The Association has simply grown gradually by personal contact. If one has to try to compress into a sentence what has been its main value, one would say it is the discovery that *the pastoral care of mixed marriages is best done by the couples themselves*.

There is now ample evidence of the enormous help many couples have received from these meetings. A "mixed" couple all too easily find themselves isolated from the "normal" churchgoers, often starting with their own families. Nobody else knows what it is like to try to live a united christian life in a two-church family. With others of the same or greater experience they can learn confidence and hope in the perhaps difficult stages leading up to their wedding. They can give and receive ideas on all the creative possibilities of joint prayer at home and joint worship in each other's churches; on every aspect of bringing up a family to experience that unity comes first, and that any necessary division can be sustained by, and as it were built on, a basis of unity. The meetings of the Association have also discussed a number of ecumenical matters apart from those directly connected with marriage, so that the couples have been enabled to see the meaning of their own experience within the wider growth towards unity of Christians, with all its difficulties and opportunities. A notable feature of the annual meetings has been the number of small children brought by the couples, to be minded by teenage girls during discussion hours, and to be a constant reminder of the realities of married and interchurch life. In 1973 the Association brought out, and itself advertised and distributed, a 40-page pamphlet, *Two-Church Families*, written by the couples themselves, to express their experience and convictions, and to serve as a guide to others similarly placed.[3]

One can confidently assert that the growing number of couples that comprise an Anglican priest with a Roman Catholic wife have been the heart and soul of the Association. The priests have a double stake in the Association, as pastors and as interchurch marriage partners. Since the annual meetings started they have been attended by Roman Catholic and Anglican bishops and by Free Church leaders. There have always been one or two Roman Catholic priests present: these may have something to contribute in the way of general knowledge of the ecumenical scene and of theological reflection, but they are the first to say that they are there to learn. A most ecumenically alert and involved Anglican bishop was heard to say that he found the week-end meeting an eye-opener. Only the couples personally engaged in living an interchurch marriage have really any idea of what it means in terms of developing personal relationship, progressive discovery, turning obstacles into means of advance, sensitivity to local ecumenical relationships, revitalising of the "merely mixed" marriage, education of the clergy, etc.

By means of close contact with the Ecumenical Commission the Association has been able to make its reflections and needs known to the bishops. Thus, in addition to providing a service of pastoral care to many, it has become a responsible influence upon the more official organs of ecumenical development.

III Pre-Marriage Course

One by-product of the Association of Interchurch Families has been a small start made, in Liverpool, on a pre-marriage course for mixed couples. The normal pre-marriage courses are unable to cater for the special needs of mixed marriages, as these have to deal with a set of tasks and problems arising, not from marriage itself, but from the division of the churches. A course of this kind is a particularly effective example of the way clergy and laity from the different churches can combine to give pastoral care to those entering on a mixed marriage. Once married, the couples themselves have proved the most effective agents of joint pastoral care.

Notes

1. As, for example, in *The Joint Pastoral Care of Interchurch Marriages in England, Wales and Scotland*. (Recommendations by the Joint Working Group of the British Council of Churches and the Roman Catholic Church in England, Wales and Scotland, put forward in December 1970, and available from the British Council of Churches and *One in Christ*).
2. Episcopal Conference of England and Wales, *Directory Concerning Mixed Marriages*, published by the Catholic Truth Society (1971).
3. *Two-Church Families*, Association of Interchurch Families, Lincoln (1973).

2. Positions and Trends in France

Joseph Hoffmann

The number of mixed marriages in France continues to grow rapidly. While the new legislation introduced for them may not have greatly accelerated the rate of increase, there are grounds for thinking that it has at least permitted the regularisation of many mixed marriages which had been invalidly contracted. Moreover, in making easier a marriage before a Protestant minister it leads to the appearance in statistics of many marriages which would otherwise have remained irregular. As a result, the clergy have become more aware of the urgent need for pastoral care of mixed marriages.[1]

The volume of such marriages varies considerably in accordance with the numerical strength in a particular region of the denominations involved. It is very difficult to establish a comprehensive set of statistics for the whole of France but some facts at least may be mentioned by way of general indication. The total number of Protestants in France is of the order of 800,000 (Reformed and Lutherans). They are scattered among 40 million Roman Catholics. Except in Alsace and Lorraine, the proportion of Protestants varies between 5% and 25% of the total population. In consequence, on the Protestant side, mixed marriages are proportionally far the most numerous, and amount to 80% of all marriages.[2]

The figures furnished by the diocese of Strasbourg, where the Protestant population is the largest in France, provide us with the following picture. Between 1965 and 1970 the office for matrimonial affairs granted an annual average of 785 dispensations from the impediment of mixed religion. From 1970 to 1973 inclusive there were on average 997 religious celebrations of mixed marriage before a Roman Catholic priest. In the course of these three years a total of 510 dispensations from canonical form was recorded. This gives a yearly average of around 1,160 religious mixed marriages. But there must be added for the two years 1971 and 1972 around 620 celebrations in a Protestant church without dispensation from the form. In the conurbation of Strasbourg alone there are some 200 religious celebrations of mixed marriage every year. It can therefore be reckoned that over a period of ten years alone in an area like the east of France, the number of Christians, parents and children, directly concerned with the problems of mixed marriage amounts to more than 40,000.

I The Present Situation of Mixed Marriage Families

This considerable number of Christians remains very under-privileged in the religious sphere. The majority of them are left to them-selves to find a solution for the family and religious problems arising from their situation. Only some large urban centres have set up groups of Mixed Marriage Families (*Foyers Mixtes*): the oldest of these began in the 1960s. The small and medium-sized towns, like the rural parishes, do not in practice offer the help which these families would need.

Young engaged couples and young mixed marriage families are still all too often subjected to strong family, social and clerical pressures. The latter are by no means the least, as it still too frequently happens that the Roman Catholic priest interprets too narrowly the promise "to do one's best" to ensure the baptism and education of the children in the Roman Catholic Church. It is also well known that mixed couples can only rarely participate as couples in the apostolic or charitable acti-vities of their respective parishes. In consequence much energy and good will are prevented from bearing the fruits which the churches could expect in a normal situation. The resultant malaise is felt all the more deeply by the couples as, on the one hand, the churches become more open to each other and denominational tensions decrease and, on the other hand, as among the better educated couples, their own faith becomes more personal. From this stem a number of concerns and experiments which attempt to find a better place in the Church for mixed marriage families and to give them the possibility of greater participation in their respective communities.

II Trends and Experiments

1 The Marriage Celebration

Concern to reduce denominational divisions makes itself apparent in the preparation and celebration of marriage. It is more and more the case, though no figures can be given, that engaged couples have at least a discussion with the minister of the other denomination when the wedding ceremony is to be a religious one. The details of the ceremony are arranged in agreement with the two ministers when both are to be present at the liturgical celebration. In this case, the minister chosen by the couple receives the vows, while the other participates in varying degrees according to the place: giving the homily, reading the prayers, presenting the Bible. The presence together of both ministers shows the couple that they can remain full members of their own churches while at the same time receiving the approval and support of the other denomination.

2 The Baptismal Celebration

This presents greater difficulties. While couples married before 1970 have in most cases, though not in all, resolved the problem of baptising their children in the Roman Catholic Church (though sometimes at the cost of pain and distress), the new generation follows an entirely different approach.

A certain number, who seem to be on the increase, delay the baptism on grounds of principle: they refuse to commit the child to a way of life he has not himself chosen. Even if the motive for this delay is, in itself, independent of the denominational problem, the latter also has an influence because of the additional difficulty which the choice of one denomination for the child involves at present.

A good number of other couples delay baptism. Some do so because of the difficulty they experience in selecting the denomination for the child – which shows that the new legislation does not make the exercising of parental responsibility any easier. Others do so in order to express their rejection of a denominational limiting of baptism as such, and to face the churches with this question. This kind of deliberate challenge to the churches is not uncommon. It reveals a deep suffering and constitutes an appeal to which the churches must listen.

A third category of couples is making a positive effort to escape this denominational rigidity. Theological reflection has made them discover in a new fashion the unique role of baptism as the unique means of entry into the Church. This is a role happily reiterated in the theological document published jointly by the Roman Catholic/Protestant Committee of France in December 1972: "It is through the ministry of our respective churches that we become members of the Body of Christ. If through baptism we become members of churches which are still separated, we affirm nonetheless that there is but one baptism, and that baptism is the sacramental bond of unity and the foundation of communion between all Christians."[3] These couples want to give this theological reality an expression which is visible and, if possible, liturgical. Various attempts have already been made: baptism by one of the ministers with the participation of the other; baptism by one minister and simultaneous registration in the records of both parishes; a child has even been baptised without the fact being recorded in either register but simply communicated orally to the churches. The problem would be made somewhat less dramatic if baptism celebrated in one denomination did not, in fact, involve the upbringing of the child in that denomination and his subsequent denominational adherence. Certain groups are expressing forcibly their desire to see on the part of the churches some concrete attitudes and signs of future development on this question of baptism.

3 Ecumenical Education

In addition to an "ecumenical" baptismal celebration, mixed couples are faced with the even more important and formidable problem of the Christian education of their children. Here we must limit ourselves to the problem of religious upbringing outside the family circle proper (where the practice of couples escapes detailed analysis). In any case, the denominational division is above all apparent at the level of institutional education, and more particularly in the area of preparation for the sacraments.

Here again certain initiatives are emerging with the aim of reducing the denominational divide to a minimum. Experiments in ecumenical catechetics are numerous in France. Almost all the Mixed Marriage Family Groups of any importance have attempted their own. Up to the present they have limited themselves chiefly to children aged between six and ten, for two reasons. Firstly, the difficulty of meeting the need for a growing number of catechists as the number of classes increases, while in certain towns the Protestant community, being very much in the minority, finds it harder to discover people who are both available and competent. Secondly, the even greater difficulty of ecumenical catechists once the point of preparation for the sacraments and the solemn profession of faith has been reached. Yet the advantages of this kind of catechetics compensate for the difficulties: freshness and originality in discovering and formulating the faith; active collaboration of parents with teachers and ministers. As a result of what was originally a specific problem of mixed marriage couples, a large number of adults have been influenced by a renewed kind of training of an ecumenical character.

In France as a whole, this catechetical teaching is given outside the school programme, as indeed is all other religious instruction. In the Moselle and Upper and Lower Rhine Departments, several experiments are taking place within State schools on the strength of a scholastic statute resulting from the Concordat between the churches and the State. Two of these experiments have a particular character.[4] The first is in the small town of Munster, where there is an equal number of Roman Catholics and Protestants. Here the lay teachers, both men and women, have taken the responsibility of ensuring ecumenical catechetics in all the classes of the community school. Regular working meetings between teachers and ministers ensure coordination on the programmes. The ministers reserve for themselves the more immediate preparation for the profession of faith at the beginning of adolescence (at age 13-14). The second is at Strasbourg. Here a small group of parents who are members of Mixed Marriage Families took the initiative in providing ecumenical catechetics in the State school. This began in September 1972 with four classes, for both boys and girls, continued in 1973/74 with three classes, and will certainly resume with four classes in September 1974. The consent of the majority of the parents was easily obtained, and parents' meetings have shown a lively interest in the experiment, precisely because of its ecumenical character. Some reservations were expressed on the part of the Church authorities, and on that of the educational authorities it was necessary to overcome administrative complications. These experiments have proved enormously enriching, in spite of some initial confusions, for they have to do with the State schools and can contribute to a reduction of the denominational separation which is at present *de rigeur* in religious classes. On the other hand, at the level of the Christian people, they strengthen ecumenical concern and the coming together of families.

4 The Eucharist

For many years, and above all since the founding of Mixed Marriage Family groups, the pain and the anomaly of separation at the moment of eucharistic celebration have been growing more intense. Many couples have for a long time loyally endured the pain of this separation in the very heart of their Christian life. Many requests have been made to the Roman Catholic authorities for at least occasional reciprocal intercommunion during meetings or retreats of Mixed Marriage Family groups, or on the occasion of family religious celebrations.

One instance among many deserves special mention because of its significance as an example: that of the general meeting of Mixed Marriage Family groups at Voirons in Savoy at Pentecost, 1971. A request for reciprocal eucharistic hospitality was sent to Pasteur Monsarrat, President of the Regional Council of the Reformed Church of France, and to Monsignor Sauvage, Bishop of Annecy. The Protestant reply was positive; that of the bishop, friendly in form and discreet in substance, offered Roman Catholic hospitality under the exceptional circumstances to those Protestant partners who wished to accept it. About two-thirds of the Protestant participants accepted this unilateral offer of hospitality; several couples practised complete reciprocal intercommunion (there were two celebrations); one couple abstained from communion entirely. All declared after the event, agreeing on this with all the Mixed Marriage Family groups, that unilateral hospitality was not an acceptable solution.

In fact, instances of intercommunion are becoming more frequent. Some couples feel that they are unable to bear any longer the pain of the impossibility of intercommunion, though they have so long accepted it in complete loyalty. For them, a situation of urgency has risen which a sound pastoral theology cannot ignore. Other couples feel that the area of common faith concerning the Eucharist and other important points of Christian doctrine, especially since the Dombes Agreed Statements, those relating to baptism, to marriage and the progress towards recognition of ministries, as well as their unity in daily life, no longer justify the forbidding of shared communion. Others again are convinced that the problem for the Church at the present time is no longer that of denominational division, but rather of survival and witness to the Gospel. They by-pass provisions which they consider as long since overtaken by other urgent requirements and as, all in all, prejudicial to the life of the Church.

Against the background of this intense effort of theological reflection conducted by groups and the more and more forceful requests addressed to the Church authorities, the decision of the bishop of Strasbourg has appeared as a normal and inevitable consequence of this powerful forward movement. This decision foresees the possibility of practising inter-communion, strictly reserved for mixed couples, and in circumstances which are clearly exceptional. The assessment of these circumstances is reserved to the bishop himself in the case of isolated instances, and to the chaplains in the case of organised groups of Mixed Marriage Families. The decision has been felt by those involved as a liberation and as a blessing. It has brought about a real easing of tension for many and a fresh impetus for ecumenical work.[5]

All this activity which is taking place among Mixed Marriage Family groups in France and among many isolated mixed couples can already be recognised after these few years as most beneficial for the progress of unity. This is an area where the unity of the Church is already being realised to a great extent in a Christian life lived in sharing, in respect for differences and in promotion of common treasures. The visible division, above all in what concerns the Eucharist, no longer corresponds to the inner reality of their lives: so many of the families tell us. Mixed Marriage Families, instead of remaining more or less isolated cells, only poorly attached to the Church, can become dynamic cells. Fully integrated into their Church as it now is, they prefigure and already realise the shape of the Church of tomorrow. Where there exists an active group of Mixed Marriage Families which is spiritually alive, there a sector of the Church is advancing towards real unity of faith and action. In virtue of their very numbers, they are more and more called to form a kind of fertile soil which will enable unity to grow in the richness of diversity – on condition that Church structures and hierarchies do not render it barren.

Notes

1. The author wishes to express his indebtedness for their help in drafting this report to his Lutheran colleague in the University of Strasbourg, the Rev. Professor Marc Lienhard, and also to the Rev. Théophane Chary, OFM who is chaplain to the Mixed Marriage Family Groups in Strasbourg. The most helpful French periodicals on the subject of mixed marriage are: *Foyers Mixtes* (2, Place Gailleton, 69002 Lyon) and *Unité des Chrétiens* (17 rue de L'Assomption, 75016 Paris).
2. *Unité des Chrétiens*, 7, p. 34.
3. The full text is to be found in *Documentation Catholique* (7 Jan. 1973) pp. 22-4.
4. Cf. *Catéchèse* (6, avenue Vavin, 75006 Paris), 54 (Jan. 1974).
5. "Eucharistic Hospitality for Interchurch Families: Mgr. Elchinger's Directives for the Faithful of the Strasbourg Diocese", *One in Christ* ix (1973) pp. 371-87. "Eucharistic Hospitality: A Statement by the

Institute for Ecumenical Research, Strasbourg, France, on Lutheran-Roman Catholic Intercommunion", *ibid*, pp. 388-401. Cf. also "Eucharistic Sharing: a Pastoral Letter of the Bishop of Superior, Wisconsin", *ibid.*, pp. 401-4.

3. Positions and Trends in Switzerland

Felix Trösch

I The Change in Roman Catholic Mixed Marriage Legislation since *Matrimonia Mixta*

On the appearance of Pope Paul VI's Apostolic Letter *Matrimonia Mixta* in March 1970, Swiss Roman Catholic and Protestant comments revealed disappointment at the traditional legalistic style of the document and the fundamentally defensive posture which still dominated it. What appeared especially shocking was the explicit rejection of ecumenical marriage ceremonies with the joint participation of non-Roman Catholic ministers. Only the trained eye of the canonist could discern that the document in fact included steps towards a significant re-orientation of previous Roman Catholic practice in regard to mixed marriage. What was now important was to make the fullest use of the possibilities given in this legal framework, and to apply them pastorally to the concrete situation in Switzerland.

It is to the credit of the Conference of Swiss Bishops that it completed this task rapidly and in an exemplary fashion. As early as 1 October 1970 its *Guidelines*[1] came into force, and in them the new legal norms were applied as far as possible in a spirit of progressive ecumenism. The most urgent pre-requisites for a resolution of the mixed marriage problem had already been formulated in 1967 in the *Joint Statement on Marriage between Christians of different Confessions*,[2] which was based on discussions of the Bishops' Conference with the Board of Directors of the Union of Swiss Protestant Churches and the Christian Catholic Bishop. Particular difficulties were raised by the unilateral requirement of Canon Law for the Roman Catholic upbringing of the children, and the non-recognition of Christian marriage celebrations outside the Roman Catholic Church. On these points the *Guidelines* gave the following new ruling:

1 The religious upbringing of the children was explicitly declared to be a matter of conscience for *both* partners, who ought through examination of their personal convictions to come to a decision which both can support. The Swiss ruling requires no written declaration from either partner on the matter, but stresses the importance of pastoral clarification of the question of conscience, which arises for the Roman Catholic and non-Roman Catholic partner alike. It is explicitly maintained that no one can dispense the Roman Catholic partner from the obligation of conscience "to endeavour to secure the Roman Catholic

baptism and upbringing of the children, insofar as that is possible under the concrete circumstances of the marriage". The dispensation from the impediment of "mixed religion" (i.e. the difference in denominational allegiance) is given by the competent parish priest. In cases of difficulty a further enquiry must be made to the bishop's office; thus the parish priest cannot decide on his own to refuse a dispensation.

2 In regard to the marriage ceremony, the *Guidelines* lay down that it is possible for non-Roman Catholic ministers to take part in a Roman Catholic celebration in prayers, readings, sermon and intercessions, but excluding the actual receiving of the marriage vows. Where a Roman Catholic ceremony raises special difficulties, the *Guidelines* see a solution in a dispensation from the canonical form, which is granted by the local bishop when there are adequate grounds. Requests for such a dispensation must be forwarded by the parish priest to the bishop's office. The Bishops' Conference particularly stresses that it welcomes it when even in such a case "a church ceremony takes place, so that the religious character of marriage between Christians is emphasised". Thus it officially distances itself from the standpoint of previous Canon Law, according to which it seemed better to have no religious marriage ceremony at all, since a non-Roman Catholic one meant excommunication. Even where a dispensation from canonical form has been given to allow a non-Roman Catholic marriage ceremony, the participation of the Roman Catholic priest is also permitted. Dialogue between the churches is expressly desired for the arranging of joint marriage preparation and the organisation and registration of such mixed marriage celebrations.

3 Apart from the new rulings on the two chief difficulties of the upbringing of children and the marriage ceremony, the bishops insist on the necessity of pastoral care for the engaged and married couples from different denominations to be given by both churches on the basis of their common belief in Jesus Christ and in baptism. Joint guidelines for the pastoral care of mixed marriages should be worked out. Thereby the hope is expressed that an ecumenical dialogue, conducted in Christian love, can contribute to the re-uniting of Christians. A summary and expansion of the episcopal *Guidelines* appeared in May 1971 entitled *Assistance for the Counselling of Marriage Couples from different Confessions*.[3]

II Further Development and Ecumenical Effect of the new Roman Catholic Ruling

As soon as the new mixed marriage regulations came to be applied practically in pastoral care, it became clear even to those outside the Roman Catholic Church that in fact a fundamental and decisive breakthrough in the direction of an ecumenical solution of the problem had been achieved. Immediately, and with new courage, the task was taken up of developing and extending this achievement through interdenominational dialogue.

The first immediate goal was the preparation of recommendations for the shaping of ecumenical marriage services, and this was tackled by the Protestant-Catholic Working Group for the Pastoral Care of Mixed Marriages in German Switzerland.[4] As a result there appeared in 1973 the volume *Ecumenical Marriage*,[5] approved by the Board of Directors of the Union of Swiss Protestant Churches, the Conference of Swiss Bishops, and the Christian Catholic Bishop. In it are offered three different orders of service enabling the mutual co-operation of clergy of different denominations. By contrast with a similar West German publication,[6] the orders are deliberately shaped in such a way that all can be used by any of the three churches. It is advised not to hold a joint Mass or Communion celebration, as the participants cannot all share equally in every part of the liturgy. In the introduction, the current marriage law of the Roman Catholic church is briefly explained, and reference is made to "the dispensation from canonical form which is still for the present necessary" if the marriage vows are not received by the Roman Catholic priest. In cases where such a dispensation has been given, the preceding civil marriage counts as valid and sacramental.[7]

In West Switzerland, opinion is not in favour of simply taking over these patterns for an ecumenical marriage liturgy in French translation. Even the expression "ecumenical marriage" is not accepted on the ground that it to some extent obscures the harsh reality that in fact there still are confessionally divided churches. The Working Group of the Roman Catholic and Reformed Churches of French Switzerland for the Study of Mixed Marriages[8] wishes therefore only to suggest a framework for such ceremonies to supplement the particular liturgies of the individual churches. It requires careful preparation by both clergy, taking account of the particular circumstances. In its "Suggestions for priests and pastors who preside together at a mixed marriage ceremony",[9] it explicitly lays down: "There is not yet a single Church, and so the marriage can only be celebrated in the one or the other in order to avoid all confusion. . . . For the moment, the marriage can only be denominational. The officiant will follow the liturgy of his own church. During this action, the other clergyman will remain apart." In the particular instance of the exchange of rings, it is noted: "In order not to offend the Protestant partner, the priest will be careful to avoid a formula which 'blesses the wedding rings'." It stands to reason that in this context no provision is made for a celebration of the Mass or Holy Communion.

An official comment on the new situation from the Protestant/ Reformed side throughout the whole of Switzerland has not yet appeared, and can scarcely be expected in view of the extensive autonomy of the cantonal churches. There are, however, statements from some Protestant/Reformed cantonal churches (for example in Bern and Zürich). These explain the new Roman Catholic regulations in detail and instruct ministers to work for co-operative and loyal partnership in the care of mixed marriages. The participation of Reformed ministers at marriage ceremonies including Nuptial Mass is explicitly forbidden. There should also be no participation in the marriage service where the marriage preparation has not from the beginning been conducted jointly with the Protestant minister, or when he discovers that the freedom of decision of the couple has not been respected. The Protestant churches in the French-speaking area published in October 1970 joint directives to all ministers; these agree in essence with the guidelines in German Switzerland. The reservations about an "ecumenical" marriage liturgy have already been mentioned.

III Trends becoming apparent on the Basis of or in Reaction to "Synod 72"[10]

The preparation and first sessions of "Synod 72" brought a fresh impulse to the development of pastoral care of mixed marriage. In the survey to discover topics for the Synods, the faithful ascribed a particular urgency to the problem. The relevant inter-diocesan fact-finding commission accordingly prepared for the very first session a draft entitled "Life in Mixed Marriage",[11] in the development of which advisers from the non-Roman Catholic churches and individual mixed marriage couples had co-operated. The proceedings in the various diocesan Synods attracted a great deal of attention. It became apparent, however, that the bulk of the membership in all the churches was still very inadequately informed about the new regulations already in force on the Roman Catholic side.

In the draft presentation, the question of the marriage ceremony is once more dealt with, and particular weight laid upon the ecumenical preparation for it. The ceremony itself should as a rule be held in the one or the other church, but in an ecumenical spirit. According to the particular circumstances, a celebration with the participation of the ministers of both churches is desirable.

Even more important in the eyes of the Synod than the making of such "ecumenical" ceremonies general is the effort to bring about a mutual recognition of church marriage ceremonies, insofar as no diriment impediment is involved. A petition on this for the whole of Switzerland was approved, and the Bishops' Conference will forward it to Rome.

On similar lines is the request to the Bishops' Conference to advocate in Rome the abolition of the present impediment of "mixed religion", which no longer accords with the new ecumenical position.

On the issue of baptism and the upbringing of the children, the importance of a joint decision by the couple is stressed once more, and any kind of unilateral promise by one partner rejected. In the individual Synods there was also discussion of the criteria which would be offered to couples to assist in their solution of this problem. On the basis of previous experiences it is regretted that the decision is often influenced primarily by merely external factors, such as family tradition or the surrounding atmosphere. There is general official rejection of the tendency in certain circles to avoid a decision altogether, and after an "ecumenical" baptism to bring up the children as members of both churches.

With reference to joint attendance of couples at worship, the Synod wishes for a declaration by the Bishops' Conference that attendance at a non-Roman Catholic service is also an appropriate Sunday observance for the Roman Catholic partner.

The granting of eucharistic hospitality to those mixed marriage couples who desire it as an expression of their common faith and life is declared by the Synod to be pastorally urgent. This problem will also be treated in connection with the question of limited intercommunion in special cases. A valuable theological preparation for these discussions was carried out by the Ecumenical Discussion Commissions of Switzerland and published in autumn 1973 as a working document *Towards a Common Eucharistic Witness of the Churches*.[12] Although this is not an official document, the foreword is signed by the Presidents of the Bishops' Conference and the Union of Swiss Protestant Churches and the Christian Catholic Bishop. It deals in detail with "The Necessity and Limits of a Common Eucharistic Witness" and "The Eucharist in the Common Understanding of the Churches". It is established there that complete agreement in the understanding of the eucharist (to which a consensus on the significance of the ministry also belongs) has not yet been reached. Nevertheless the document holds eucharistic hospitality to be justifiable in particular individual cases, especially for mixed marriage couples who desire in their common faith to encounter the Lord in the visible sign of unity. In spite of the theological difficulties which stand in the way of mutual intercommunion (particularly because of the question of ministry) efforts in this direction ought to continue. It would be disheartening for committed Christians in mixed marriages if advances were not soon achieved in this area. By contrast, less can be said in favour of eucharistic celebrations with two or three ministers of different denominations officiating and the corresponding receiving of communion in different ways: there in effect only an illusion of unity is achieved, and the status quo consolidated.

The *Dombes Agreement: Towards a single eucharistic Faith*[13] by a group of French and Swiss theologians naturally had a good reception in Switzerland. The permission for intercommunion granted by Bishop Elchinger and the Lutheran Church in Alsace was warmly greeted, and not infrequently quietly imitated.

Various recommendations for joint pastoral care of mixed marriages by the churches were also discussed in the Synods. Here it was explicitly maintained that this is not merely a question of co-operation between the clergy; the congregations too ought to make more efforts for a brotherly reception of the couples. In this entire area the churches are only at the first tentative beginning of authentic ecumenical behaviour. There is no lack of outlines for joint recommendations for pastoral care, but tactlessness by clergy and continuing defensive reactions at the grass roots still cause many a setback.

IV The Ecumenical Expansion of Mixed Marriage Groups

In German speaking Switzerland since 1970 the main focus of ecumenical concern has been directed towards the shaping of the marriage ceremony and the organising of official pastoral care by the churches. In the French part, however, more stress appears to be put on the exchange of religious and spiritual experience by the mixed marriage couples in small circles. According to our information there are about 12 such groups in the canton of Vaud, 15 in Geneva, and more in Valais and in Jura. They are mostly attended by a Protestant minister and a Roman Catholic priest, or are at least in contact with clergy. They are only loosely connected to each other, but draw a common inspiration from the bulletin *Foyers Mixtes* which is published in Lyons. In it, concrete problems of the religious life and upbringing of children of mixed marriages are discussed, but fundamental theological material on matters ecumenical is also offered. There is no comparable publication in German Switzerland. Unfortunately such mixed marriage groups are only to be found in larger conurbations, while couples in the countryside often still remain in difficult spiritual isolation.

The spiritual experience of these couples has exerted a positive influence on the development of the ecumenical dialogue, since both pastors and lay people from such groups have been delegated to the various Commissions for ecumenical questions. Through this contact with life at the grass-roots, the dialogue was preserved from the danger of theological intellectualisation. The actual experience of life showed that purely canonical or dogmatic "solutions" do not dispose of the problem of mentalities and sensitivities which are so differently stamped by the different denominations.

The vote on the special denominational clauses in May 1973 demonstrates furthermore that the grass-roots have as yet scarcely appropriated the ecumenical openness of the theologians and church leadership.[14] Switzerland too must seek her own way of overcoming her denominational past. Depending on the people who occupy the leading positions in the churches – both Roman Catholic and Reformed – there come to the fore now hopeful openness, now cautious hesitation. The work of the Synods, where the voice of the laity carries weight, may however have strengthened on the Roman Catholic side the will and the courage for an authentic ecumenical solution of the mixed marriage question.

Of particular importance in all ecumenical questions is the significance of the difference between the generations. While the middle and older generations still have great difficulty with these problems, the younger generation has scarcely any interest left for controversial theological debates which seem to it, in view of the real issues, to be abstract and outdated.[15]

Notes

1. "Directives de la Conférence des Evêques suisses pour l'application de la lettre apostolique du Pape Paul VI sur les mariages mixtes du 31 mars 1970" in *La Semaine Catholique* (1 Oct. 1970).
   "Richtlinien der Schweizerischen BischofsKonferenz zum Apostolischen Schreiben Papst Paul's VI, *Matrimonia mixta*", in *Schweizerische Kirchenzeitung*, 138 (1970), pp. 541-3.
2. "Déclaration commune sur le problème des mariages mixtes", Zürich (1967).

"Gemeinsame Erklarung über die Ehe zwischen bekenntnis-verschiedenen Christen", in *Schweiz. Kirchenzeitung*, 135 (1967) pp. 386-7, 395-6.

3. "La préparation et l'inscription des mariages mixtes dans les paroisses" in *La Semaine Catholique* (27 May 1971).
"Die pfarramtliche Vorbereitung und Eintragung von Mischehen" in *Shweiz. Kirchenzeitung*, 139 (1971) 358-9.

4. *Evangelische-katholische Arbeitsgemeinschaft für Mischehenseelsorge der deutschen Schweiz.*

5. *Oekumenische Trauung,* Verlag Benzinger & Theologischer Verlag, Zürich (1973).

6. *Gemeinsame Kirchliche Trauung,* Verlag Friedrich Pustet, Regensburg (1973).

7. The normal practice in Switzerland is for a civil marriage ceremony to precede the religious one. In the case of Roman Catholic marriages according to the canonical form, this previous civil ceremony is not regarded by the Roman Catholic Church as the actual marriage: that only takes place when the priest asks for and receives the marriage consent in the church ceremony. In the theology of the Protestant churches, the preceding civil ceremony is the actual marriage; the subsequent church ceremony is a blessing upon it. When a Roman Catholic partner has received a dispensation from the canonical form, the marriage is regarded by the Roman Catholic Church as occurring at the civil ceremony where this precedes a religious one in a Protestant church; thus the attitude of the Roman Catholic Church *in this instance* parallels that of the Protestant churches. Hence this reference to the civil ceremony, rather than to the non-Roman Catholic Church one.

8. *Groupe de Travail des Eglises catholique romaine et réformées de Suisse romande pour l'étude des mariages mixtes.*

9. "Directives provisoires a l'intention des prêtres et pasteurs des Eglises catholique-romaine et réformées de Suisse romande" – document sent to priests and ministers (Oct. 1971).
"Quelques indications a l'intention des prêtres et pasteurs qui president ensemble une ceremonie de mariage mixte", – document sent to priests and ministers (1974).

10. By "Synod 72" we mean the diocesan Synods which have been held simultaneously in Switzerland since 1972, at which material prepared on an all-Switzerland basis is dealt with. The necessary coordination is sought through extra joint meetings, or by a proper all-Switzerland Synod in which the dioceses are represented by groups of delegates in proportion to their size.

11. "Oekumenischer Auftrag in unsern Verhältnissen: 1. Teil: "Leben in der Mischehe", in *Schweiz. Kirchenzeitung*, 40 (1972); "La vie chrétienne dans les foyers mixtes" in *Projet de la Cospei* 5, Fribourg (1972).

12. "Pour un témoignage eucharistique commun des Eglises" in *Evangile et Mission* (Oct. 18 1973).
"Für ein gemeinsames eucharistisches Zeugnis der Kirchen" in *Schweiz. Kirchenzeitung*, 141 (1973) pp. 629-638.

13. *Vers une même foi eucharistique?*, Editions du Seuil, Paris (1971).
14. The "special denominational clauses" of the Federal Constitution rendered illegal the restoration of suppressed convents and the foundation of new ones (Art. 50), and the establishment and maning by the Jesuits of churches and schools (Art. 51). These discriminatory regulations were imposed on Roman Catholics after the civil war of 1848, and grew in severity by virtue of a constitutional revision after the struggle with Catholicism in 1870. They resulted initially from the political strife between conservative federalists and radicals in the 19th century, but were subsequently understood by the Protestant majority as "precautionary measures" against the threat of "aggressive political Catholicism". Since World War II the Government had applied these anachronistic articles of the Constitution with the utmost tolerance, and exerted itself to prepare for abrogation by vote of the people.

Officials of the Protestant churches, as well as nearly all political parties, approved of the abrogation proposal. Parliament voted, with only a few dissentient voices, in favour of abrogation. But as the plebiscite drew near, emotional prejudice and anti-Catholic feeling proved to be still very much alive, and the flames were fanned by the "Committee for the Maintenance of the State's Protective Clauses". Numerous Protestant leaders, both pastors and lay, who displayed their ecumenical spirit were dubbed as traitors to Protestantism by their opponents. Certain sects saw in ecumenism the hidden and dangerous dagger of Rome.

The results of the plebiscite were in doubt up to the very last moment. It was noteworthy that the younger generation did not greatly interest themselves in the outcome. The final result of 790,799 votes for abrogation and 648,959 votes against, while positive to be sure, yet was so close as to warn the churches against assuming that their ecumenical endeavours were bearing immediate fruit.

15. The author wishes to express his thanks to the Rev. Werner Heierle, S. J. who represented him at the Dublin Consultation and to the Rev. Claude Reverdin of the Swiss Reformed Church who was also present at the Consultation and who helped in the preparation of this paper.

4. Positions and Trends in Germany

Joachim Lell

I Social Background

It is hardly possible for a German to describe the legal situation of mixed marriages and the development of the ecumenical discussion in Germany without some preliminary remarks on the social background in that country.

1 Marriage and the Family

No German can at present speak on the situation in Germany as a whole. The country was both reduced in size and divided after the last war. I will, therefore, confine myself to the western part of Germany. Here some 62 million people live in roughly half their former living-space: 247 inhabitants per square kilometre, as against some 58 per square kilometre in the Republic of Ireland. In the industrial areas the concentration is even greater: in 1957 about 477 inhabitants per square kilometre. Industrialisation, with all its own anthropological and social problems, has, however, also had its effect on agricultural and forested areas. High-rise buildings have changed the appearance of even the smallest towns. Social upheaval, so marked a feature of all western countries, has had especially serious consequences in West Germany, right down to marriage and the family. The small family with one or two children is becoming the norm. In spite of the large families of foreign workers, the population is declining. Particularly significant is the increase in the divorce figures. In 1970, 11.4% (in 1962, 7.4%) of Evangelical[1] marriages were dissolved, and 7.9% (in 1962, 5.2%) of Roman Catholic ones. Today roughly every fifth marriage ends in divorce.

Before one moralises about this, one should remember that in a society based on the division of labour men and women often live more closely together at their place of work than at home in the family. In addition, there is the general sexualisation of life; contraception, everywhere advocated and certainly effective, makes premarital and extra-marital intercourse "safe"; traditional moral standards are disappearing in all levels of society: the *Bundestag* is relaxing the criminal law on abortion. Many radical groups are calling marriage itself into question as an antiquated structure for the ordering of life. Their criticisms and their new suggestions are carried by the mass media into almost every family, and supply fuel for fierce arguments. Not a few – and those not only young people – are attempting a kind of life together similar to marriage on trial, or are doing so as part of a group or commune, which can indeed be understood as a sort of contemporary "extended family".

Nevertheless – it seems almost a contradiction – marriage and family have remained astonishingly stable up to the present. In the mind of society as a whole, marriage is still understood as a sharing of life and home which is life-long and juridically regulated. There is an increase in the number of marriages among younger age-groups. Under discussion at the moment is a reduction in the minimum age for marriage from 18 to 16 for women, and from 21 to 18 for men. 70% of all divorcees remarry, 40% marry other divorcees. Marriage law is moving from the traditional patriarchal structuring of the institution towards an equality in partnership of both sexes. As a result, the husband's one-sided rights and duties of protection and representation are being removed. In divorce law the principle of breakdown has replaced the older one of culpability.[2]

2 The Churches and Society

It is in this area of social tensions, which is marked by other contradictions as well, that the denominational problems must be sketched in. As a result of the enormous movement of refugees after the second world war and the continuing industrial movement of population, while there are indeed still areas which are denominationally coloured, there are no longer any States which are denominationally defined. The West German population lives in a kind of large-scale "mixed marriage", with some 45% Roman Catholics and 49% Protestants side by side. This means that the denominational oppositions can no longer escalate into political conflicts. Even as Germans began together to rebuild their shattered cities and factories, a wartime experience was repeated in their conversations: "After all, we have the same God" – or, "We have it in common that we have no God, at least not the one we had previously imagined, learnt or dreamt of." At the same time the social contrasts between Protestants and Roman Catholics are fading more and more. Even theological pluralism, up till now a feature of Protestantism is finding its way into Roman Catholicism and tends to relativise denominational disagreements. The characteristic German concern for fundamental issues is leading to new polarisations within the churches and among a public which is growing more critical of the Church.

Our people are experiencing the march of secularisation in ever new waves. Even if the number of those who leave the churches appears today to be falling somewhat, nevertheless some 70,000 Roman Catholics and 190,000 Protestants left their churches in 1970. Certainly that adds up in all to less than 1% of the Church membership. The falling-off of church weddings, however, by around 23%, depicts more clearly the decline of Church and religion. The laicising of many priests (at present around 10% and the decline in vocations from 777 in 1962 to 315 in 1972 (and of these perhaps 25-30% will proceed to ordination) forebode, in many eyes, a bleak future for traditional forms of ministry.

This rather dark picture is reflected again in the public debates about the churches. Although, according to a recent survey, they still enjoy a considerable amount of confidence, their status as established churches is under attack. Liberal forces are demanding the radical separation of Church and State – in concrete terms, the abolition of State collection of Church tax, of religious teaching in public schools and of theological faculties in the universities; also among other things the removal of all Christian symbols from public buildings. They insist that the churches should no longer have any influence on politics and society simply because of ancient privileges, but only as much as corresponds to their actual strength without any State assistance. Reality itself has been "dedenominationalised", and should, accordingly, be declericalised.

The churches themselves and groups within them are asking why this decline is occurring. Confessional movements on both sides accuse the Church leadership of giving in all too much to the spirit of the times. In the eyes of ecumenical groups, on the other hand, the leaders seem too traditional and backward. These groups demand honest analyses of the effect of cultic and charitable action, the democratisation of church structures, and an energetic attack – with no backward glances – on the areas of political, social and racial tension in the world. While the former groups demand strict confessional loyalty, among the latter respect for doctrine retreats in favour of ecumenical action, which they practise to the point of eucharistic sharing in spite of all prohibitions. To these ecumenical groups, the official ecumenical contacts between the churches and their tentative agreed statements appear as nothing but ecclesiastical political tactics. The general body of Church people, who are still loyal, however, stand by their bishops, are thankful for their clear position, and desire, at most, a little more freedom in matters ecumenical. Depending on the attitudes of the clergy, local Roman Catholic parishes develop associations with the neighbouring Evangelical congregations – although, of course, such associations do not only develop and grow: they can and do also decline or even die out.

3 The Development of the Mixed Marriage Situation

It is against this background that the development of the situation of mixed marriages is to be seen. Their number has more than doubled since 1933. In 1970 they amounted to 27.5% of all weddings. If they continue to increase at the same rate, they will be as numerous in about ten years as the purely Roman Catholic or Evangelical marriages. In 1971 about 40% of all mixed marriages were celebrated in the Roman Catholic Church, and about 36% in the Evangelical. The remainder did not have a church wedding.

The attention given to the problem is apparent from the flood of publications on the subject. The bibliography contains 249 titles from 1918-1926; 293 from 1926-1959; 302 from 1959-1966; and 705 from 1966-1970. Working parties on mixed marriage have been formed in Germany since the Second Vatican Council. These have challenged the churches not to work out the problems of church division on the backs of couples and families any longer. Through numerous reports of actual experiences they have confirmed the discovery of well-known psychologists that there are scarcely any marriages "which were unsuccessful simply because they were denominationally mixed" (Bovet); or, again, that "the marriage counsellor extraordinarily rarely – not to say as good as never – meets breakdowns that are primarily caused by denominational difference" (Groeger). Unfortunately, this reality is scarcely reflected in the pastoral literature; for it is more concerned with disputing or justifying ecclesiastical warnings and prohibitions than with the people affected. This has led the mixed marriage groups to criticise the churches for confusing milieu and denomination. At the Augsburg Whit Meeting, 1971, an occasion jointly organised by the Roman Catholic *Katholikentag* and the Evangelical *Kirchentag*, 700 participants (out of 8,000) expressed their wishes in 47 resolutions to the following effect:[3]

> The churches should no longer generally discourage mixed marriages, but rather advise young people and their families in an ecumenical spirit.
> The impediment of "mixed religion" – an ecumenical stumbling-block – should be abolished; likewise all legal restrictions should be removed without replacement.
> On the question of the baptism and upbringing of the children in a mixed marriage, no normal pressure ought to be exercised by either side. The parents' responsible decision in conscience ought alone to be decisive.
> Pastoral care of mixed marriages must be exercised jointly by both churches. Such care involves ecumenical services, joint seminars on marriage and family, shared Bible groups, and the admission of the marriage partner from the other church to Communion as a guest so long as intercommunion is not yet possible.
> Just as the principle of indissolubility forbids the churches to co-operate in the dissolution of marriages, so too does their office of forgiveness require them to receive again to full sacramental fellowship those who in awareness of their fault before God wish to live a Christian marriage with a new partner.

These and similar statements were well received among the laity – admittedly with an underlying feeling of resignation that, in the long run, everything would nevertheless remain as it was, and that mixed marriages would continue to be driven out into indifferentism.

II The Juridical Status Quo

The explanatory statement of the Roman Catholic German Bishops Conference of 23 September 1970 interprets the papal *Motu Proprio Matrimonia Mixta* of 31 March 1970 relatively liberally.[4] It does, however, begin (by contrast with the Swiss Bishops' Conference, which speaks principally of the married couple) with the "difficult problems" of denominationally mixed marriages, with their steady increase, and with the growth of ecumenical awareness. It concedes, nevertheless, that the new regulations can deal with only a part of the problems and can merely moderate the effects of church division for mixed marriages. By doing so, it hints that the last word has not yet been spoken.

Priests are empowered to dispense from the impediment of "mixed religion": there are "sufficient reasons in the German situation for the granting of a dispensation in every case". Only if difficulties arise must the local Ordinary give a decision; he also dispenses from the canonical form if the couple do not wish a Roman Catholic wedding. A precondition is that the Roman Catholic partner in the examination before the marriage gives a positive answer to the following questions: "Will you live in your marriage as a Catholic Christian and witness to the faith? Are you conscious of your duty as a Catholic Christian to have your children baptised in the Catholic Church and brought up in the Catholic faith? Do you promise to exert yourself, according to your power to fulfil this moral commandment, so far as that is possible within your marriage?" This promise means, in particular, that the Roman Catholic partner will actively share responsibility for the Christian shaping of marriage and family life; that he will promote the religious upbringing of the children and through exemplary conduct bring the Catholic faith home to them; moreover, that he will deepen his own faith through further religious education in order to conduct fruitful discussion of the faith in his family, together with prayer, especially in order to foster the grace of unity.

The Evangelical partner does not have to make any promise. He should, however, come to the pre-marital meetings (the *Brautgespräch* and *Brautexamen*) for instruction. If he does not, the bishop must be informed.

If a dispensation from canonical form has been granted, the civil marriage ceremony or the wedding in the Evangelical Church counts as valid and sacramental. Double wedding ceremonies are forbidden, but joint ones permitted: the minister of one church may take part in the wedding in the other. If the wedding is in the Roman Catholic Church, the Roman Catholic priest must ask for and receive the marriage consent. Provision is made for the registration of the marriage in the Church records. In order to re-admit to the sacraments those excommunicated before 1 October, 1970, the priests responsible may undertake a *sanatio in radice* under the usual conditions.

The Council of the Evangelical Church in Germany welcomed these new regulations, though it would have preferred "if it had been found possible to abolish the impediment of mixed religion entirely. That would have left the way clear for a really radical reform of the mixed marriage problem." It hopes, however, "that a liberal application of the present regulations in an ecumenical spirit may open the way to a more comprehensive solution". At the same time it requested all member churches – the *ius liturgicum* rests with them – to review their rules and remove all regulations which disadvantage an Evangelical Christian who agrees to a Roman Catholic wedding and to Roman Catholic upbringing of his children.

This has since been done. It must, of course, be said that Protestantism has never known mixed marriage regulations of the kind represented by the Roman Catholic *Codex Iuris Canonici*. No Protestant was excluded from the sacraments or denied church burial simply because of a mixed marriage. Some established churches made marriage conditional on a promise of Evangelical baptism and upbringing of the children – as a reaction to the *Codex* and as a safeguard against later interference from the other side. As a rule, church offices (godparent, religious teacher, member of the church council) were not assigned to those who had been married in the Roman Catholic Church; but plenty of room was left for dealing pastorally with individual cases. Even the minister was not "forbidden" to marry a wife of another faith; only his remaining on in his parish had then to be reviewed. This rule is still in force.

Congregations were informed of the new regulations through a joint pamphlet published in a large edition by the Institute of the Evangelical Union for Denominational Research and the Johann-Adam – Möhler Institute for Ecumenics of the Roman Catholic Church.[5] Two commissions were appointed. One had to draft an Evangelical and a Roman Catholic marriage service, and to indicate the parts which are assigned to the minister of the other church in a mixed wedding. The Roman Catholic form is a compilation based on the current pattern in the *Collectio Rituum* and the 1969 revised edition of the *Rituale Romanum*. The Evangelical rite is a compilation from the nine wedding liturgies of the member churches of the Evangelical Church in Germany. The two orders have been made to resemble each other in language and rubrics, and came into force in 1971.

The other commission needed considerably more time. Finally, however, on 10 December, 1973 the "Joint Church Recommendations for the Marriage Preparation of Couples from different Churches" were cleared for publication.[6] Their starting point is "that what unites Christians of different denominations in the faith is stronger than what divides them"; they refer to seminars in preparation for marriage and marriage counselling centres, and deal as well with the content of pre-marriage instruction and examination. This too can be conducted jointly. It must be made clear that "the Church wishes to be there for this couple and this marriage"; for this reason, clergy must be fully acquainted with the teaching and regulations of the other church, so as neither to remain fixed in denominational one-sidedness, nor to behave as if nothing any longer divided the churches.

The two understandings of marriage are then presented. On the Roman Catholic side texts of the Second Vatican Council, the *Motu Proprio* and the explanatory statement of the German bishops are quoted. The Evangelical side takes as a basis the "Considerations on the Evangelical Understanding of Marriage by the Marriage Commission of the Evangelical Church in Germany" (1970): marriage is a divine gift and institution, which contains within itself the freedom to give the marriage personal shape. Because marriage is seen between these two poles, Protestantism knows "no conceptually complete marriage doctrine". The communion in love which opens itself to the believer as an image of the relationship of Christ to his Church "is not to be grasped in the structures of law and order". These, like the public protection of marriage, are a matter for civil law and thus the concern of the State. This is why the Evangelical churches "as a matter of fundamental principle recognise marriage contracted according to civil law as valid". They are of the opinion "that in the law of contraction and dissolution of marriage they need to take no juridical initiatives so long as the State recognises and protects the preconditions and the essential content of marriage. This includes free choice of partner, the contract of marriage as a life-long partnership, and monogamy". By contrast to the civil ceremony, which is a legal matter, the Evangelical church wedding is a public service of worship, in which the couple are asked, after Bible reading and preaching, if they wish to accept each other as given by God. The congregation takes up their answer and God's pledge in prayer and intercession, so as to receive God's blessing together with the couple.

The "Recommendations" then attempt to find the right balance between respect for the freedom of conscience of the couple and their denominational allegiance. Denominational difference ought neither to be overstressed nor understressed, and ministers should help the couple to come to their own decision on the place of the wedding and the baptism of their children, free from any un-helpful influence of third parties.

In the laborious discussion on services and Eucharist, the Commission did finally struggle through to the point of formulating the differences. In the marriage preparation, it is suggested, understanding should be awakened for the fact that in Evangelical Churches the Roman Catholic partner is admitted to Communion as an expression of pastoral responsibility, whereas the Roman Catholic Church holds such a practice as impossible for reasons of faith. The Church authorities were unable to accept the statement in this form; nevertheless, the Roman Catholic Church has come to accept that a Roman Catholic may be dispensed from his duty to attend Sunday Mass if his presence is either impossible, or possible only with serious difficulty.

If one compares the two understandings of marriage, the differences are not so great that the one must view the other as a danger to the faith. Such is, however, the case so long as the impediment of "mixed religion" applies, and the resultant regulations only manage to be maintained through an ingenious system of dispensation.

III The Further Dialogue

Consequently, further dialogue is pushing towards the abolition of Roman Catholic mixed marriage law. It poses the question – which arises even on purely formal grounds – whether extensive dispensations do not bring the law itself into disrepute. A sign that this is the case can be seen in the decline in church weddings. To many it no longer matters very much to be "canonically invalidly" married. *Sanationes in radice* are requested disturbingly rarely. Many Roman Catholic canon lawyers are unhappy with the position: some would like to see the relaxations once more removed; the others would prefer to abolish the entire canon law on marriage, on the ground that it does the Church more harm than good.

Evangelical criticism has always insisted that the revision of this law must show how far Rome recognises the *Oikumene*, and is itself becoming ecumenical.

Roman Catholic criticism of the Evangelical understanding of marriage directs itself chiefly at the absence of the sacramental character of marriage and the marriage contract; secondarily, at the lax attitude to divorce – a criticism also often previously formulated in bishops' utterances.

Indeed the Evangelicals, while unambiguously teaching that marriage is life-long, do reckon with the power of sin which can destroy it. For this reason they cannot refuse their agreement to a divorce where the legally compelled continuance of a broken marriage would put those affected – parents and children – in greater danger than a divorce. "Anyone who wishes to uphold indissolubility in every instance by juridical means, overestimates the capacities of the law". Anyone, however, who must agree to divorce – no matter how narrowly he limits the exceptional cases – will not be in a position to forbid a new wedding, unless of course he were to hold that, in this particular case, sin and guilt cannot be forgiven.

Over against the Roman Catholic criticism, the Evangelical side – recently strongly supported by Roman Catholic canon lawyers – has cast doubt on the moral ambiguities of annulment, and indeed on the ecclesiastical categories of validity and invalidity themselves. In these, according to the Roman Catholic canonist, Neumann, the Message appears "as a cup of wrath".[7]

Those who are affected, both Roman Catholics and Protestants, ask why the church uses such a patchwork of rules; what the much-praised relaxations really amount to; why the Church does not admit "that the whole mixed marriage problem is an artificial one" which the churches hold on to because they wish to secure the allegiance of the children. However understandable such a posture may be on psychological or sociological grounds, it is tragic that such closed-shop thinking should be justified by appeal to the Gospel of Jesus Christ.

The criticism is thus that the official debate is concerned less with people, their questions, needs and conflicts, than with the churches and their self-preservation; and that underlying it, in spite of the verbal insistence to the contrary, is the ultimately unchallenged tendency to see one's own church as having a monopoly of authentic Christianity. Such thinking, however, makes the minister a group-functionary and, as such, incapable of genuine pastoral care. Where God is concerned it is the Church's task to issue a summons to obedience; where men and institutions are concerned, however, it is her task to issue a summons "to partnership and hence also to compromise, to concession, to the discovery of the new, to authentic sharing of differing experiences, traditions and families". Nowhere in the documents have the churches spoken of their own failure, not even where they bemoan the massive exodus of the faithful into indifference. They are still overdrawing the ecclesiastical account, and building "with theological concepts Potemkin villages, in which one cannot live" (Vinçon).[8] Indeed, neither ecumenical weddings nor ecumenical baptisms are of help here. Rather they hinder the essence of catholicity and ecumenism, because they anchor life firmly in the arena of denominational rivalry. The help which the Gospel offers for the recognition and overcoming of conflict in the family is as a result actually withheld from the faithful. A family which cannot go together to the Lord's Supper, the most central and intimate expression of community, is cheated of the essence of community itself, and must needs seek it elsewhere. It is only "with great difficulty imaginable that children can experience the sacrament as a means of grace when either father or mother remains excluded from taking part by church decree" (Vinçon).

Whatever one thinks of such questions, which are being raised in many places by theologians, psychologists, canon lawyers and pastors, but above all, by the mixed marriage couples themselves, one thing does seem to be certain. If the commissions drafting material for the pastoral care of mixed marriage at national and regional level do not address themselves to them, the Church itself will have to bear full responsibility for its further "ghettoisation". The Gospel, said Martin Luther once, is a "driving storm". It does not have to remain with the churches. It can seek new disciples and witnesses outside them.

Notes

1. "Evangelical" is used throughout this paper to describe the various Protestant churches within the federated *Evangelische Kirche* of Germany (E.K.D.).
2. An excellent survey of the recent changes in marriage law against the background of wider social change is given by Hans Dombois, *Kirche und Eherecht* Studien und Abhandlungen (1953-72). Forschungen und Berichte der Evangelischen Studiengemeinschaft, Band 29, Stuttgart (1974).
3. Cf. *Oekumenisches Pfingsttreffen Augsburg 1971, Dokumente*, Paderborn, Stuttgart-Berlin (1971) pp. 275-8.
4. Documentation on the present position of Roman Catholic and Evangelical law can be found in Reinhard Frieling, " 'Mischehe' -aber wie?" in *Bensheimer Heft* 41 [3], Göttingen (1971) pp. 57 ff.
5. *Informationen über die konfessionsverschiedene Ehe*, Bensheim-Paderborn, March 1971, March 1974[3].
6. *Gemeinsame kirchliche Empfehlungen für die Ehevorbereitung konfessionsverschiedener Partner*, Würzburg-Gütersloh (1974).
7. "Ehescheidung und Wiederverheiratung nach katholischem Kirchenrecht" in *Frankfurter Allgemeine Zeitung* (8 Jan. 1970); "Unauflösliches Eheband? Eine Anfrage zum kanonischen Eherecht", in in *Theologische Quartalschrift* 151, Tübingen (1971), pp. 1ff.

8. Herbert Vinçon, "Christliche Erziehung in der Mischehe?" in G. Kiefel, O. Knoch, *Anregungen and Modelle für ökumenische Zusammenarbeit*, Katholisches Bibelwerk and Calwer Verlag Stuttgart (1973) pp. 113 ff.

5. Positions and Trends in Australia

Paul Duffy

Australia is a religiously pluralist society, with more than 15 denominations and sects. Interchurch marriages have always been a fairly common practice, particularly among adherents of the four main churches,[1] and over the past ten years the number has increased significantly. The pastoral problems associated with the nature and number of mixed marriages received added emphasis when in 1971 the Joint Working Group of the Australian Council of Churches and the Roman Catholic Church met to plan co-operative pastoral care in this area. The first steps in co-operation have been taken, while the chief obstacles to closer collaboration have been frankly acknowledged, particularly those relating to the religious upbringing of the children and to Eucharistic sharing.

In the 1971 national census 85% of Australians declared themselves Christian. More than 75% comprise the membership of the four main denominations: Anglican (32%), Roman Catholic (27.6%), Presbyterian (8.5%), and Methodist (7.6%). A sociological survey conducted in 1966 with a limited sample from three States indicated the following mixed-marriage rate: Anglican (20%), Presbyterian (29%), and Methodist (26%).[2] However, these figures also revealed a growing trend among younger adherents of these denominations to marry across denominational boundaries.[3] The author of this survey considered that religious affiliation remained "a formidable factor" in the choice of a marriage partner.[4] If a later study of the Roman Catholic rate of mixed marriages[5] indicates a general trend, then this judgement of the force of religious affiliation in marriage-partner selection may have to be revised. By 1971 the national mixed-marriage rate for the Roman Catholic Church was 48.1%: between 1961 and 1966 there was an overall rise of 10.2%.[6]

Figures for the largest Roman Catholic metropolitan diocese indicate the dimensions of the problem. This diocese, with the second lowest incidence of mixed marriages throughout the nation, had over the 20-year period, 1941-61, a growth rate in such marriages of only 2.4%. Yet over the next 10-year period, 1961-71, the growth rate was 1% for each of the ten years. Even these figures may mask the real rate of mixed-marriage increase: large numbers of in-faith marriages have been between migrants marrying within their ethnic and cultural groups.[7] Pastors in areas of migrant concentration suggest that many such marriages are based less on religious affiliation than on ethnic associations. They predict that second-generation migrant children will detach themselves from the ethnic connection sufficiently to follow the general pattern of Australian-partner selection, in which the factor of religious affiliation will be seen to be less the formidable force that it has been assumed to be.

Church leaders of several traditions agree that the mixed-marriage situation accents the need for joint pastoral care. The need is felt more acutely as all churches recognise the force of the secular humanist attack on the Christian concept of marriage in general, and the tendency among the young especially to accept the view of marriage as a civil contract only.[8]

Official Positions

1 Roman Catholic

The official position was stated by the Australian Catholic Episcopal Conference in 1970 and is based on the Roman regulations of *Matrimonia Mixta*. Within his own diocese each bishop is left with considerable discretionary powers in applying the regulations, particularly with regard to Eucharistic sharing and to dispensation from the canonical form of marriage in a Roman Catholic church.

The discipline rests on the premise that mixed marriages are to be discouraged because they impede "perfect union of mind and full communion of life" of the spouses, and as a sign of division among the churches they do not aid the re-establishment of church unity.[9] However, the Church recognises the fundamental human right of each person to choose his own marriage partner, and so it allows for dispensations from the norm of in-faith marriages.

Chief interest in the Bishops' statement centres on four points: dispensation, the religious upbringing of the children, canonical form, and Eucharistic sharing.

a. The local ordinary's dispensation is needed for a marriage between a Catholic and a non-Catholic Christian to be recognised as licitly performed. For a marriage between a Catholic and a non-christian a dispensation is needed for it to be recognised as valid and licit. Dispensations will ordinarily be granted for a "just" cause (previously the requirement was "a just and grave" cause).

b. For a dispensation to be granted the Catholic partner must declare that he/she is ready to remove all dangers of falling away from the Catholic faith that such a marriage might occasion; and shall sincerely promise to do "all in his/her power" to have all the children baptised and brought up in the Catholic faith. The non-Catholic partner is to be informed of this promise; due respect is to be paid the non-Catholic partner's rights and conscience in this matter.

c. Canonical form is necessary for the validity of such marriages: the marriage will normally be conducted in a Catholic church according to the Catholic rite. Dispensation from canonical form may be granted by the local bishop in cases where there is a blood relationship between one partner and a non-Catholic minister, or where a refusal of dispensation is likely to endanger the Catholic's faith or harm the peace and harmony of the spouses and the family home. In such a marriage the ceremony may be conducted by a non-Catholic minister in a non-Catholic church according to the rite of his tradition. A Catholic priest may attend to give a final blessing. Likewise a non-Catholic minister may attend a Catholic ceremony and give a blessing and add prayers at the end. However, there is not to be a joint celebration of the rite by both ministers; nor are there to be two ceremonies, one in a Catholic church and another elsewhere. The Bishops conclude by declaring that "for the present" dispensations from canonical form should be "relatively rare".

d. A mixed marriage in a Catholic church may be celebrated with a Nuptial Mass, according to the local bishop's ruling; this does not automatically imply permission for the non-Catholic spouse to receive the Eucharist: "The situation of a non-Catholic spouse during Nuptial Mass does not, generally speaking, meet the requirements . . . set down in n.55 of the *Directory of Ecumenism*".[10]

The bishops instruct pastors to encourage the intending spouses to discuss openly the problems they anticipate, and to work in open consultation and co-operation with non-Catholic ministers for the better pastoral care of mixed-marriage couples.

2 Anglican

In response to the Catholic Episcopal Conference's statement on mixed marriages, the bishops of the Church of England in Australia issued their statement on the matter in October 1970. This was a brief statement of guidelines, but "it is necessary to bear in mind that while Anglican dioceses are within one communion of the Christian Church and subscribe to certain common formularies, they have virtually independent jurisdiction under their Bishop and Synod. Jurisdiction regarding marriage discipline is in the hands of the Bishop".[11]

The Anglican bishops' decisions specify certain conditions for their clergy's participation in mixed marriage ceremonies: the conditions are not imposed upon their laity entering a mixed marriage. It is clear from their statement that the fundamental point at issue with the Catholic approach is the Catholic insistence on its laity promising to raise all the children of a mixed marriage in the Catholic faith.

The Anglican bishops urge that both parties to a mixed marriage should discuss their mutual problems, especially those relating to religion, with the ministers of both denominations concerned; rather than simply with the Roman Catholic priest (as the Catholic Episcopal Conference statement indicated).[12] They welcomed the Roman Catholic provision for dispensation from canonical form, but "would look forward to discussing with the bishops of the Roman Catholic Church the wider basis for the granting of dispensations" than the present "very limited circumstances".[13] Meantime they affirmed that the bride should be free to "follow the custom of choosing the church" for the wedding.

While welcoming the Roman Catholic relaxation of the previous requirement for the non-Roman Catholic partner to promise to help in the Catholic upbringing of the children, the Anglican bishops had "grave reservations" about the requirement that the Roman Catholic party alone should make this promise. They considered divisive the demand that one party alone should be committed to a particular direction in the children's religious education: the exclusion of the other partner from a positive share in such education "is a serious obstacle to true union".[14] Both parties should be left free to make together a decision that satisfies the conscience of both. They therefore recommend that, where a promise has been required and made by the Roman Catholic partner according to the Australian Episcopal Conference instructions, no Anglican priest should participate in a mixed marriage ceremony – whether in an Anglican or a Roman Catholic church – unless both partners have freely agreed to bring the children up in one of their churches.

3 Presbyterian

The Presbyterian Church has issued no official instructions of the kind which the Anglican Bishops presented. In relation to the Roman Catholic partner's promise to raise the children as Catholics, it is left to the individual Presbyterian Minister to decide whether he will participate in a mixed marriage ceremony, either in his own church or in a Roman Catholic church. Likewise it is left to him to decide whether and to what extent he may permit a Roman Catholic priest to share in the Presbyterian ceremony. The Presbyterian Church offers a general sharing of Communion to members of other denominations who ask for it.

4 Methodist

As with the Presbyterian Church, there is no official set of instructions for Methodist ministers on conditions for participating in a mixed marriage ceremony where the Roman Catholic partner has made the promise to raise the children as Catholics. This decision is left to each minister. The same freedom is left to each minister in the matter of Roman Catholic clergy sharing in a Methodist ceremony. The Methodist position of sharing Communion is much the same as the Presbyterian.

Practice:

1 Roman Catholic

The dispensation from canonical form is left to the local bishop, so the practice varies from diocese to diocese. In a few small rural dioceses dispensations would be rare, if granted at all. However, in the two largest metropolitan dioceses the practice is much more liberal: in one no request has been refused since the 1970 instructions came into effect;

in the other, the church official who processes applications for dispensation has said that a refusal is "very rare". This would be the general practice in most other dioceses. By far the majority of requests for dispensation is based on the claim that a refusal would harm the peace and harmony of the spouses: this ground is interpreted fairly widely. The request for the wedding to be in a non-Roman Catholic church is most likely to be made where the non-Roman Catholic partner is the bride. One reason why requests are rarely refused is that they must be accompanied by the Catholic celebrant's recommendation: where the priest endorses the request the bishop usually accepts his judgment. Relative to the total number of mixed marriages, the number performed in non-Roman Catholic churches is still small. This is a function, not of episcopal refusal, but of the fact that there is not much known about dispensations from canonical form, among the laity generally, and many who might seek such a dispensation do not do so because they are unaware of the availability of it.

There is no variation on the Roman Catholic partner's promise to raise the children in the Catholic faith: the bishops declare this is an obligation from which no one can dispense the Roman Catholic partner. However, there is some variation in the practice of intercommunion at a Roman Catholic marriage ceremony. Most dioceses would refuse Communion to the non-Roman Catholic partner, except where there is evidence of full faith in the Eucharist in the Catholic sense. But in one of the largest dioceses, and in a few others, a much wider practice is allowed. Here the Directory of Ecumenism is interpreted so that the non-Roman Catholic partner and even members of the immediate family, if baptised, may share in the Eucharist, on the grounds that a wedding is an important occasion in the family's life and there is a "moral impossibility of family members receiving the Eucharist from one of their own clergy". One bishop also interprets the Directory to mean that where the non-Roman Catholic baptised partner has been consistently attending the Roman Catholic liturgy prior to marriage, such a person may be considered a catechumen and therefore may be admitted to communion during the marriage ceremony.

At the local parish level there is increasing collaboration between Roman Catholic and other clergy in pastoral care of mixed-marriage couples, and a good deal of inter-denominational co-operation, at diocesan levels, in training courses for clergy.

2 Anglican

A recent survey of practice in seven Anglican dioceses, including the four major metropolitan dioceses, indicates considerable variation.[15] In three dioceses there are no specific regulations: the bishops' joint statement of October 1970 is taken as episcopal policy in specific cases. In a fourth diocese written permission from the bishop is needed for a non-Anglican clergyman to participate in an Anglican marriage ceremony, and he may only offer prayers and a blessing after the closure of the Anglican service. Until now, this permission has been granted to Roman Catholic priests only where there is special consideration, such as blood relationship. In a fifth, an Anglican clergyman may participate in a non-Anglican service on condition that he pronounces a blessing and specific prayers over the spouses. Where a non-Anglican clergyman participates in an Anglican service he is excluded from participation in the central part of the ceremony, and the Anglican priest must conclude the service.

In the other two dioceses, emphasis is laid on the need for the clergy of both denominations involved in the mixed marriage to discuss the religious problems of the spouses together. One bishop seeks wider and closer sharing of the marriage ceremony between Anglican and Roman Catholic clergy, with each taking a "real and active" part, whether in an Anglican or Roman Catholic church (e.g. in the Anglican ceremony the Roman Catholic priest should be permitted to conduct, in the words of the Roman Catholic rite, the exchange of vows and to preach). In the seventh diocese the bishop adopts a liberal position on most aspects of mixed-marriage participation by clergy of other denominations; but, in his concern over the Roman Catholic requirement for the Roman Catholic partner to make a promise for the Catholic education of the children, he refuses permission for an Anglican clergyman to participate in a Roman Catholic ceremony, where such a promise has been made, and for a Roman Catholic clergyman to participate in an Anglican ceremony. Since, in fact, all Roman Catholics in mixed marriages are required to make this promise formally, the episcopal instruction in this diocese effectively rules out interchurch participation by the clergy in the wedding ceremony.

3 Presbyterian

As indicated, the absence of specific official instructions leaves the local Presbyterian minister free to decide on the level of participation of a non-Presbyterian minister in a Presbyterian service, and of a Presbyterian minister in a non-Presbyterian service. There is a general sharing of Communion with the other churches in the Presbyterian service; in particular cases there are some difficulties on the part of some Anglican ministers on sharing in the Presbyterian Communion.

4 Methodist

The Methodist minister is left with comparable freedom in practice to that of the Presbyterian minister, in the matter of interdenominational sharing by non-Methodist clergy. Communion is now generally shared with Anglican, Presbyterian, and Congregationalist adherents.

Trends

From the experience of recent years church leaders have recognised that social changes "have led to a vast increase in the number of mixed marriages".[16] Ecumenical dialogue has produced a more sensitive awareness, on all sides, of the kinds of tensions affecting such marriages. These include markedly different attitudes to ecclesiastical authority, to moral questions such as family planning methods, to the religious education of the children, and to worship in the home. There is the problem of the elderly couple for one of whom religion has now become a central interest – an interest that cannot be fully shared with the other spouse. And there are problems of religious indifferentism where both partners are weak in religious belief and practice, or where for the sake of peace both decline to discuss religious differences openly. Yet the signs of more fruitful ecumenical pastoral co-operation in this important area are hopeful.

The changes in Roman Catholic practice on two matters that previously vexed interchurch relations – canonical form and inter-communion – have clearly reduced tensions and have opened the way to closer co-operation. The availability of dispensation from canonical form is a major breakthrough: the fact that it is now possible for a Roman Catholic to contract a valid (Roman Catholic) marriage in a non-Roman Catholic ceremony, and the fact that this is no longer un-common, have made for easier ecumenical relationships that can assist pastors of various denominations to co-operate in the pastoral care of a mixed-marriage couple. The Joint Working Group of the Australian Council of Churches and the Roman Catholic Church reported the hope that "the dispensation from canonical form be granted uniformly throughout the different Australian dioceses [of the Roman Catholic Church] with the liberality required to meet actual pastoral needs."[17] It also expressed the hope that before long the condition of canon-ical form for validity would be no longer required. Since dispensations from form rest very much on the celebrant's recommendation, it may be assumed that the growing ecumenical understanding and co-opera-tion at the local level will lead to more priests being less reluctant to support requests for dispensations from form. Some Catholic experts in this field predict that as the practice becomes more widespread the laity will put stronger pressure on bishops to make such dispensations more easily available.

The application of Roman Catholic regulations on inter-com-munion, such as that made by the bishop of the large diocese cited above, likewise indicates an opening towards a wider practice of inter-communion. A leading Roman Catholic expert suggests the trend may be towards a Roman Catholic sharing of the Eucharist at mixed marriages with all who are validly baptised and have full faith in the Eucharist, as already happens with adherents of the Orthodox tradi-tions.

What clearly remains as the major obstacle in interchurch mixed-marriage relations is the Roman Catholic insistence on the Roman Catholic partner's undertaking to raise the children in the Catholic faith. It is generally agreed among Australian Roman Catholic canon-ists and theologians that, with the abolition of the requirement of the non-Roman Catholic partner to make this promise, the Roman Catholic Church has gone as far as it can go. The requirement for the Roman Catholic partner to make a formal *promise* may be abolished eventually, but, they say, the *obligation* on the Roman Catholic "to do all in his/her power" to ensure a Catholic education of the children will remain.

Roman Catholic canonists envisage future tensions in a widespread practice of dispensation from form, when a couple seeks a church dissolution of a mixed marriage. Where previously, with the application of the "Ne Temere" decree, such marriages would have been regarded as invalid, and dissolution or nullity was therefore less a problem, now they consider the problems for a couple seeking a declaration of nullity for a mixed marriage conducted with a dispensation from form will be greater.

Among the Protestant churches there are decreasing difficulties in the pastoral care of mixed marriages, especially with the recent decision of the majority of Presbyterians to come together with the Methodists and Congregationalists to form, in 1976, the Uniting Church of Australia.

All church leaders acknowledge the need for closer pastoral co-operation in the care of mixed marriages, for three reasons in particular. One is so that the full value of the contribution that mixed marriage couples can make to the life of the churches may be realised. A second is connected with the sociological changes occurring in modern society, in which young people especially are often led to absorb the secular humanist concept of marriage as merely a civil contract. The third is the accelerating rate of divorce which aids the breakdown of the concept of Christian marriage as life-long.

The collaboration of the Churches, begun at the official level in the meetings of the Joint Working Group of the Australian Council of Churches and the Roman Catholic Church, gives promise of considered and positive co-operation in the area of pastoral care of mixed marriages. The understanding, good will, and acknowledgement of what the churches share in common along with a frank appreciation of differences, have prepared the ground for true ecumenical work together. What remains to be done particularly is to bring these achievements to the local pastoral level, for the further stage of effective pastoral collaboration.

The desire to make this local-level collaboration effective is expressed strongly in the recommendations of the ecumenical conference held in conjunction with the Fortieth International Eucharistic Congress at Melbourne in February 1973 (see Appendix 1). Stressing the positive and creative aspects of mixed marriages the conference Workshop Group on "Christian Marriage and Pastoral Responsibility" argued the potential of these "cells of ecumenical growth" for bringing the families of an interchurch couple closer together, and for deepening understanding and co-operation between the pastors and congregations of the local denominations. The Group recommended "the responsible, calculated risk of experiment" in intercommunion and in fostering the interchurch family's loyalties to both denominations represented in the family. It urged action for the joint pastoral care of interchurch marriages through ecumenically structured pre-marriage courses for couples. The Group's Roman Catholic members specifically asked that the present requirement of canonical form be retained for the lawfulness, only, of a marriage, and that its requirement for the validity of a marriage be dropped.

The same Workshop Group sought an advance in understanding the Catholic partner's promise on the education of the children in an interchurch marriage. It emphasised that the Catholic's promise was to *try* to bring the children up in the religious tradition he believed was authentic for him. It is unexceptional for a committed Christian to promise to attempt this; any Christian should be able to appreciate the intent of such a promise, and, according to his conviction, to share it. The manner of honouring the promise had, in each case, to be worked out by the couple within the context of the unity of the marriage and the rights of conscience of each.

In a similar quest for ecumenical initiatives the Eucharistic Congress Conference Workshop Group on Baptism sought a more pronounced affirmation of the basis for interchurch co-operation, that bears directly on the pastoral care of interchurch families. It recommended that church bodies explicitly acknowledge in their baptismal liturgies "that its baptized person is received into membership in the whole Catholic Church, and into the fellowship of all baptised Christians" (Appendix 1).

These recommendations, and the Eucharistic Congress setting in which they were made, represent a significantly bolder approach to the growing demands for pastoral care of interchurch families than has yet been made. They reflect the trends in two strong grass-roots movements among the laity. One is the rapid development of Christian family life movements of couples seeking a deepened spirituality of family life. From denominational beginnings these groups are now expanding into an ecumenical development. The second is the formation of a powerful inter-denominational family action movement operating on the socio-political plane. It is the response of married couples of several religious traditions to what they consider is a coalescence of diverse social forces threatening the stability and integrity of Christian family life. The inspiration of the movement is the common Christian faith the members share; they see the strength needed for their task coming from their shared experiences of prayer and worship. In both these movements the laity have been the chief pacesetters. Their initiatives for interchurch co-operation spring from a conviction that the consolidation and renewal of family life depend on the full shared use of the spiritual resources of all churches. In this mood the laity show little patience with an official juridicism which they see as deepening divisions in interchurch families, at a time when all positive means need to be used to strengthen their unity. It may be expected that increasing pressure by the laity for intercommunion will be placed on Church authorities. It is likely, too, that the movement for the joint worshipping by interchurch families will gather momentum. Some church authorities will not respond too enthusiastically to the recommendations of the Eucharistic Congress Conference. There are already signs of a groundswell among the laity for more direct and more closely co-ordinated pastoral care of interchurch families. If the laity feel that action by church leaders is inadequate or too slow in coming, they may no longer wait for their leaders.

Notes

1. The Anglican, Roman Catholic, Presbyterian, and Methodist Churches. Practising members of the smaller sects marry almost exclusively within their own tradition.

   In the preparation of this Report the author has been generously helped by: Reverend Frank L. Cuttriss, Rector of St. James (Anglican) Church, Sydney, N.S.W.; Reverend Dr. H. D'Arcy Wood, Parkin-Wesley Theological College, Wayville, South Australia, and former co-secretary of the Joint Working Group of the Australian Council of Churches and the Roman Catholic Church, and Reverend Frank Engel, of the Australian Council of Churches, Sydney, NSW.

   The author wishes to thank them warmly for their valuable assistance and courtesy, and particularly the Reverend Frank Cuttriss for permission to quote from his "Anglican Approaches to Mixed Marriages" in H. D'Arcy Wood & P. Dougherty (eds.), *Christian Marriage and Pastoral Responsibility*, Reports and Papers from the Fifth Session of the Joint Working Group of the Australian Council of Churches and the Roman Catholic Church, Sydney (May 24-28, 1971).

2. Hans Mol, *Religion in Australia* (Melbourne, 1971) pp. 230-1.

3. Ibid., 233-4.

4. Ibid., 230.

5. Paul Duffy, S.J., "The Sociology of Mixed Marriages" in *Australasian Catholic Record, XLIX* (1972) pp. 40-54.

6. Ibid., 42-3.

7. Australia's postwar migration programme has built up a population of which one-sixth was born outside Australia. Very large numbers of migrants come from Southern Mediterranean countries, who form densely concentrated ethnic and cultural communities in Australia.

8. Cf. Ladislaus Örsy, S.J., "Mixed Marriages: New Instructions" *Dublin Review* (Winter 1966-7) p. 375.

9. Cf. Thomas J. Connolly, D.C.L., "Mixed Marriage: A sign of Division Among Christians – The Catholic Decisions of 1970 and the Reactions to Them" in H. D'Arcy Wood & P. Dougherty (eds.), *Christian Marriage and Pastoral Responsibility*, Reports and Papers of the Joint Working Group of the Australian Council of Churches and the Roman Catholic Church (Sydney, 1971) p. 108.

10. Connolly, "Mixed Marriages: A Sign of Division Among Christians", 112-113.

11. Frank L. Cuttriss, "Anglican Approaches to Mixed Marriages" in D'Arcy Wood & Dougherty (eds.), *Christian Marriage and Pastoral Responsibility*, p. 87.

12. "Statement on Mixed Marriages by the Bishops of the Church of England in Australia" (October 1970) Appendix to Cuttriss, "Anglican Approaches to Mixed Marriages", p. 91.

13. Ibid., p. 91.

14. Ibid., pp. 91-2.

15. Cuttriss, "Anglican Approaches to Mixed Marriages" in D'Arcy Wood & Dougherty (eds.), *Christian Marriage and Pastoral Responsibility*, pp. 87-90.
16. Report of the Joint Working Group of the Australian Council of Churches and the Australian Episcopal Conference of the Roman Catholic Church, 24-28 May, 1971, in *Ecumenical Dialogue in Australia* (Australian Council of Churches, Sydney, 1973) p. 25.
17. Ibid., p. 23.

Appendix

Recommendations of the Workshop Group on "Christian Marriage and Pastoral Responsibility"

From a Conference on "Eucharist, Ecumenism, Community" held at Monash University, Melbourne, 13-16 February 1973, in Conjunction with the Fortieth International Eucharistic Congress

That a more positive attitude should be taken by the churches to *interchurch* marriages, understanding these as marriages of *committed Christians* of different denominations. The group regarded such families as cells of ecumenical growth in which the convergence of the churches as a whole can find a special assistance; they are a privileged area of ecumenical development.

For this reason the group recommend that there should be special experimentation in the interchurch situation, involving enhanced pastoral care and the responsible, calculated risk of experiment in intercommunion and the fostering of loyalties within the family to both the denominations represented.

That the potential of interchurch marriage as a unifying factor should be recognised and developed. They can serve, as marriages, to draw the families of the couple together, and the congregations of both churches should be encouraged to welcome the brother or sister who has married into their fellowship.

It is on the ministers of the two churches involved that a special responsibility rests to make interchurch marriages an occasion of co-operation and mutual acceptance and understanding involving the couple, themselves and the congregations they represent.

That the joint pastoral care of interchurch marriages should include special preparation for couples entering on their unions. The group recommend the establishment of ecumenically structured preparatory courses, such as are to be found in parts of the U.S.A. at present.

That the true implications of the new Roman Catholic regulations for mixed marriages should be explained to all concerned, both inside and outside the Catholic Church. A dispensation from form (i.e. the Catholic Rite) should not mean the priest washes his hands of the marriage ceremony, but be prepared to co-operate in the rite of another denomination in the same way that other ministers are prepared at times to participate in a Roman Catholic ceremony.

The group noted that the promise concerning the education of children, rightly understood, was in terms that any Christian should appreciate, and would – according to his conviction – share. It is a promise to *try* to bring up his children in the religious tradition that he recognises as authentic for him. To what extent this will be *possible* depends on the particular case, and the unity of the marriage and the rights in conscience of each partner must be respected as they attempt to reach a solution acceptable to both.

The Roman Catholic members of the group expressed a desire that the requirement of canonical form for the *validity* of a marriage should be dropped in favour of the arrangement that already prevails in marriages between Catholics and Orthodox adherents – that canonical form should be a matter affecting the lawfulness of a marriage rather than its validity in the eyes of the Church.

The Workshop Group on "Baptism – Basis of Ecumenism" included the following among its recommendations:

That appropriate church bodies be encouraged to include within the baptismal liturgy explicit acknowledgment, that its baptised person is received into membership in the whole Catholic Church, and into the fellowship of all baptised Christians.

V Intermarriage and the Irish Clergy: A Sociological Study

John Fulton

The purpose of this study is to focus attention on the theory and practice of the Irish clergy with regard to intermarriage – a term which will be used restrictively in the following pages to indicate marriage between a Roman Catholic and a Protestant, the latter including members of the Anglican communion. However, it would be of little use to list the variety of attitudes which prevail among the clergy of the different churches unless an attempt were made to *understand* them. As a consequence, it was felt to be a much more profitable enterprise to concentrate on a small group of clergy of one church, so as to enter into the basic problematic of what constitutes such attitudes. After all, attitudes are complicated realities, made up of beliefs which have both religious and cultural dimensions and it is impossible to make sense of such realities unless their structure is unfolded.[1] Thus, what follows does not represent the results of quantified research and cannot be taken as a mirroring of the Dublin clergy's views on intermarriage. As a pilot project, the study was designed to produce indicators of the manner and content of the clergy's social construction of the intermarriage phenomenon. It may be possible to investigate these indicators more substantially in the near future.

The subject of the study is a group of Roman Catholic clergy working in the parishes of the Archdiocese of Dublin. The diocese itself has a population of just under one million, three-quarters of whom live in or around the Greater Dublin area. Ninety-one per cent of the adult population of the diocese is considered to be Roman Catholic. There are no official (government or church) figures available on the extent of intermarriage. Our own rough estimates suggest that these numbered about three per cent of approved Roman Catholic marriages in 1960 and that this figure increased to about six per cent by 1970. Hence, though the population of Dublin and Dublin County increased by only 20% from 1960 to 1970, the average annual number of intermarriages in the area went from about 200 to 400 over the same period and is still on the increase.[2]

The working-class Protestant population is very small. For the whole of the Republic, this was only 6.2% of the total Protestant population in the 1961 Census.[3] As a consequence, Irish intermarriages in the South are between a middle-class Protestant and a middle-class or working-class Roman Catholic. What is more, a large number of these are between a Protestant male and a Roman Catholic female.[4]

For over a year and a half dispensations from canonical form have been granted in the Dublin diocese with the requirement that a Roman Catholic priest be present at the wedding. The Roman Catholic party in an intermarriage is normally required to express in writing the promise with regard to the Roman Catholic upbringing of the children.

The archdiocese had 142 parishes in December 1973. Only a handful of these were run by religious orders. 101 of the parishes run by the diocesan clergy were within a nine mile radius of the city centre and involved just under 400 priests. This was roughly the area covered by the urban complex. A selection of both large and small parishes in the urban area was made, fifty in all; and then twelve parish priests and thirty-eight curates, each from a different parish, were asked to help. Only three of these declined the invitation and they were replaced by priests from similar type parishes.

Interviews were loosely structured and tended, where possible, to follow up those lines of questioning which seemed productive and relevant both to the priest's own situation and to the inquiry at hand. Usually, very few questions were asked as priests would naturally flow on to discuss related aspects of the problematic. The help of the clergy in this research was given willingly and they showed great kindness and openness during the interviews.

The Clergy's Experience of Intermarriage

The clergy's direct experience of intermarriage varied. Some older priests, for example, had rarely met intermarried couples and handled very few intermarriages. The average number per priest was two to three a year, though some were experiencing dramatic increases at the present time. In one or two instances, these increases amounted to 30% of the total number of marriages dealt with over the previous year.

Its Marginality: A number of priests interviewed admitted that they had not given much thought to matters and discussions concerning intermarriage. This response was most common when questions referred to the pastoral care of interchurch marriages.[5] It could be implied that a lack of reflection of this sort is mainly due to unfamiliarity. However, the handling of two or more intermarriages a year cannot be considered insignificant. What is more likely to be the case is that such events were marginal to the priests in terms of meaning. As Mary Douglas says, "Human thought serves human interests".[6] It is possible that the reference made by a group of priests to the present stir in Ireland over the intermarriage issue as being "exaggerated out of all proportion" has a relationship to this marginality of meaning.

The Experience of the Legislation: The legal dimension appeared to be of considerable importance to the clergy's experience of intermarriage. The majority of those interviewed had had the pre-1966 experience of "sacristy weddings" and the same written promises for both parties. These weddings had been experienced by the majority as sad affairs: "tragic" was a word frequently used. Nevertheless the regulations concerning them had been rarely called into question by any of the priests interviewed. Even until quite recently legal concerns had been, for the majority, the first things they had encountered and taken for granted. It also seemed that such matters had not been experienced as irritants, impeding the essential pastoral task, but as part and parcel of what intermarriage was supposed to have been. In general, their chief pre-occupation had been to obtain the dispensation. It was said by some that a sense of danger and insecurity had pervaded pre-1966 procedures, even though a dispensation had not generally been refused. In the words of one interviewee, "All [priests] felt embarrassed [about mixed marriages]; some had a drowning man's fear of it. . . . There was a very definite opinion that this sort of thing was damaging to your career. The whole thing was so disapproved of that the fact that it had a spiritual dimension never occurred to me".

Opposition to Intermarriage: The majority saw intermarriage as a fact that had to be accepted and coped with. It was generally agreed that it was a good thing that nowadays people could make up their own minds about whom they wanted to marry even though one might disagree with their choice. In fact, a large minority of those interviewed would have preferred intermarriage not to take place at all. Some affirmed that they knew colleagues who had refused to handle intermarriage out of conviction.

As priests spoke of their general experience of intermarriage, their basic orientations towards it were emerging. It was with direct reference to this context that the relationship between the interpretation of the law and the way in which Christian belief was conceived assumed particular importance.

To justify a hard line on intermarriage, an explicit appeal was made by some to divine law which, via Canon Law and other directives of authority, was seen as extending of necessity to the requirement of an explicit promise as regards the Roman Catholic upbringing of the children.

A larger number though still less than half of the clergy stressed, as a motive for opposition, the need to safeguard the most treasured possession of all: the true faith. As one priest said, "I am not trying to be pompous, but we have the fullness of the truth". This gift of "the faith" was seen as something with which the vast majority of Roman Catholics were born. They did not go through an intellectual consideration of it; they were simply brought up in the truth while Protestants were not. As a consequence, intermarriage was a situation in which the Church, as guardian of the "deposit of faith", had to make the Roman Catholic partner guarantee his own faith and that of the eventual children.

Most of those stressing possession of the truth found the recent changes in legislation on intermarriage very disturbing, even though they expressed some sort of external approval. As one priest said, "On the one hand we are claiming to have the fullest truth; on the other hand, we are conceding an awful lot of it by, in fact, giving away [perhaps one could say] our rights."

In this respect, intermarriage and the new legislation were seen as a "watering down" of the demands of the faith. In this opinion, the old legislation and to an extent the present one were designed "to preserve the faith".

Those who operated within such boundaries of meaning were also the ones who opposed joint prayer in each other's church (sometimes quite strongly) and any participation by ministers in the preparation or celebration of the wedding. Opposition to dispensation from canonical form was particularly marked. In the words of one priest, "We are conceding and we are diluting our full commitment and giving the impression, well, it does not make any difference".[7]

Interpretation of the Reality of Intermarriage: In the view of the author, the above boundaries of meaning constituted, for the minority to which we have referred, interpretative dimensions for the experience of meeting intermarrying Protestants, particularly in matters concerning conscience and the promises, and for the understanding of the very nature of intermarriage itself.

The Priests' Evaluation of Conscience

The 1970 directives had brought about a change in lay attitudes which did not always meet with approval. Some thought that, rather than "appease" the Protestants by removing the requirement of a promise from them, the new directives had stimulated them into a realisation of their "rights". Sometimes, priests referred to the increased activity of Church of Ireland ministers who encouraged their laity to stand up for these rights. This was resented. As one priest put it, it was an attempt "to twist the arm" of the Roman Catholic Church.

What is perhaps of greater importance is the *way* in which the "rights" of the Protestant party were frequently conceived. It is true that such "rights" were seen to have some legal content, in so far as it was thought that they could be signed away in a promise. The overall impression was, however, that for those whose theory and practice were characterised in the above manner the rights of the Protestant partner were not theoretically formulated, and hence an evaluation of them, and when encountered, was rendered problematical.

At the theoretical level, the nature of the moral consciousness of the Roman Catholic appeared to be evaluated differently from that of his Protestant counterpart. It is, of course, possible that such an evaluation is closely allied to the basic concern which many of these priests had for the Roman Catholic partner and the children of an intermarriage. In the philosophical language of principles and rules (the former being those ultimate human values which penetrate into every human action, and rules being the actual ways of realising those principles in a given human situation)[8], the Protestant was seen as having principles but no rules relating himself to his future bride and children on a religious level. The Roman Catholic was regarded as having to operate such rules, but, instead of these being seen as expressive of moral consciousness, they tended to be considered as objective realities: as the re-translation of an external revelation mediated by the Church and formulated in canonical terms.

From this point of view, the Roman Catholic Church as a legal institution was seen to be more relevant to the Roman Catholic's conscience than were the moral dictates of the Protestant's conscience. In these cases, the Protestant was not seen as a person to communicate with in terms of genuine moral concern. Equally, the laws of the Church were seen as moral conscience *simpliciter.* In the words of one priest, "I do not believe in conscience, as a Catholic, which I suppose, is the essence of the Protestant religion, that is that every man makes his own decision, but a Roman Catholic does not. It is not a question of conscience. It is a question of what is objectively right or objectively wrong. . . . Their [the Protestant] conscience, you see, may not be right: that is the point. Every man's conscience differs and if we all followed our own conscience, society would be uncontrollable". However, when it came to an actual consideration of the problem at hand, the same priest firmly planted himself on the horns of a dilemma by affirming the need for the Church to respect a non-Roman Catholic conscience: "I find it a very big problem. How we can solve it, I just do not know".

We must add that when objective legal structures predominate in the evaluation of moral conscience and where intermarriage is viewed only from the angle of the Roman Catholic partner, there can be no way out of dilemmas of this nature. [9]

The Promise: Over half the priests interviewed saw the Roman Catholic upbringing of the children of an intermarriage as a serious obligation for the Roman Catholic partner. For some priests, all of whom were characterised by the general orientation we have been describing, unless there was a promise to this effect, the marriage could not possibly take place. Yet some of them found it hard to make such a demand on an intermarrying couple when it came to confronting them. One of them felt that the clergy in general were very Roman Catholic in their actions but not very Christian: "We are so taken up with Catholic laws and regulations – the Church teaches this and the Pope says that – that we forget . . . that we have got to be kind to the [Protestant] partner involved and consider him. And very often we do not bring it into practice. I feel a terrible sort of cloud. I feel constricted by the whole thing. And I was talking to the other priests this morning and they were saying they do not know what to make of it. They see that the Protestant partner should have . . . full rights as regards the children, the marriage and his conscience and they also think that the Catholic should follow the teaching of the Church." [10]

Another priest expressed this difficulty in a peculiar fashion, as the following conversation illustrates:

Q. "Do you think that [the promise] is a fair thing to demand, a right thing is a better word?"
I. "No, I don't think it is fair."
Q. "But do you think it is right?"
I. "As a Catholic myself, I think it is right."

The same priest spoke of himself as being a sort of schizophrenic. He had reached convictions at the theoretical level about the rights of non-Roman Catholics, but felt incapable of translating such convictions into action: "Just when I am going to jump into the water, I say 'Ah, I won't'. I am afraid in fact to take the plunge. This is how I feel towards the whole ecumenical marriage [problem]."

The Nature of Intermarriage: Some priests were not sure what sort of a marriage an intermarriage was. It was certainly not a "Catholic" one in the view of one priest. For others, it was a marriage from which something was missing. They asserted that there was no union on the level of faith. This factor, together with undefined cultural diversity, was sufficient for one priest to affirm that partners in an intermarriage could not possibly have a basic understanding of each other. Those who admitted to this orientation in their thinking considered the spiritual life of the intermarried couple as a separate reality in each spouse. A meeting between the two on this level could not be seen as taking place, because the spiritual life was viewed in terms of practices and channels of grace which were not possessed by the other denomination. The spiritual life of the Roman Catholic children was also seen as cut off from that of the Protestant parent.

There were those priests who positively approved of the Protestant being uncommitted to his belief, because, in this case, there were "no problems" and the spiritual side of the marriage was seen as more firmly in the hands of the Roman Catholic partner. The more committed the Protestant party, the more problems there were. Other priests admitted that indifference "made things easier" but stated that there was something wrong with this situation.

Even when interviewers probed for it, a consciousness of the possible existence or promise of a profound Christian union between husband and wife did not appear among this group of priests, though it was only a minority who saw husband and wife as resolving their problems by going their separate ways. Although mention was frequently made of the great love which the spouses often had for one another and for their children, none of them explicitly indicated that there was anything very Christian about it. In this sense, the possibility of a united spiritual life (an existential relationship between their religious knowledge and commitment and their knowledge and commitment to each other) was a horizon which exceeded the boundaries within which many of the priests interviewed moved.

Positive Evaluation: Half the clergy interviewed either stressed a positive pastoral approach to intermarriage or saw something positive in it. This evaluation did not always come from the appropriation of a different theology from that which insisted on the "possession of the true faith". There were old priests among their number. In our opinion, their common bond lay in their various experiences which had led them to move away from a more traditional interpretation of intermarriage and from the rigid application of the norm.

They were frequently of the opinion that two major forces had played their part in masking what they considered to be the human reality of intermarriage. These were their seminary training, which had viewed marriage in general only from within a canonical framework, and the directives of ecclesiastical authority, whose pronouncements on intermarriage were seen as being principally negative and concerned in the main with purely legal procedures. As one priest said, "I certainly was concerned in the beginning that everything should be followed to the letter, but afterwards, when you get involved in the humanity of the thing, you kind of see things in a different light."

For several, the legislation of 1966 had only signalled a switch from a conversion attempt and from sheer reluctance to deal with intermarriage to the provision of an information service for intending couples. The 1970 decree only increased the legal problem as now the way was open for non-Roman Catholics to raise matters of conscience and still marry the girl (or boy) they wanted. This rendered all the more striking for them the paradox that it was the committed Christian who experienced the greatest difficulty in obtaining ecclesiastical approval for an intermarriage.

It was only now, in recent times, that these priests were beginning to see a *pastoral* dimension to the problem, particularly as they were under pressure from an increasing number of intermarrying couples. Several felt that the transferral of spiritual matters to the Roman Catholic partner was not a solution to the spiritual aspects of the intermarriage problem. If considered a solution, said one, "It is wrong, it is very short-sighted, of course. What you are really doing is failing to face the thing; you are just brushing it aside. It would be a disaster, I would say, for the after-growth of the marriage. I think it is common enough though. I found myself doing it often enough when I started off".

Some priests had even formulated a fairly definite pastoral approach, as in the following case: "I really try to sort out which of them has the deeper religious conviction. Now, if one of them were a deeply committed member of the Church of Ireland or Presbyterian or Methodist or whatever, if the Catholic party were just nominal and indifferent towards [his] religion then I would say, 'for God's sake get married in the church of the committed party and bring the children up that way, much better'." If the Protestant was uncommitted to his church, this priest saw it as "making it easier for the bookwork . . . [but] when you think of the deeper side to the marriage, then it begins to worry you a little bit".

The majority of those who belonged to this current referred to their own experience, even to one or two particular cases, or to events within their own family circle which had affected their outlook. Some of them had Protestant relatives to whom they were close; others had worked abroad and had experienced a more positive pastoral approach and a broader interpretation of legal requirements. This experience was brought to bear on the application of legal directives. Many of them disapproved of the Church's official "disapproval" of intermarriage; others swept aside the theoretical issues and simply took the intermarrying couples at their face value, beginning with an assessment of "what they have in common". This was seen not as a lowest common denominator but in terms of a common genuine commitment to human values. Specifically in the interchurch marriage context, they stressed the word "Christian" or fidelity to Christ as a common ground of experience. One priest spoke of intermarriage in terms of a special vocation from God and another of "the unique nature of this Christian experience", though, on the whole, perspectives of this kind were limited to a small number of the clergy.

In the case of both parties being committed, joint prayer in both churches was advocated by several. One priest said that the so-called crisis of identity which children of an intermarriage were supposed to experience was more than likely the result of the external pressures coming from educators rather than from the marriage itself.

On the whole, these priests were not sure how such marriages would develop especially in their relationship to the denominations; they were however sure that true Christianity could be found there.

Religious Indifference: We have already said that it was a view of a number of the clergy that intermarriage diluted the faith or weakened it. There was at least the opinion that intermarriage, of itself and without the support of the Church's legislation, led to religious indifference. However, the question of religious indifference was one which even those most favourably disposed to intermarriage were asking. It merits particular attention before we attempt to relate the experiences described to broader theoretical perspectives.

The clergy's evaluation of the actual intermarriages they had handled varied considerably. Some were at pains to point out that the couples they had known had been of above-average commitment. Others said that the Protestants involved were generally uncommitted to their churches.[11]

When priests were asked about the intermarried couples they had known for some period of time, cases of "lapsing" among intermarried parishioners were said to be rare. By and large, the couples the priests knew were "good" Christians and fulfilled their (separate) religious obligations, even to the point of the Protestant partner looking after the children's Roman Catholic education when the Roman Catholic partner proved to be indifferent. Some suggested that intermarried couples settling in Ireland as opposed to England would be relatively "safe" from religious indifference. All the same, they admitted to feeling a genuine fear when they saw a young married couple just starting off their married life, despite the presence of exemplary intermarried couples in their own parishes.[12]

One group of priests in particular referred to the increasing numbers of intermarrying couples who had hardly any attachment to their churches at all. For several, this was a new kind of intermarriage which they had not come across before. Others seemed to be unconsciously examining the legislation on intermarriage to see if it had any potential as a weapon against the incursions of "neo-paganism". However, it was precisely in these terms that they saw the legislation as being either too weak or irrelevant. The question for them was now whether or not the time had arrived for priests to distinguish between the committed and the uncommitted, and to refuse a church wedding when they thought it necessary *and* to be supported in this by higher ecclesiastical authority.

One who saw the present legislation as futile and who felt the need for a more definite framework to his practice considered his pastoral procedure satisfactory in the case of a couple who were "tuned in to Christianity". But, "with a couple who are using [the Church and its facilities] for a public convenience, as is often the case, I would be nervous [of taking the liberal approach]. . . . I begin to wonder am I on the right lines, you know. We have our kind of fidelity, the training we got; and yet our experience does not quite measure. No, it does not. We are left in a kind of grey area there.''

Priests experiencing indifference in this way gave the impression that they did not know which line to take, a strict or a weak one. Traditional views of what constituted Christian boundaries of commitment and of what was the content of the priest's role were considerably obscured. There can be little doubt that the priest's clerical role, in which he dispensed the social function of marriage broker and witness, was in conflict with his pastoral and prophetic roles, though this must be seen as only part of the problem. These priests were very much in search of new boundaries of discrimination with which to make sense of a growing situation whose comprehension the old schemes of knowledge did not contain.

Reflections

Relevant reflections from within broader sociological perspectives can help to situate the experiences of the group of clergy we have been considering.

In the present context, we are not directly concerned with the significance intermarriage may have in strictly theological terms, though what we have to say has theological implications. Our concern is with the sociologist's task of unravelling the complexity of the meaning conferred by the thought and action of the clergy on intermarriage. In other words, we are concerned with *interpretations* of reality. When such interpretations are shared, they tend to have durability and to mediate experience.[13] In fact, their own terms of reference only permit a certain experience of reality.[14] They have cultural parameters which are established by the relevant institutions, in this case the Church, and by the general socio-cultural milieu. We will now briefly examine what seems to us to be the most important mediating influence which the Church's legislation and its institutional nature on the one hand and the general cultural environment on the other have had on the meaning which intermarriage has for the clergy.

The Church as an Institution: The Roman Catholic Church, by legislating on intermarriage, has thus presented priests (and the faithful in general) with a legal structuring of the phenomenon. The way it is to be dealt with has been laid out and a definite interpretation of such events has been provided; intermarriage is disapproved of and it is broadly indicated as a threat to continued religious adherence; divine law demands the Roman Catholic upbringing of eventual children and parental moral obligation in this respect must be rendered explicit by means of a promise on the part of the Roman Catholic parent. If and when applied, this legislation enters into the social and familial orders and is operative in personal encounter as an interpreter of present and future relationships. From the description of the priests' experience we have given, it is apparent that the mediating influence of this legislation was sometimes profound.

One of the reasons for this type of legislation is that the Church as an institution relies in the main on the families of its members for its self-perpetuation. From the point of view of its life as a community, the Church faces in intermarriage the issue of its separate social identity over against other socio-religious groupings. The set of relationships which constitute intermarriage do not square with those which maintain the institution and this factor affects the way in which the institution relates to those who intermarry. The institutional Church can be seen therefore as coping with this ambiguity in social identity by legislation, prescribing the ways to maintain the correct identity in this "abnormal" situation and thus somehow bringing this different form of behaviour back into the scheme of things.

Cultural environment: Other elements mediating the meaning of intermarriage are derived from a whole range of social relationships which are not strictly limited to those explicitly associated with the religious institution. Attitudes towards, and the manner of dealing with, intermarriage are bound to be dependent on the alignment of social groupings, which may be on political, economic, traditional or other grounds. It is evident that a mixed marriage in Ulster has a different meaning from one in Hamburg, even for the religiously committed. As a social reality, therefore, intermarriage can assume various configurations of meaning according to the cultural framework into which it is inserted. In the case under consideration, we would suggest that the Roman legislation on intermarriage and the type of theology which lay behind its original formulation[15] has combined with the particular circumstances of the Irish scene and resulted in the intermarriage phenomenon achieving a higher degree of importance than probably anywhere else in Europe.

The present antagonisms throughout Ireland between Roman Catholics and the Protestant population as a whole are very much a product of the economic developments of the eighteenth and nineteenth centuries. After the Plantation period, there were times when alliances might have been made on non-sectarian lines, with the result that the present politico-religious division might never have come about. However, the end product was a community divided not on economic but on religious lines which have consistently provided the material for sectarian strife. The idea that the interests of capital and property owners led to the (conscious or unconscious) manipulation of religious divisions by the privileged classes is not to be lightly dismissed. Without the possibility of an alliance with any economically powerful group the "dispossessed" Roman Catholics developed a culture in which they had to find both political and religious meaning, if they were even to survive at all against the real religious, political and economic enemy, the Ascendancy.[16]

One result of this situation was that the working-class community of Ulster emerged into the twentieth century split in two diametrically opposed groups, with Protestant workers in an uncommon alliance with property and capital owners.[17] Many members of these groups may well have been prepared to allow the necessary encounters of social life and the results of industrial development to lead to an eventual economic merging of the communities. But the strict interpretation of social identity which required that one belonged to the one group or to the other did not permit this and intermarriage in particular became the forbidden fruit.

Another development was the way in which the Republic of Ireland as a State developed its relationship with the Irish Roman Catholic Church. There was, in fact, a substantial amount of interaction between the two in matters relating to certain political decisions (such as the Mother and Child scheme in 1951) and to the problem of education especially in the first forty years of the Republic's life.[18]

History thus provides information of great importance to the sociologist's inquiry. For, if we examine the thrust of the general cultural environment and that of the institutional and legal framework, not only do we see opposition to intermarriage but we also begin to perceive a powerful influence in the direction of a simplification of social structure. There is the pressure to eliminate the complex identities which come from operating in the political, economic, religious and other spheres of social experience and to institute a basic identity principle in terms of Catholic and Protestant. This lies behind the peculiar power which sectarianism has in Northern Ireland where, despite the size of the Roman Catholic population, there is comparatively little inter-marriage. At the same time in the Republic, there is a certain clarity in the division between Church and State, politics and morals, with the clergy being accepted in their role of authoritative interpreters in this regard. The presence of Protestant clergymen in the political arena in Ulster can be considered a parallel development.[19]

From a sociological point of view, the accent in such a society is on clearly defined directives, authoritatively given. Hence, the less com-plicated a society is, the more important become its rules and the more easily definable are social realities. In this context, it becomes more evident that the manner of interpreting reality is closely related to the overall structure of society and to its official ideology. In fact, the simpler a society, the less likely is the existence of an alternative system of belief because such a society, or those of its members who move within that universe of meaning where the central cultural and religious identities tend to merge, does not easily tolerate the shading over of the boundaries of clarity or the violation of its symbols. For these create unease and produce ill-defined areas at the level of meaning.[20] Where this is the case, a strange power inheres in the margins of the framework of society and when the rules and symbols are violated, that power arises to threaten the accepted social order, the ideas that go with it and the type of social action it institutes.

The relevance of this perspective to the intermarriage question is borne out by the conflict arising in the clergy's own understanding and handling of the issue. Intermarriage was experienced by some members of the clergy as a threat to the uniqueness and possession of the faith. It was considered a threat to the integrity of Roman Catholicism. The violation of established patterns of behaviour towards intermarriage, even on a small scale, brought about the same unease, as in the case of those priests who felt "shaky" about separating the canonical form of marriage from the Roman Catholic priest and allowing a Protestant minister to officiate. Some of the clergy had handled such marriages with fear and trembling in the past. Uncertainty over the rights of Protestants and about the "nature" of intermarriage had been a frequent experience. The occurrence of intermarriage is one of the few occasions, sometimes the only one, in which the Roman Catholic clergy meet Protestants; and it is precisely here, in this context, that institutional and cultural interpretations on the one hand and direct experience on the other clash. In these terms, intermarriage is more than just an illustration of the existing divisions between the churches; it lays bare basic orientations in the perception and handling of social reality.

At the risk of expressing a common opinion which rarely finds itself in print, we cannot but affirm the emergence of two separate types of theory and practice.[21] The various members of the clergy gravitated towards one or other of these. One group of clergy tended towards a rigid attitude of thought and had a desire, rarely satisfied, for a clear course of action. From within this perspective, intermarriage was and had to remain a marginal phenomenon. The other group was characterised by elements of openness at the cognitive level and was influenced by personal experience, particularly from within the family or from abroad. However, each group in its own way was characterised by an experience of intermarriage as problematical, and both evidenced a similar theological training which had subsequently received conflicting interpretations. All the same, the thinking surrounding intermarriage and the very handling of it tended to bring such overall dimensions of theory and practice into focus. Whereas the attitude of one group appeared more direct and mathematical and more consonant with the cultural parameters which have been described, that of the other appeared more dialectical in its interpretation of reality and more critical of the same cultural milieu.

The Problem of Religious Identity: One result of these opposing orientations was that the personal spiritual relationship of the intermarried couple was divergently interpreted, although with a degree of uncertainty in both cases. The presence of "religious indifference" compounded this difficulty considerably. One broadly anthropological reflection which throws light on the subject concerns the relationship between religious belief and religious affiliation and the way the two are associated. Belief in a set of propositions is linked to belief in the transcendent. In the Christian case, belief about Christ and his Church is linked to belief in Christ and, already in a different way, to belief in his Church as a living community. Religious affiliation is, in fact, derived from the interpersonal relationships existing within the community. Though, in cognitive terms, we perceive propositions and affiliation first, in experiential terms the intersubjective element (our relationship with God, Christ and our fellowmen) is decisive. It is precisely at the intersubjective level of experience that meaning arises to – subsequently – inform and transform the cognitive.

The present study has indicated a close relationship in the minds of several of the clergy between the idea of faith and of the possession of that faith. This appeared as part of a theory and practice in which the cognitive and affiliative levels of religious belief were assumed to be meaningful before they were constituted by intersubjectivity. Equally, possessing the "deposit" of faith, in the way this term was used was somehow seen as meaningful of itself rather than as mediating meaning, especially in the strong formulation "we have the faith and others have not". This was particularly apparent in the way in which intermarriage was considered by some to lead to a "watering-down" of the faith, putting the Roman Catholic partner "at risk" and, from the point of view of identity, placing the eventual children (and possibly the Roman Catholic parent) in an ambiguous situation.

The secondary role conferred upon the intersubjective may well be the reason why there appeared to be a frequent failure to encounter the Protestant "other" who did not for many priests constitute a person with whom to communicate on a religious level. Together with the influence of the legislation, this may explain why, in several cases, the handling of a religiously committed couple was experienced as "more difficult" and why the objections of the Protestant partner to the promise were seen as hostile action.

Importance of the Family Today: The problem of religious affiliation and religious belief is bound to occur again in any attempt to define the relationship between denominational and family identity. Though peripheral to our theme, this problem deserves attention in the light of recent sociological studies. According to these,[22] in a growing pluralist and industrialised society, the family is becoming a fundamental source of meaning for its members. If this is the case, it follows that the family is a primary source of *religious* meaning. This thesis finds support in an analysis of the meaning of the family in a contemporary industrialised society. Urban life is, of course, the first place where the cultural resonances of economic change are felt. In a world of service to the machine and to bureaucracy, faced with the dividing up of self in role performances, members look to the family as a locus for authentic self-expression and fulfilling relationships.[23] The shift in identity which marriage in any case brings about is, therefore, of particular significance. For it is now precisely in terms of the family that an experience of meaningful existence emerges. Such an experience is underpinned by its religious dimension.[24]

As society becomes more industrialised and pluralist, the inter-married family in particular must assume an even more special significance. Sociologically speaking, the new intermarried family unit constitutes the affirmation of a new community and identity and a fundamental source of meaning. Hence the intermarriage itself is being pushed towards the centre of meaningful religious experience. Given the relationship between the inter-personal and the structural, the kind of community which has sprung up is bound to affect the continuing relationship and identity of the two partners with their respective religious denominations. They are a couple sharing a religious experience *before* they are members of (separate) denominational communities.

Such a structural modification to denominational identity does not yet seem to be recognised by these same denominations. The signs are that intermarried couples living in Ireland are only now coming to an awareness of this modification, that is if we are to take notice of increased activity by them for a consideration of their situation by ecclesiastical and even civil authority.[25] Some of the clergy interviewed showed that they were becoming increasingly aware of the same, though even they did not feel at ease in their pastoral activity, because of the obstacles they encountered when it came to advising couples on such matters as intercommunion, whose practice in extreme circumstances is not allowed by the hierarchy in Ireland.

The Religious Importance of the Woman: An additional reflection was suggested by the research. The majority of priests came to the conclusion that it was better from a Roman Catholic point of view if the female partner was Roman Catholic; then her faith would be more secure and so would that of the children. The implication went beyond the simple indication of the woman's role in the family. She was considered (and even said) to be "more religious by nature". In the words of one priest, "Inevitably if the girl were the Catholic, it made things easier from one point of view because girls are inclined to have a more mature outlook. . . . As well as that, the depth of religious commitment is usually greater . . . and you discovered that there was a greater Catholic outlook on the marriage if it was the girl who was the Catholic." There is at least the conviction that the woman is of special significance in the religious dimension of society and this conviction would seem to enter more profoundly into the consciousness of priests than is generally admitted. We are in no position here to develop a theory of the identification of the religious in the Irish context. What is important is to see the relevance of this for the intermarriage question. For more Church of Ireland males marry Irish Roman Catholic females than do Church of Ireland females Irish Roman Catholic males. If the identification of the religious in Ireland is of some objective social significance, then it is not only the present Roman Catholic legislation on the upbringing of offspring which must be blamed for the diminishing size of the Church of Ireland (due account having been taken of the variables of emigration and of the higher age-structure of that community). The cultural context of female religiosity will remain even if the legislation is removed. Some light could again be shed on this by a study of intermarriage in Ireland in the nineteenth century, when the religious affiliation of the children was decided according to sex and where, presumably, fathers would have been involved to some degree in the religious education of their sons.

Conclusion:

In examining intermarriage, the role and position of the clergy is of considerable importance. For this social reality receives a definition from the institution which attempts to mediate the significance of the event to the people through its pronouncements, legislation and the attitudes of its clerical representatives. However, perhaps sociologists have in the past identified the rank and file clergy too closely with the religious institution and have not nuanced the distinction enough. The clergy have been seen to interpret intermarriage in anything but a uniform manner. Their "reading" of intermarriage has shown the manner in which culture can provide an interpretation which can in varying degrees be assimilated; but it has also shown the way in which man through his experience can grapple with meanings for which culture may have provided inadequate tools and be spurred on to search for new boundaries of religious meaning.

In particular, the study has highlighted the common threat of any religious praxis, namely that, in attempting to relate experiences to schemes of thought, it is all too easy to transform the experience without transforming the schemes also. One can internalise doctrines and ecclesiastical statements as recipes for action and take for granted one's own cultural milieu as God-given for the purpose of unfolding one's faith and religious practice. Such a recipe approach leads either to a pragmatic attitude in pastoral activity or to the formulation of ideological interpretations of faith by disconnecting the essential bipolarity of meaning between self and the world of others. It is a human tendency to prefer clarity of thought and action to the insecurity of the critical stance, but it always ends with the imposition of a particular interpretation of reality upon other people.

Finally, the tentative results of our analysis are themselves suggestive of the sociological orientation on which they are based and towards which they have attempted to move.[26] Sociological analysis of this kind is able not only to go back to re-consider the presuppositions on which it is based (a necessary philosophical exercise, rarely recognised in sociological circles,[27]) but can also incite the believer and the theologian to a re-examination of their *own* religious belief. If modern theology has sometimes gone to extremes in interpreting the sociological dictum that culture mediates human experience, it has done so either by ignoring empirical analyses or by supporting the view that the entire content of (social) reality is culturally relative. It is believed that a more conciliatory approach will benefit the theological and sociological spheres of thought and it is hoped that this approach may have shown its benefits in the present study.[28]

Notes

1. The type of analysis here employed attempts to reflect the concerns of a sociology of meaning. Cf. N. Kokosalakis, "The Problem of Meaning in Religion", *The Human Context* iv: 2 (1972) p. 506-18.
2. The above (rough) calculations were based on our own data, the 1961 Census, the 1966 Census, the first two volumes of the 1971 Census (the remaining five are not yet published) and B. M. Walsh, *Religion and Demographic Behaviour in Ireland*, Economic and Social Research Institute no. 55, Dublin (1970) pp. 26-8.
3. B. M. Walsh, op. cit., p. 25.
4. Ibid., p. 28.
5. They were asked such questions as: did they see positive elements in the faith of Protestants? Had they thought of involving ministers in the wedding? What did they think of joint prayer (in each other's

church)? "It is only now that you ask me that I have to think", was a frequent answer.
6. M. Douglas (ed.), *Rules and Meanings*, Harmondsworth (Penguin), 1973, p. 11.
7. The priest quoted above changed his opinion, however, when asked if the same answer was appropriate in the situation where the parent of the Protestant was a clergyman. Here, one can recognise the entry of a new set of rules of interpretation derived from the situation and in opposition to the previous set.
8. Cf. J. B. O'Malley, "Morality as a Style in Action", *Philosophical Studies* xvi (1967) p. 165f.
9. It may be of significance that some of those whose Roman Catholicism was expressed in the above terms did not see any significant change coming about in the workings of the social system in the event of a united Ireland. Their notion of democracy was that of the imposition of the "rights" of the majority, rather than the recognition and granting of the "rights" of the minority. However, this was itself a minority opinion.
10. The conflict experienced between belief in the legislation and actual rights of Protestants should also be situated in the broader context of Protestant – Roman Catholic relationships; some priests combined personal warmth in their own friendships with Protestants with harsh views about their religious convictions. One priest used satirical language about Protestants in general but yet his personal contacts with them were excellent.
11. The question of what criteria were being used by the clergy to assess commitment was not followed up. Occasionally it was clear that the same criterion was being used both for Roman Catholics and Protestants, namely, attendance at Sunday mass or service. Again, the desire which many Anglicans showed to have their children brought up as Christians, caring little for the exact denomination, seemed to be interpreted sometimes as a sign of commitment and at other times as a sign of indifference. It is recognised, of course, that the use of such criteria would probably only form part of a more global evaluation of character, which would also depend on the type of relationship established between the priest and the Protestant partner.
12. It could be asked how far back the tradition of associating religious indifference with intermarriage might be. In the Irish context, it is known that in the nineteenth century the children of intermarriages were quite simply divided according to sex, the sons assuming their father's denominational identity and the daughters their mother's. It is doubtful if the mental association of religious indifference with intermarriage was the same then as it is now. The present association may be connected, at least in part, with the introduction of the restrictive Roman legislation on intermarriages at the turn of the century. As a generalised view of intermarriage, this tradition may have performed the function of justifying the legislation. Such conjecture is without the backing of historical research and may prove false; however, it is still worth bearing in mind.

The theory that today, at least, intermarriage *leads* to religious indifference has yet to be proved. Many members of the clergy are of the opinion that the growth of religious indifference is a wider problem. We consider the expression "decline of church-oriented religion" to be more appropriate, if and where this is occurring. The phenomenon is connected with changes in the socio-economic structure of society and, if anything, the corresponding rise in the intermarriage rate, is a result of this decline in church-oriented religiosity. Cf. T. Luckmann, op. cit., p. 37ff.

13. We thus enter the sociological discourse on social facts. Such social facts may be called symbols. cf. H. J. Helle, "Symboltheorie und religiöse Praxis" in J. Wössner (ed.) *Religion in Umbruch*, Enke Verlag, Stuttgart 1972, p. 200f. (*The Invisible Religion*, Macmillan, London 1970).

14. For an excellent collection of readings on the mediation of reality by culture, see M. Douglas (ed.) op. cit.

15. This paper is not the place to discuss "post-Vatican 1 theology". We are particularly concerned in this context with those developments which gave rise to the idea of the Church as a "perfect society".

16. An aggressive sense of inferiority to that Ascendancy still survives. One or two of the clergy interviewed in this research identified the Church of Ireland with middle and upper class income groups *tout court* and appeared to accept with ease all the myths about their economic dominance.

17. The subject is of course a hotly debated one. For a brief historical analysis *cf.* Liam de Paor, *Divided Ulster*, Harmondsworth (Penguin), 1971: for a sociological (and neo-Marxist) analysis *cf.* Anders Boserup, "Contradictions and Struggles in Northern Ireland" in *The Socialist Register* (1972) pp. 157-92.

18. Cf. J. H. Whyte, *Church and State in Modern Ireland* 1923-1970, Gill and Macmillan (1970) passim.

19. Whyte, (op. cit. 21 ff.) emphasises the traditional importance of authority in Ireland. It is important to add to this that authority tends to perpetuate the existence of well-delineated modes of thought and institutional relationships because they are easier to cope with.

20. Mary Douglas calls this experience "pollution". The danger of pollution, she says, "is not likely to occur when the lines of structure, cosmic or social, are clearly defined". (M. Douglas, *Purity and Danger*, Harmondsworth (Penguin), 1971, p. 136.)

21. With the terms "theory and practice", we are referring to what constitutes an *effective* world-view for the clergy, as opposed to a set of abstract opinions.

22. Cf. P. L. Berger and H. Kellner, "Marriage and the Construction of Reality" in *Diogenes*, xlvi (1964) p. 1-24.

23. Berger and Kellner (ibid., p. 23) suggest that the high divorce rate in industrial societies may be due to the family having to bear a disproportionate burden of self-authentication, more than it can really take.

24. We accept in part Luckmann's contention that the processes of development of personal identity have a religious texture and the contention of N. Kokosalakis that the experience of meaning in life emerges from the deeper or mythical level of experience, namely from the religious level. Cf. T. Luckmann, op. cit., pp. 41-49 and N. Kokosalakis, op. cit. passim.

25. Recently, lobbying by the Irish Association of Inter-Church Families has led to the introduction of a Bill in the Dail to change the obnoxious legislation forbidding intermarried couples the right to adopt children.

26. The hermeneutic-dialectical approach to the human sciences, to which the author subscribes, not only requires the complementing of attitudinal research, but also a stepping beyond subjective meaning context. Such a limitation of inquiry leaves out the all-important question of the double tension of meaning which, on the one hand, exists beyond the subject and the world he interprets and which, on the other, exists between the social scientist and the reality he himself is interpreting. Any "reading" of findings implies a dialectic between a social scientist, subject of study and situation which can only be sustained if *some* kind of trans-cultural referent is involved in the exercise, Cf. G. Radnitzky, *Contemporary Schools of Metascience* New York (Humanities Press), 1970; J. Habermas, *Knowledge and Human Interests*, Heinemann, (1972); J. B. O'Malley, *Sociology of Meaning*, London, Human Context Books (1972); N. Kokosalakis, *op. cit.*

27. For example K. Dobbelaere and J. Lauwers, "Definitions of Religion – A Sociological Critique" in *Social Compass* xx/4 (1973), pp. 535-51, who restrict the definition of religion to the subjective views that people have of it on the grounds that, to do otherwise, would be to interfere with the philosopher's task.

28. The author wishes to thank Maura Wall, Noel Dalton, James Donleavy and Redmond Fitzmaurice for their help in interviewing the clergy and for their contribution to the project as a whole.

VI Conclusion

Baptising the Children

John Coventry

In response to the request that I should write a concluding chapter to this book to round it off, a chapter written after the Consultation and therefore not considered during it, I have thought it better not to try to "report everything". This would make a very bitty chapter, and one probably of minimal value to the majority of readers. I thought it would be of more value if I chose a single topic, one important in itself, one that was fully considered during the Consultation, and one that allows me to bring in (usually without acknowledgment) at least some of the more telling points made in the course of very varied discussions. I have chosen the question of the baptism of children of an interchurch couple, i.e. a father and mother who are devoted and practising members of different churches and intend to remain so. As a Roman Catholic I am thinking mainly of a Roman Catholic married to an Anglican or Protestant; and I put forward the following reflections in my own name, and not merely as one reporting the views of others.

Background to the Question

Elementary and basic to the question of baptism is a true understanding of the sense of the promise about the children made by the Roman Catholic. This is spelled out by paragraph 2 of the joint statement issued at the end of the Dublin Consultation (below p. 186). It is variously treated in the reports from different countries (*Positions and Trends*) given above, notably by the Swiss *Guidelines* (see p. 128). In this connection one must take to task the report from Australia for repeatedly referring to the promise as one "to raise the children as Catholics". It is not. In 1966 Rome *changed the content of the promise* required from the Roman Catholic, before it ceased in 1970 to require any assurance from the other partner. So the matter of the baptism and upbringing of the children is one for father and mother to decide together. It is well to recall here, as it is not quoted in the earlier papers, the sentence of *Matrimonia Mixta:* "The problem of the children's education is a particularly difficult one, in view of the fact that both husband and wife are bound by that responsibility and may by no means ignore it or any of the obligations connected with it."

The changing of regulations leads one to realise that *Matrimonia Mixta* is itself not final, but represents a rather middle position arising from the Synod of Bishops in 1967: the whole matter is still under discussion internally in the Roman Catholic Church and also with other Churches. The existence of such regulations at all leads one to reflect more deeply that Church authority has over the years been too prone to legislate for christian marriage. The Church entered the field of legislation by the historical accident of its being heir to Roman law in the so-called Dark Ages. With the emergence of the secular state as an independent reality there has ceased to be the same need for ecclesiastical law. No one denies the right and to some extent the need of a Church to translate its ideals and its teaching into disciplines. And alone of the western Churches the Roman Catholic Church has retained a sense of overall responsibility for christian marriage. But in our modern society rules less and less attain their desired end of securing the values on which they are based. The Church's authority today will be greater when it is seen as spiritual authority; when it is seen to speak to marriage rather than to drill it; when it is seen to offer christian values as gift. And in particular the Church needs to give priority to the interpersonal values of marriage, and to be seen as caring for and sanctifying the human attachment which is the vehicle of God's love, rather than to be focusing primarily on the institution – either the institution of marriage, or the Church itself as institution. These general reflections have their application to, and are part of the background to, the matter of baptism.

Next, as Dr Heron's and Mr Fulton's papers bring out, the perspective of the couple is as valid as that of either church. Any "demand for capitulation" by either church or by either partner is a denial of the self-gift which is the heart of marriage: the spouses "plight their troth" or give their integral selves; and it is christian marriage that wishes to assert this over and against less than christian forms of marriage. In anthropological terms, for the interchurch family the family itself is a "centre" of religious experience that is prior to the centre-function o either church. Hence it is the (divided) churches that are a problem for the interchurch family, and it would be wrong for the churches to regard such a family as simply "a problem" for their own self-definition.

It was the perspective of the couples themselves that came across clearly during the Dublin Consultation in the course of what must have been for all present the most revealing experience of the week, the public meeting at which two couples, one English and Anglican-RC the other Irish and RC-Presbyterian, told the audience of their own personal christian lives. Through this touching and searching experience of listening to the people involved it became manifestly obvious in quite a new way that it is quite impossible for the truly interchurch couple to decide the religious upbringing of their children at a stroke, and in advance. (Hence they should certainly not be pushed to such a decision before they marry by pastorally concerned clergy, but only helped to begin to face up to the issues and the best means of coping with them.) First of all, one has no real idea of what it is like to be a parent until the child is there. Then, each partner can only progressively come to appreciate the Christian tradition of the other, be enriched by it, and grow thereby in appreciation of his own tradition. The actual dynamics of this growth towards union must depend on the two real people involved. But a growth towards union it is, a growth in the spirituality of their own married life precisely as two-church, a growth in the ability to break through beyond tensions to positive achievements, which may well take some years before, for instance, each is ready to share Holy Communion with the other. And it is a discovered and created union that the father and mother are principally concerned to pass on to their children, a new kind of union that can exist in the "domestic church" and that will precede in the children's experience any awareness of division. It is therefore clear that the whole process of creating and experiencing a christian marriage must enter into decisions that have to be made about the religious upbringing of children. It is further clear that it is a matter, not of *a* decision, but of a whole process of step by step decisions involving prayer at home, shared churchgoing, joint instruction, association of parents and children with church groups, schooling, etc. It is into this process, into the realities of life and of interpersonal relations, that baptism fits. Furthermore, the interchurch couple plans for union, hopes for union, prays for union. It seeks to defend the experienced christian unity of the family from the divisive pull of the two church communities. It cannot make a string of decisions well in advance of the realities encountered. It must plan for the two churches being at least far closer to each other by the time the children reach their late teens. The children's religious future must remain always to some extent a matter of faith and of hope.

It is no part of these reflections to deny to interchurch couples the propriety of jointly and responsibly deciding to bring up their children exclusively or almost exclusively in one or other church. (To let the boys follow the father and the girls the mother – the other way round might be more psychologically sound – is an evasion rather than a solution of the problem, a surrender to the possessiveness of communities and institutions.) And, given such a decision, more particular choices such as those concerning baptism would then more easily fall into place. But a significant number of couples have already discovered that it is possible to bring up their children "within both churches", to use the phrase of the joint statement given below. It is a phrase which purposely avoids saying "as members of both churches", as this raises questions both theological and canonical that have as yet no full answer. In the interchurch family the churches are coming to discover a reality for which they have not yet got an adequate theology. And to speak of "membership" is to view the children principally from the perspective of the two communities and institutions involved; whereas here, as essential background to the question of baptism, we are trying to highlight the perspective and experience of the family and of the children themselves.

Those who are not personally involved are inclined to make the mistake of imagining that some reductionist or sieved version of Christian tradition is intended: no, it is the fullness of both traditions that the parents seek to give, because it is this fullness they seek to share.

Similarly, "outsiders" always ask, "But won't it confuse the children and bring to bear on them adult tensions they should not be asked, and are not able, to support?" The only available evidence, namely from the children themselves (and not much is available because the inter-church attempt is mainly recent) is that what is not found confusing by the parents does not confuse the children: to them it is normal, and even a standard by which to judge one-church allegiance. Similarly, it is only tension between parents (which children are quick to perceive) that generates tension in children. Hence any feeling by one partner that he has been ousted or forced to capitulate is at least as likely as the interchurch attempt to produce tension in the children. It is extremely good for them, in both human and Christian terms, to be brought up in a milieu of firm and contrasting convictions that are held together not by mere toleration but by conjugal love.

In all this context and background, then, one is able to see how, and with what force, the question arises; "Cannot our children be baptised into the One Church of Christ, as it exists in our two churches, and not exclusively into one or other church?" It is a very good question for ecclesiology to face.

The Ecclesiological Question

The Dublin Consultation brought out into the open that it is naïve and pre-ecumenical for Protestants (as "other Christians" are usually termed in Ireland) to say to Roman Catholics: "For heaven's sake change your one-sided ecclesiology and then we can all start being ecumenical." Roman Catholic theology finds itself since Vatican II with a plurality of ecclesiologies on its hands, a plurality that remains obstinately pluralist and refuses to be reduced tidily to one. The Roman Catholic Church has at least pertinaciously adhered to an ecclesiology of unity. It seems fair to say that Protestant traditions have in the main offered ecclesiologies of division, except that there are new patterns to be studied in the Church Unions that have actually come about in different parts of the world. (And in this matter the Orthodox, too, are central.) So it is not only Roman Catholic thinking that has to change or to grow. And if what has predominated in Roman Catholic eccles-iology is unacceptable to Protestants, then it is only in dialogue together that we can discover a mutually acceptable ecclesiology of unity.

One dimension of all ecclesiologies must be the eschatological, the realisation that the Church on earth is the effective sign of the future. The visible and historical Church "is already" the Kingdom of Christ, by the life and power of the Risen Christ present and active by his Spirit in its midst; is already one, holy, catholic, apostolic. Human history in this world is the stuff out of which the Kingdom is made: this is what the incarnation reveals. But at the same time the Church "is not yet" the Kingdom; not yet in any absolute or perfect fashion, one, holy, catholic, apostolic; always receiving from God, and never simply possessing; always striving in response to God's self-gift to become more perfectly what his gift has already made it to be. As far as unity in particular is concerned, the Roman Catholic Church believes it has a position of pre-eminence among christian churches, but at the same time recognises that the unity bestowed by Christ on his Church from the beginning must grow and increase in time (*Decree on Ecumenism*, n.4), and that the Holy Spirit, the principle of the Church's unity, dwells and operates in other churches too (*Decree*, nn.2-3). In this eschatological perspective the interchurch marriage can be seen as anticipatory of the coming Christian unity (as all exogamous marriage is anticipatory of the union between social groups), a realisation of the future in our midst, a better fulfilment of the Church's vocation to oneness. In this perspective, whatever their need of an ecclesiology that defines their identity and their special christian insights, the churches must also see in the interchurch marriage a challenge to their thinking *merely* in terms of their present identity, or their present state of imperfect communion with each other. They must hear a call from Christ's Spirit into the future. They cannot simply govern or discipline the interchurch family in terms of present internal norms.

In the West, communions other than the Roman Catholic have never thought of themselves as "the Catholic Church". So, though with various ecclesiological models operating (the branch theory is only one such model), they have more readily accepted that baptism is primarily into "the Church of Christ" or "the Catholic Church", and only secondarily into their own denominations. (Hence, too, they have not understood that a Christian is under an obligation coming from Christ, obliged by "divine law" or institution, to rear his children in his own denomination, but only to rear them as believing Christians.) In Methodist thought, owing to the origin of Methodism as a Society within the Church of England, baptism is into "the Church", and membership of the Methodist Society is only attained later by an act of personal commitment and community acceptance. Yet in most western reformed thought it is clear that the Church of Christ in fact only exists in designable christian communions or denominations; and that baptism is an entry into and a reception by a visible believing community. Hence, while those in this tradition more easily accept that a child could by baptism become a member of more than one church, they would normally reject the idea that he could simply be baptised into "the Church" without any specification of what denomination he belonged to.

The mutual recognition of baptism that has been formally achieved between churches in a number of countries is in the first instance simply a recognition that a person has been truly baptised. It does not of itself imply a particular ecclesiology beyond the recognition that, as Vatican II puts it: "By the sacrament of baptism, whenever it is properly conferred in the way the Lord determined, and received with the appropriate dispositions of soul, a man becomes truly incorporated into the crucified and glorified Christ and is reborn to a sharing of the divine life" (*Decree*, n.22). This is, of course, a crucial recognition, and it is worth noting that it differs greatly from the view that prevailed after the fourth and fifth century controversies: then baptism in schism was regarded as unrepeatable, but not as regenerating; it was not "valid" as we understand the term; it was thought only to have its effect when the schismatic rejoined the true Church in which alone the Spirit dwelt and vivified. However, in our time the mutual recognition of baptism has been achieved by prescinding from particular ecclesiologies, and so the interchurch couple cannot appeal to it as presupposing a particular ecclesiology. On the other hand, it does have implications for all ecclesiologies, and to this we shall return in at least one context.

What then does Catholic theology say to the request that a child be baptised simply into the One Church of Christ? I think it can be shown that there is no one simple answer, and that this fact itself should suggest to Church authorities that they could be right, in a situation of some uncertainty, to respond favourably and in hope to the theology of the family.

As is well known, Vatican II rejected the proposition that the One Church of Christ is simply to be identified with the Roman Catholic Church. That is the one certain thing that can be said about the Council's statement that the single or one (*unica*) Church of Christ "subsists in the (Roman) Catholic Church" (*Constitution on the Church*, n.8). The Council itself gives no exegesis of the word "subsists", nor can an authoritative exegesis be drawn from any other source: all that is clear from the change of an original "is the Catholic Church" to "subsists in the Catholic Church" is that identification is excluded. This leaves various ecclesiological models open.

In the same passage of the *Constitution on the Church*, and in the corresponding passage (n.3) of the *Decree on Ecumenism*, use is made of a theology of "elements", elements constitutive of the Church as Church, existing in other communions separated from the Roman Catholic Church and belonging by right, not to the Roman Catholic Church, but to the One Church of Christ. It can be argued from this careful choice of language that the Council's position is: *not* that all baptisms are into the Roman Catholic Church, such that those baptised in other communions are simply as individuals in imperfect communion with the Roman Catholic Church and called by the inner meaning of their baptism to return to full communion, as some preconciliar theology held; *but* that baptism is primarily into the One Church of Christ, and secondarily into separated churches, among which the Roman Catholic Church is the centre of an at present imperfect communion, though destined by Christ's call to be the centre of full communion.

From this ecclesiology there are two implications for baptism. The secondary one is that an individual cannot be baptised simply into the One Church of Christ, and not at the same time into a particular believing community: either/or; either into the Roman Catholic Church, or into a community in imperfect communion with the Roman Catholic Church. The One Church of Christ does not exist as a visible and historical entity separable from the believing communities. If it "subsists" in the Roman Catholic Church, then it also exists in a somehow reduced form, according to this ecclesiology, in the other churches. (Some find that the language of sacramental theology is the one that best clarifies this position. The Roman Catholic Church understands itself as the fullest sacramental sign of the Body of Christ and his

Kingdom: fullest as sign, not necessarily with fullest effectiveness or presence of every reality signified. Other churches too are sacramental and therefore efficacious signs of the Kingdom, though less full or adequate precisely as signs.)

But the primary implication of this ecclesiology remains, and is of immense importance both for the understanding of baptism and for the very starting point and launching-pad of Roman Catholic ecumenism. It is, quite simply, that the One Church of Christ is logically and theologically prior, just as it is chronologically prior, to the divided churches; and that the one Church of Christ is to be seen and understood as *visibly united in our midst* before it is to be seen as visibly divided. For it is not the heavenly and invisible reality of the Kingdom, or the Body of Christ precisely *as* transcendent and as *not* embodied in historical reality, that is said to subsist in the Roman Catholic Church, but the *Church* of Christ. The scriptures, the creeds, the sacraments, and many other elements – including the way Christians behave towards each other or act together, and including the interchurch family – are visible bonds of unity. There is great significance in the Council's statement (*Decree*, n.22) that "baptism constitutes a sacramental bond of unity linking all who have been reborn by means of it". A sacramental bond is of its nature a visible bond, a sign and an effective sign of the Kingdom in our midst. Baptism manifests the One Church of Christ as it exists in tangible reality on earth prior to its divisions. It manifests the unity that Christ gives to his Church, which all human inadequacies are unable to destroy.

Therefore, though that ecclesiology of the Roman Catholic Church which is predominant (but not alone in the field or all-inclusive, as we have seen in considering the eschatological aspect) defines in the way explained the meaning of baptism *within* itself and within other churches, it seems that the interchurch family can press that their own question remains unanswered. Can their children not be baptised into the One Church of Christ *as it visibly exists in both their Churches*? This precisely corresponds to what they are: a two-church and not a one-church family; a two-church couple who wish progressively to do their best to rear their children in both churches. Will the churches allow them to do this, and signify their acceptance in baptism? The Roman Catholic Church cannot take the same attitude to this question as churches with an ecclesiology that allows parity of denominations (nor can the Orthodox churches). But it is not clear that the Roman Catholic Church, having stated its own position, but also having then left the upbringing of the children to the responsible decision and subsequent co-operation of both parents, is unable to bless their decision to be two-church, and to accede to the request. It is a point where the nature and needs of the family challenge the need of the social structure to translate its convictions into disciplines and rules.

I am not one normally addicted to drawing theology from canon law. But it is interesting in this connection to note that some uncertainty prevails in Roman Catholic thought, deriving from the preconciliar mood of identifying the Church with the Roman Catholic Church, about what constitutes baptism into the Roman Catholic

Church. The point arises in practice for canonists when, for example, it has to be decided whether a baptised person is bound by the law of canonical form for marriage. Doubt can arise if a baby is baptised in hospital in danger of death. Canonists seem to be agreed that in the case of infants incapable of expressing their own intention it is the intention of the parents manifested by their requesting baptism from the competent Roman Catholic authority that principally determines entry into the Roman Catholic Church. It is noteworthy that it is not primarily the place (which might be a hospital or the scene of an accident), nor the minister (who may not even be a Christian), that are the main determining factors, but the parents' intention. But, of course, minister and place can be further determining factors, and are so in the great majority of cases. It is a nice point whether Church authorities are *able* to baptise an infant exclusively into one church when it is the manifest intention of the parents that he should be baptised into two! – and this is not a perspective that has been envisaged in the Roman Catholic formulation of promises.

Practical Possibilities

We all know, but sometimes need to recall, the axiom that there are no perfect solutions to the problems raised by mixed marriages short of the disappearance of church division. Nor is it for the theoretical ecumenist to lay down a new kind of law, an ecumenical law, for interchurch couples: they have enough laws to contend with already. Rather, because each couple is precisely that couple and no other, two real people with their own mutual christian relationship and development, and with their own situation and external relationships, it is desirable that the maximum variety of possibilities should be open to them, from the baptism in which only one church is involved to that in which both are equally involved.

To avoid complications of language, let us just for this concluding section use the prevailing Irish symbols, and consider a Catholic (= Roman Catholic) husband with a Protestant (= all other western Christians) wife.

In some countries churches have set about devising an ecumenical rite of baptism. Others think it more ecumenical for the churches as a confirmation of their recognition of each other's baptism to use the existing rites, supposing these contain nothing of offence to others. The modern Catholic rite lends itself to a great deal of participation by ministers, parents, godparents, and has been chosen for this reason by some couples. But the main point here is that the couple should be allowed the maximum freedom in the choice of rite, rather than that clergy should needlessly dicatate to them. (The same goes for wedding ceremonies.)

One form that goes some way to express the two-church nature of the couple and of their intentions is baptism by the Catholic priest in the Catholic church with participation by the Protestant minister and family, e.g. in welcoming the child, reading lessons, conducting intercessions, preaching. The full involvement of both churches and families is what mainly counts, as it exhibits welcome of the interchurch family by both churches. The Protestant mother will otherwise feel she is "losing her child" or surrendering the child to the Catholic Church precisely as institution. One has heard too much of Christian baptism being an occasion of anguish for Protestant parents, instead of one of happiness. A really generous attitude by the baptising church can make the ceremony a source of great encouragement to both parents, manifesting both the partial communion of the churches and the special situation of the family, and one which can be treasured in memory more than a normal baptism in a one-church family. Further, such a celebration helps the perspective of the parents by bringing out that baptism is first and foremost into the Church of Christ as visibly one and undivided. And this is also true of the forms that follow.

The reverse process, baptism by the Protestant minister in his church with participation by the Catholic minister and family, runs into difficulties deriving from the inequality of Protestant and Catholic ecclesiologies. Even supposing the Catholic authorities have fully and really accepted that the decisions must rest jointly with the parents, and therefore truly accept the personal decision of the Catholic to have the child baptised by the Protestant minister, there remains something publicly unacceptable and in conflict with the conviction that the Church of Christ subsists in the Catholic Church, in the child of a Catholic parent being baptised in this form; and the Catholic authorities will hesitate to give public approval for it by the priest's participation. Some evidence of making headway with the problem is, however, shown in the report given above from France (p. 120), and in the joint declaration of the Protestant and Catholic Churches in Holland in 1971 that: "To express the fact that the baptism is recognised by the two churches of the parents, it may be registered also in the parish or chapel where it has not been administered." This declaration does not say anything about Catholic participation in a Protestant baptism, or vice versa; but mutual registration of the fact that it is a true baptism, which we shall consider further, would certainly be a psychological help to the Catholic parent.

Intermediary between these two forms is the possibility of baptism by the Catholic minister in the Protestant church, or vice versa, with participation by the other church. These variations do not raise special questions not already dealt with, or arising from what follows.

A further alternative is baptism in the home by Catholic or Protestant minister, with participation by the other church. By this is not envisaged some private or hidden-away affair, but a gathering in the home for the occasion of relatives from both sides of the family, and of friends (clerical and lay) of different churches from round about. This does not merely exhibit the two-church nature of the family, but preserves the essential idea that baptism belongs within and is a celebration of the community, and not a private matter. It brings together what can properly be called the real Christian community of this particular family, an ecumenical one drawn from both kinship and locality. This form also gives expression to the idea that the interchurch family can be a sign of coming unity and an actual force for unity.

But there are no perfect solutions. Some two-church couples dislike the idea of house baptism because it sets them up as unusual, special, even affected. They want above all to be, and to be accepted as, a perfectly normal and ordinary marriage, and a perfectly normal Christian marriage, and not, at least principally, as ecumenical pioneers.

House baptism would avoid this suggestion of the interchurch family's being "special" in any unacceptable sense, if it were also fairly common for one-church families. And is this not a possibility to be looked at? Is it not perhaps already pointed to by the house Mass? Serious consideration of this question would take us too far afield, raising as it does the whole relationship between Church and world (i.e. society other than Church) as it is experienced today. The house Mass does, and the house baptism could, give expression to the awareness of the believing community that it is in and part of the world; either would perhaps be felt to be more appropriate, the more a given society is pluralist and dechristianised.

Finally, the question of the registration of the baptism by both churches comes up for consideration in any of the forms of baptism outlined. Mutual registration is of considerable psychological importance to the parents, as it assures them, not basically of any theological truths, but of the personal acceptance of themselves and of their child by both churches. What it means beyond that, and beyond the fact that both churches recognise the child as truly baptised, is somewhat difficult to unravel. If Protestant churches generally regard baptism as simply "into the church" without specification of denomination, they also vary in the further steps required, even when they avoid distinguishing "membership" from "full membership", before a person is admitted to Holy Communion, or to an electoral roll, or regarded as an adult member. The Roman Catholic Church, however, regards baptism as either into the Roman Catholic Church or not, and as deciding membership; and membership of the Roman Catholic Church of its own nature is oriented to, or presses for, Confirmation and Communion in the Roman Catholic Church. So there can be no simple answer to the question of what the churches would mean by their both registering one child's baptism. The statement of the Dutch churches quoted above commits the Churches by the fact of their registration to regarding the child as truly baptised, but not to their regarding him as a member.

In any case, one has to recall that registration of baptism is a canonical act, not a sacramental act. In any church, what matters is how the child is reared and comes personally to fulfil the promise of baptism.

From the Roman Catholic side one might tentatively suggest the following. Baptism into the (Roman) Catholic Church is normally signified by the parents' asking the priest to baptise the child – a dialogue now built into the new rite of baptism. If the baptism is performed by a priest in the home or in a Protestant church, the two facts that the parents had asked the bishop (or competent authority) for this form, and that he had approved, would themselves signify and determine baptism into the Roman Catholic Church. Indeed, if the parents express the desire for baptism into the Roman Catholic Church, it is hard to find a reason why the bishop could not agree to this being performed by a Protestant minister: if he did so agree, then his agreement would again manifest baptism into the Catholic Church, as would its registration as such at the local parish. If the Protestant Church then also registered the baptism, and wished by this act to mean, not only recognition of baptism, but acceptance as a member, this need not be the concern of the Roman Catholic authorities. Inevitably, owing basically to different ecclesiologies, it will be possible for Church authorities to put different interpretations on the same event.

We have got very involved and anomalous, the reader may well be feeling, possibly with some impatience. Those involved in trying to run ecumenical parishes will recognise the anomalies that do arise over common baptism and Church membership. And if some attempt has been made here to unravel them for the interchurch family, it is not just out of love for speculation, but because many such families have asked for them to be unravelled.

The major anomaly from which all minor anomalies arise is the division of the churches. In speaking during the Dublin Consultation to his paper given in this book, Dr Wainwright urged the principle that minor anomalies should be resolved in the sense that diminishes rather than reinforces the major anomaly. It is another way of saying that the churches are a problem for the couple, and should not think of the couple primarily or solely as a problem for them.

Appendix I

Final Statement of the Dublin Consultation

The International Consultation on Mixed Marriages, organised by the Irish School of Ecumenics, from September 2 to 6, 1974, wishes to share with a wider public some of its reflections and conclusions.

The participants experienced together during the week a deeper sense of fellowship in Jesus Christ, and therefore felt all the more the scandal of disunity as revealed especially in the problems of mixed marriage. They were moved by a spirit of repentance and conversion and a desire to express this in a reform of attitudes and practices with regard to mixed marriage.

The Consultation considered many questions, such as those of the social and political context of marriage, the interfaith marriage, legislating for marriage, baptism for interchurch families, etc.; but wishes to put forward for immediate consideration only the following more limited reflections. In doing so the Consultation felt it more helpful to concentrate on the "interchurch" marriage, namely that in which both partners are committed to their churches, as is generally the case in Ireland.

1. The members came to appreciate more fully
   a. the Christian reality of such a marriage;
   b. how it can provide an enrichment for the partners, for both their churches, and indeed for society as a whole;
   c. how it can help the mutual understanding and coming together of these churches.

2. In the case of marriage between committed Christians, the obligation to transmit their faith to their children bears equally on both partners. While many people felt that the abolition of all legislation in the matter would be desirable, the Consultation welcomes the very considerable change brought into this field by the *Motu Proprio Matrimonia Mixta*, of 1970, with its recognition that a Roman Catholic partner cannot commit himself in advance to the Roman Catholic upbringing of the children, but only to the will to communicate his own faith within the structure of joint marital responsibility. (The promise "to do all in his power" to ensure a Roman Catholic upbringing is not a promise that his children will in fact be brought up as Roman Catholics.) The Consultation hopes that this change will be widely understood.

Consequently, *both* partners have a duty in conscience to advance towards joint decisions about the religious upbringing of the children which *both* can conscientiously cooperate in fulfilling.

It is of particular significance that many parents do find themselves able to bring up their children within both their churches. There was much debate about the ecclesiological significance of this and many of the participants from all churches regarded this joint upbringing as theologically acceptable. Moreover, a widespread hope was expressed that partners in an interchurch marriage should be permitted a measure of continuing sharing in the Eucharist.

3. The Roman Catholic Church causes deep resentment among other Christians in that it does not generally recognise the marriage of a Roman Catholic in their churches. As Rome has extended recognition to the celebration of these marriages in the Eastern churches, it is hoped that a similar arrangement might soon be made with the churches of the West.

4. In the light of a full understanding of the assurances to be given by the Roman Catholic partner in a mixed marriage (cf. para. 2) the Consultation hopes that other churches will reconsider any rulings they may have made against participation by their ministers in Roman Catholic weddings.

5. Effective commitment to joint pastoral care by ministers of the participating churches to the couple involved, before, during and after the wedding, is urgently required.

6. The existence of Associations of Interchurch and Mixed Families was particularly welcomed, and their development should be further fostered and officially endorsed.

7. The formal presentations to the Consultation revealed that statements on mixed marriages in many countries had been based on joint consultation between the churches, or that at least a statement by a particular church, before being finalised, had been submitted to other churches for comment and possible modification.

Appendix II

Address by Dr Garret FitzGerald, T.D., Minister for Foreign Affairs to the International Consultation on Mixed Marriage

I have a triple interest in your deliberations, which I have followed from a distance, but with close attention during the past few days.

First, as one of the progeny of a mixed marriage, I have a personal interest in these matters – and, no doubt, a personal bias. You will at any rate find it easy to understand that it would be hard for me to assent to a proposition that asserted that such marriages are inherently undesirable, for by doing so I should in a sense be negating my own existence!

Second, as a Roman Catholic layman I am interested in the current evolution of the general theology of marriage, some aspects of the traditional expression of which have since my schooldays seemed to me to have been imperfect and incomplete. Accordingly, I value some of the insights on the institution of marriage itself which have emerged incidentally from your consideration of one particular type of marriage.

Third, as the Minister for Foreign Affairs of Ireland I am deeply concerned about the political implications for this island of the present ecclesiastical provisions with respect to mixed marriages. It is of this latter aspect of the problem that I shall speak today.

You have, quite properly and understandably, not adverted in any detail to this aspect of the problem in the course of a conference which has been international and theological, rather than national and political. But in inviting me to speak I presume you must have been prepared for the possibility that I might address myself to the political implications of this matter as they seem to me to arise in this country at this time, and may perhaps even have adverted to the improbability that I would confine myself to the theological area, in which I am little qualified!

The inter-action of theology and politics is often, perhaps almost always, controversial, and I know that in addressing myself to the twilight zone between the two I am taking some risks. However, I have done so before on occasion without fatal consequences, and shall hope to survive on this occasion also! I recognise at once that it is not, of course, possible to segregate the political from the theological aspects, and that someone with another theological perspective might see the political aspect of the problem somewhat differently. I also recognise that to someone primarily concerned with the theological aspects of mixed marriage, my political approach may seem at best to be somewhat lopsided, and at worst to involve putting the cart before the horse. Nevertheless, I feel that without doing violence to theology, and even perhaps within a broadly theological context, it is possible and worthwhile to consider the political aspects of this problem.

These political aspects arise from a unique combination of circumstances that exist in the Republic of Ireland, and as between the Republic and Northern Ireland. Within the Republic 96% of the population are Roman Catholics, and of these something like nine out of ten practise their religion and take its obligations seriously – many, indeed even tending to implement these obligations with almost legalistic zeal. In Northern Ireland the religious balance is much less uneven – 35% being Roman Catholics.

The effect of this very unbalanced ratio of religions in the population of the Republic has been that, despite considerable social pressures in favour of confining inter-marriage within the Protestant group of Churches, about a quarter of Protestants – at least in the 1946 to 1961 period for which a reasonably full analysis of data is available – have married Roman Catholics, and in the vast majority of cases during that period at any rate the children of these marriages were baptised into the Roman Catholic Church and brought up as Roman Catholics. The problem is complicated by the fact that the proportion of Protestant men contracting mixed marriages is higher than in the case of Protestant women and where the mother is Roman Catholic the likelihood of the children being brought up in that faith is especially high. The inevitable statistical or demographic consequences of this – in conjunction with a higher age level and consequently higher death rate amongst the Protestant population, although this is a relatively minor factor – is an erosion of the Protestant population by about 25% per generation – or around 1% per annum. No similar phenomenon appears to exist, at any rate on such a scale, anywhere else in the world.

In Northern Ireland the social pressures in favour of marriage within one's own religious group have always been stronger – some individuals, indeed, have in recent years even paid the penalty of losing their lives because they committed the offence of a mixed marriage.

Moreover, in the North the opportunities for marriage within one's own religious community have also, because of the much less uneven ratio of Protestants and Catholics in the population, been much greater. The consequence has been that relatively few Protestants in Northern Ireland have married Catholics, and the erosion of the Protestant population through the mixed marriage mechanism has been negligible in that part of Ireland.

The consequence of the existence of these two very different situations in the two parts of this island, has been that Protestants in Northern Ireland have observed a continuous decline in the number of their co-religionists in the Republic, and, because the conditions leading to this erosion do not exist in Northern Ireland such an erosion has thus not occurred there, they have not attributed this decline in Protestant numbers in the Republic to mixed marriages but have instead assumed that some other more sinister force has been at work. The common assumption of Northern Protestants has seemed to be that conditions of life in the Republic are uncongenial for Protestants and that they therefore have emigrated in such large numbers as to decimate the Protestant population, and the less well-informed amongst the Protestant population have even assumed that this emigration has been forced on Protestants by a form of job discrimination similar to that which they have observed working in their own favour within their own part of the island. In fact this interpretation is quite false – the emigration rate of Protestants from the Republic has in fact been significantly lower than that for Roman Catholics as their generally higher socio-economic status has made it easier for them to secure employment in Ireland.

The political consequences of this misconception have been incalculably great, and the misconception has proved immune to all debunking, partly because people so often believe what their prejudices lead them to want to believe, and partly because the differential demographic impact of mixed marriage in the two areas is in any event a concept too statistically complex to be readily grasped.

The fact is that more than any other single factor the observed decline in the Protestant population in the Republic has confirmed Northern Protestants in their prejudices and fears. Even members of the Protestant community otherwise moderate in their views, and generally well-disposed towards their Roman Catholic co-religionists, are frequently moved by this phenomenon to fear a closer political association with the Republic lest such an association should spread the virus of Protestant demographic decline to the North.

Moreover, even the tiny number of sophisticated and demographically-informed people amongst the Northern Protestant community who may understand that the virus in question is of its nature non-contagious (being a function of radically different religious population ratios in the two parts of Ireland) are nonetheless discouraged from being willing to accept a closer political association between North and South because they find distasteful a society in which the influence of the Roman Catholic Church in a given population situation has the observed effect of decimating the Protestant population there.

Now if the effect of this demographic situation upon the views and attitudes of Northern Protestants were merely to be that it discouraged them from agreeing to political re-unification, it could well be argued that this purely political consideration is theologically quite irrelevant. Whatever the views of the average Irish Roman Catholic on the subject of re-unification may be, the issue of whether Ireland should be politically united is obviously not a theological one or one that theologians should have to concern themselves about. Unfortunately, however, the effects of this situation run much deeper than this – very much deeper.

First of all, the fears of re-unification thus confirmed or reinforced, are so powerful as to pose today a threat to the very lives of a large proportion of the Roman Catholic population in Northern Ireland. There have been many pogroms of Roman Catholics in Northern Ireland over the years – within the past five years tens of thousands of Roman Catholic families have had to leave their homes. The proximate cause of these tragic events lies in the IRA campaign of the past four years, but the ultimate cause is the fear amongst Protestants of absorption in a predominantly Roman Catholic Ireland in which, they believe, they would disappear as rapidly as Protestants have been disappearing in the Republic for decades past.

There is thus the paradox that the Roman Catholic Church's policy with respect to mixed marriages when it operates in the kind of conditions that exist in the Republic, though presumably having the intended effect of maximising the Roman Catholic population in that area, also has the effect of helping to threaten the very existence of the Roman Catholic population in parts of Northern Ireland.

Of course it can be argued that the part played by the demographic impact of mixed marriages in the Republic upon Northern Protestant thinking is so intangible and incalculable, that it does not provide a compelling reason for changing the Roman Catholic Church's policy in this matter in Ireland. I would, however, tend to draw the opposite conclusion – that, given the risks now facing the Roman Catholic community in Northern Ireland, none of us is entitled to add to these risks or to aggravate them, even immeasurably, by pursuing a policy the direction of whose effects upon Protestant thinking in Northern Ireland is known, even if these effects cannot actually be quantified. I would feel in fact that in the situation that now exists one is not entitled to leave unturned any stones whose uprooting might in any degree minimise the risks that now threaten Roman Catholics in Northern Ireland.

It may be noted that the argument here put forward is not met by an assertion that the Roman Catholic Church has greatly modified its requirements in respect of mixed marriages in recent years, and that it no longer imposes an obligation on the Protestant partner. The simple fact is that the fidelity of Roman Catholics to their Church's teaching is so great in Ireland that even the simple maintenance of an obligation on the Roman Catholic partner to do his or her best to bring up the children as Roman Catholics, imposes a major demographic distortion, in the Republic, which has most dangerous consequences for Roman Catholics in Northern Ireland. The solution to this and to other similar ecclesiastical problems that is often found in other countries – viz. not to take the obligation too seriously – is ruled out in Ireland by the character of the religious observance of Irish Roman Catholics.

So far I have been dealing with one political aspect of the problem – the impact on Northern Protestant opinion of the religious demographic situation created in the Republic by the present position with respect to mixed marriages, and the threat that this poses to the Roman Catholic community in Northern Ireland. There is, however, a much more fundamental question that has to be raised. The very existence of the problem of inter-community strife in Northern Ireland derives from the fact that despite the disappearance of linguistic barriers several centuries ago, and despite the absence of any clearly-marked physical differences between them, the two sections of the community in Northern Ireland – native Irish on the one hand, and Ulster Scots and English planters on the other – have largely retained their separate biological and cultural identities because of the religious barrier to inter-marriage and because of that alone. All previous groups of settlers – Danes and Norwegians, Normans, and English prior to the Reformation – became assimilated with the native Irish because they inter-married, and no lasting problems of racial or cultural divisions were created. It was only when the Reformation set up a barrier to inter-marriage between later arrivals and the native Irish community, that the division between newcomers and older inhabitants became indefinitely perpetuated.

To be fair, the failure of the new settlers in the north-east and the native Irish in this area to assimilate was not in earlier centuries due to particular ecclesiastical legislation with regard to mixed marriages, for this legislation became a significant factor only after Ne Temere was promulgated in Ireland in 1908. But it is arguable that this application of these new and stringent requirements with respect to the religious upbringing of the children of mixed marriages in the early years of the twentieth century, came at a crucial point in Irish history and probably contributed to continuing the division of two sections of the community at a time of particular political tension. Certainly positive encouragement to mixed marriages, rather than discouragement, would have been more likely to have improved community relations in Northern Ireland during this century, although another important factor in the maintenance of the lethal division between two sections of the Northern Ireland community can also be argued to have been the segregation of children for educational purposes. That, however, is another question that does not concern this Conference!

The question I wish to pose, therefore, is whether the deep, and for many people fatal, division of the community in Northern Ireland, and the mutual antipathy of the Roman Catholic and Protestant sections of that community, is not in some degree at least attributable to past and present ecclesiastical legislation with respect to mixed marriages, and whether, if this is so, the problem thus created is not one of which theology must take cognisance. If it is right that theology should concern itself with the creation of conditions in which individuals will be brought up as Roman Catholics rather than Protestants, is it not also right that it should concern itself with the creation of conditions in which these Roman Catholics can survive in peace within a genuine social community, and be free of the threat of assassinations and pogroms and of the threat – a reality for tens of thousands of families in recent years – of being intimidated out of their homes. It is a characteristic of Christian theology that it rejects the liberal individualist view of society and is concerned with social effects as well as with the lives of individuals; Roman Catholic theology lays great stress on these social effects – *vide* the arguments put forward in recent times as to the possible effects on the "quality of life" in the Republic of changes in the laws relating to contraception. Why, in the case of mixed marriages, should theology suddenly become individualistic, concerned only with the particular case of the individual child of a mixed marriage, and not with the overall impact of its teaching on the character of society?

These are questions which as Christians we are not merely entitled, but I feel required, to ask ourselves. They are questions which those of us who are politicians, concerned to secure peace and justice in this island, have an especial obligation to pose. I am grateful to you for having given me the opportunity, at the end of your Conference, to raise these questions.